GROWTH OF
AMERICAN STATE
CONSTITUTIONS

Da Capo Press Reprints in

AMERICAN CONSTITUTIONAL AND LEGAL HISTORY

GENERAL EDITOR: LEONARD W. LEVY

Claremont Graduate School

GROWTH OF AMERICAN STATE CONSTITUTIONS

From 1776 to the End of the Year 1914

By James Q. Dealey

DA CAPO PRESS • NEW YORK • 1972

Library of Congress Cataloging in Publication Data

Dealey, James Quayle, 1861-1937.
  Growth of American state constitutions, from 1776
to the end of the year 1914.
  (Da Capo Press reprints in American constitutional
and legal history)
  Bibliography: p.
  1. Constitutions, State — U. S. I. Title.
KF4550.Z95D42 1972   342'.73'02   75-124891
ISBN 0-306-71985-1

This Da Capo Press edition of
Growth of American State Constitutions
is an unabridged republication of the first edition
published in 1915.

Published by Da Capo Press, Inc.
A Subsidiary of Plenum Publishing Corporation
227 W. 17 St., New York, New York, 10011

Manufactured in the United States of America

GROWTH OF AMERICAN STATE CONSTITUTIONS

GROWTH OF AMERICAN STATE CONSTITUTIONS

FROM 1776 TO THE END OF THE YEAR 1914

BY

JAMES QUAYLE DEALEY, Ph.D.

PROFESSOR OF SOCIAL AND POLITICAL SCIENCE IN BROWN UNIVERSITY

GINN AND COMPANY

BOSTON · NEW YORK · CHICAGO · LONDON
ATLANTA · DALLAS · COLUMBUS · SAN FRANCISCO

The Athenæum Press

GINN AND COMPANY · PRO-
PRIETORS · BOSTON · U.S.A.

PREFACE

The basis for this study was a series of articles prepared at the suggestion of President E. Benjamin Andrews and syndicated to the newspapers in the year 1899 under the heading "Tendencies in Recent State Constitutions." In 1906 the articles were revised and published in the Galveston *Daily News* and the Dallas *Morning News*, and later were published as a pamphlet for general circulation. In 1907 the series was enlarged and published as a supplement number in the *Annals of the American Academy of Social and Political Science*, March, 1907. This pamphlet has now been revised so as to include the changes of the last seven years, and ten additional chapters have been added, more than trebling the original material.

Part I traces the history of the state constitutions so as to show the trend of nearly a hundred and forty years in the constitutional development of the commonwealths of the Union. Part II is in general the revision of the supplement to the Annals, but with many omissions and additions. Part III includes constructive suggestions as to the probable trend of changes in state constitutions during the next few years. The work as a whole aims to call attention to the great importance of these fundamental laws, and hence to the necessity of devoting to their improvement far more attention in the future than has been given to them in the past. In many respects these laws concern more vitally the interests of the average citizen than does the national constitution, so that the increasing attention paid to them in recent years is an excellent illustration of a growing civic interest in local government and in the principles of democracy. This interest is greatly stimulated by the increasing attention given to state constitutions and government by the departments of history and political science in so many American colleges and universities. For such classes this work possibly may be considered worthy of introduction as a textbook. The author furthermore hopes that citizens and members of legislatures and constitutional conventions may find these chapters to some slight extent helpful in furthering a knowledge of our state political institutions.

Acknowledgment is cheerfully given to the Legislative Reference Bureau of the State of Rhode Island for kindly and frequent assistance in securing information in respect to constitutional amendments, and to the *Annals* for permission to republish its Supplement revised.

J. Q. DEALEY

BROWN UNIVERSITY

CONTENTS

PART I

HISTORY OF STATE CONSTITUTIONS

PART II

PROVISIONS OF EXISTING STATE CONSTITUTIONS

PART III

TREND IN STATE CONSTITUTIONS

GROWTH OF AMERICAN STATE CONSTITUTIONS

PART I

HISTORY OF STATE CONSTITUTIONS

CHAPTER I

STATE CONSTITUTIONS IN RELATION TO THE FEDERAL GOVERNMENT AND THE "UNION"

In writing about or discussing American constitutional history there is a tendency to magnify unduly the importance of the federal government in comparison with the governments of the states. This tendency was natural enough in those years marked by heated discussions of states' rights, nullification, and secession, and has even its modern justification in view of the vast powers wielded by the federal government in the formulation of national and international policies. The idea of a federation is even yet so unfamiliar, that almost unconsciously a writer tends to fix his attention on what may be considered as the spectacular aspects of federal government, to the neglect of the more prosaic activities and powers of the constituent states. These, in consequence, seem to be mere provinces or administrative districts, that through some inscrutable act of Providence, have somehow managed to acquire powers which interfere with, hinder, and obstruct the nationalizing, centralizing, and unifying policies of the federal government.

THE STATES AND THE UNION [1]

Unquestionably in any discussion of the American governmental system, the federal government with its great general powers and its control over international affairs should never be slighted; yet on the other hand it should not be forgotten that, while any particular state may seem relatively insignificant, the states unitedly perform by far the largest part of governmental activities, and raise through taxation an amount much larger than that levied under the authority of congress. Furthermore, the states do not derive their powers from the federal government, as, for example, the departments of France do from their national government, but instead, both the states and the federal government derive their powers directly from the Union and in their relationship are coördinate one to the other. Because of this fact it is really impossible to understand the American constitutional system as a whole, unless one has a knowledge of the constitutions of the several states in the Union, so as to comprehend their attitude and policy towards the political problems arising in the government of the states. Moreover, the several policies of forty-eight different states towards the numerous problems of government are in many respects so diverse, and have so widely varied at different periods, that the state constitutions, which embody these variations, are in themselves full of interest, as a sort of cinematoscope of the times, and hence do not deserve the neglect which up to quite recent times

---

[1] See, Johns Hopkins Studies, Introduction to the Study of the Constitutional and Political History of the States, by J. Franklin Jameson. Series IV. Also, article by Woodrow Wilson, referred to at end of Chap. XXIII.

has been their portion. For it must be remembered that federal powers and federal problems are widely different from those that occupy the attention of the states. The really distinctive feature of the federal government by contrast with the states is that its powers are carefully enumerated and delegated, so that any power whatsoever, rightly used by any one of the three federal departments of government, must be based on an expressed or clearly implied authorization in the national constitution. By contrast all other governmental powers not thus delegated to the federal government are by constitution declared to belong "to the states respectively or to the people" excepting a few prohibitions plainly stated in the constitution itself.[1]

Thus the great mass of governmental powers in regulation of purely domestic affairs within the borders of the several states, such as the detail of local government, education, sanitation and policing, is by constitution delegated to the states themselves; and in addition some extremely important sovereign powers fall to their share. In fact the states under the constitution are so powerful in their collective capacity that the federal government by comparison seems impotent. By the terms of the national constitution the

---

[1] Readers of constitutional history are familiar with national struggles over the doctrines of implied powers and strict interpretation. The older issues of this sort are practically settled. In recent years the discussion assumes a newer aspect: the United States of America, being a sovereign state, has in its possession all possible national powers. Since the federal government has by delegation certain fundamental national powers of the Union, such as the war and treaty powers, by implication it may use, when necessity arises, any other national power that may be shown to be for the general welfare, even though in so doing, it seems to trespass on powers supposedly in the possession of the states. An opponent to this newer doctrine of implied powers would argue that particular powers only are delegated to the federal government, and that others if desired must be obtained by the consent of the coördinate partner, the states, through an amendment to the constitution.

states formulate their own fundamental law and derive their powers directly from the Union. The federal government therefore by no constitutional possibility can add to or diminish the powers of the states,[1] or deprive any one of them permanently of its equal status in the Union.[2] The Union under the constitution is itself indestructible and is composed of indestructible states,[3] but the federal government has no such status. Two thirds òf the states have the right to have a convention called for the purpose of proposing amendments to the constitution, and these when ratified by the affirmative votes of three fourths of all the states become part of the constitution. Such amendments might alter or even destroy any part or all of the federal government, substituting for it a new form of government, organized on such principles and in such manner as would seem best to the states and most likely to effect their safety and happiness.[4] Such a contingency is in no respect anticipated, and legally, as already said, the federal government and the states collectively are in theory coördinate, since each traces its powers to the national constitution and neither is authorized to interfere with the rights of the other as defined by the constitution and umpired by the

---

[1] It is understood that there are certain concurrent powers, such as that in respect to bankruptcy, in which the extent of a state's jurisdiction seems to be determined by the action of the federal government, but in fact the state's *authority* to act in the matter is derived from the constitution, not from any act of congress. The federal government cannot delegate to the states any power exclusively given to it, but in the case of concurrent powers it has the right to determine how these may be best shared so as to insure the general welfare.

[2] A rebellious state when conquered may have its affairs placed into the hands of a military governor as a sort of "receiver," but only for the purpose of reorganizing a constitutional form of government, so that the state may resume its place in the Union.

[3] Texas *vs.* White, 7 Wallace, 700 (1868).

[4] Declaration of Independence, first two paragraphs.

supreme court of the United States.   Yet if by any possibility there should arise friction or open antagonism between these coördinate parts, the states so obviously control the really important sovereign powers of the United States, that the federal government is seen to be a mere governmental agency, organized to serve the states and to assist them in expressing the national will.   In short, the states collectively could destroy at short notice the entire federal government, but this by contrast, with all of its powers, could not deprive even Nevada (our pettiest state) of any one of its constitutional rights, nor of its place in the Union.

This coördinate relationship between state and federal government is best seen when their respective laws seem to be in conflict.   If by chance a state constitution or some legislative statute in harmony with it happens to conflict with an act of congress, the national supreme court does not assume that *ipso facto* the state law is unconstitutional; nor on the other hand that the act of congress is unconstitutional.   Rather it turns to the national constitution, which is the fundamental law for both state and federal government, and determines from this whether congress or the state has exceeded its powers in legislation, and then renders its decision accordingly.   Thus the states in the performance of their legal powers, pass statutes, administer the law, supervise local government, and adjudicate cases, without interference from the federal government, which in its turn performs its duties without hindrance from the individual states, even though, as already explained, these collectively are autocratic and may wield at will the full sovereign powers of the nation.[1]

[1] The relationship indicated in the preceding paragraphs between the Union, the States, and the Federal Government, may be illustrated by the three following diagrams, explanatory of these relationships: —

The Priority of the States

From the preceding part of this chapter one might be prepared to admit that from the legal point of view at least, the study of American state constitutions ought not to be neglected. There is however another aspect of this question that should not be ignored. From the historical standpoint state constitutions have a real significance since they preceded in time the present national constitution, which in fact embodies in its most essential features a type of governmental organization already familiar to the states of the revolutionary period through their colonial governments and their first constitutions. For, by the time the federal convention met in 1787, the dominant features of American constitutionalism were fairly well

I. The constitution, or fundamental law of the United States of America was

(a) *formulated* by (1) the federal convention of 1788, coöperating with and acting in place of the continental congress; (2) the several ratifying state conventions, made up of representatives of the people, coöperating with and acting in place of the state legislatures.

and may be

(b) *amended* by the joint action of (1) congress (or, if two thirds of the states so prefer, by a national convention), and (2) the state legislatures (or, if congress so prefers, by state conventions).

II. The United States of America is a sovereign state, organized as a federation, which is made up of

(1) The federal government,
(2) The forty-eight states or commonwealths.
(These two parts are coördinate one to the other, but are both subordinate to the United States of America, or the "Union.")

established in most of the thirteen states. Fundamental law had become or was becoming differentiated from statutory law; and was formulated into a definite, written document, amended by a more complex and difficult procedure than that used for ordinary legislation; the constitutional convention had become a familiar institution and through the example of Massachusetts the principle was

III. From another standpoint the government of the United States of America may be considered as divisible into four branches or departments.

(1) The executive: consisting of (a) the president and the heads of the administration, (b) the forty-eight state governors and the heads of their administrative systems.

(2) The legislative: consisting of (a) the national congress, and (b) the states' lawmaking agencies (legislatures, constitutional conventions, the electorate when using powers of "initiative" and "referendum").

(3) The judicial: consisting of (a) the supreme court and the inferior courts of the United States, and (b) the supreme and other courts of the states.

(4) The electorate (using executive powers in the choice and recall of officials, legislative powers through the initiative and referendum, and judicial powers through jury service): consisting of (a) the electorate in national elections, and (b) the several electorates in the states.

(Note). It will be remembered that the qualifications of both the national and the state electorates are determined by the states, subject to the few regulatory provisions of the national constitution.

gaining ground that fundamental law needed for its validity a ratification by the electorate on referendum. Moreover, the three great departments of government were separated in accordance with English and colonial custom, a much more important influence than the much-discussed theory of Montesquieu ; [1] the governor's veto was coming into use ; state judiciaries had on several occasions assumed the right to declare acts of state legislatures to be unconstitutional ; [2] and formal bills of rights were regularly incorporated into the constitutions as checks on possible legislative tyranny.

The federal convention, therefore, in formulating a national constitution did not on the whole originate anything really new in government, but rather carefully culled from the customs and experiences of the states those provisions that seemed to work best in practice and united these into as logical a document as the necessity for compromise permitted, with such additions as seemed necessary for the rounding out of a national system.[3] It is incorrect, therefore, to say, as some do, that the national constitution has been to any considerable extent the model followed by the states after the formation of the Union, as they assumed statehood or revised or amended their constitutions.

[1] Spirit of Laws, Book xi. The theory of Montesquieu would really separate the three departments so that each would use those powers that properly belong to it, the harmony of the whole being secured by a carefully devised "check and balance" system. This theory finds its best exemplification in the federal government, in which system the executive powers are for the most part really in the possession of that department of government. In the states by contrast, as in the English parliamentary system, the division of powers is formal and rather nominal, since as a rule the lawmaking department has a quite complete control over administration (an executive power), and shares with the executive in the exercise of most of the few powers confided to him by constitution.

[2] See, Bondy, Separation of Powers, chap. vii.; and Haines, American Doctrine of Judicial Supremacy, especially Part II.

[3] See, Bryce, American Commonwealth, Vol. I. pp. 670–3, note to chap. iv.

For, a state when revising its constitution rarely departs to any considerable extent from its previous type of organization. Even when the first state constitutions were formed, they were in the main merely the colonial charters and governmental organizations, translated with necessary modifications into state constitutions.[1] This same statement would hold true also of the first constitutions of Connecticut (1818) and Rhode Island (1842), which in substance are modifications of the charters obtained from King Charles in the seventeenth century. So likewise the Southern Confederacy, in formulating a constitution in 1861, merely adapted the national constitution to the new order of things. A similar principle holds in respect to the constitutions of new states. These are largely determined by their former historical connection,[2] or by their territorial framework of government, or by the influence on a constitutional convention of prominent members who are familiar with the constitutions of the states of their birth.[3] Thus the real models consistently followed in making or revising constitutions have been the constitutions of existing states and territories. In the case of states created from national territory, the great model contained in the famous Ordinance of 1787 became the basis for later territorial organization and thus impressed its principles on the states of the northwest and later on the region west of the Mississippi River.[4]

[1] See, *Annals*, Vol. I. April, 1891, Article by Professor Morey on the Genesis of a Written Constitution.

[2] As, for example, Kentucky and West Virginia with Virginia, or Maine with Massachusetts.

[3] The constitution formed, for instance, in Texas, in April, 1833, was an almost verbatim reproduction for the most part, of the constitution of Tennessee. Houston, the chairman of the Committee on Constitution, had also been governor of Tennessee.

[4] The Ordinance, for example, required that the territory have three departments of government; a governor, a court, and a legislature, and

On the other hand, it might be said in behalf of the theory of the imitation of the national constitution by the states, that in so far as certain features found in the constitutions of the states under the confederation were selected for insertion in the national constitution, these, so to speak, became *standardized*, thus forming natural patterns for later imitation.

FLEXIBILITY OF STATE CONSTITUTIONS

There is, finally, another reason why state constitutions are deserving of larger study. The national constitution is a rigid document amended only with great difficulty, so that of necessity needed alterations, if made at all, must usually come through legal interpretation and judicial decision. This method of modifying fundamental law by what is virtually judicial legislation has its natural limitations, and in consequence the fundamentals of federal organization and jurisdiction remain practically the same as they were one hundred and twenty-five years ago. On the other hand, the older states have for the most part, freed themselves from difficult amending processes, and the newer states invariably prefer a simple method of amendment and revision. In consequence, the meaning and development of the national constitution is best traced through the many authoritative decisions made by the national supreme court in interpreting the constitution; but by contrast the interpretations given by state supreme courts of their respective constitutions are of far less permanent importance, since the real history of the constitutional

that the last named should be based on a "proportionate representation of the people." It also provided for religious liberty, a system of education, and the guaranties of jury trial and habeas corpus; forbade slavery, and insisted that in the formulation of any future constitution, the government should be republican in spirit and in form.

development of the states can best be traced decade by decade in the many amendments and revisions made so as to satisfy popular demands for reforms in existing systems. Thus from state constitutions far better than from the national constitution can be traced the really important stages in the march of American democracy since 1776, seeing that the states are the agencies through which the ordinary daily life of the citizens is regulated and hence they are much more closely in touch with popular demands. Through the varying decisions of the national supreme court one may study the movements of national unity, expansion, centralization, imperialism, and foreign policy; but in the state constitutions can best be studied the class struggle between the intrenched conservatism of propertied interests and the advancing radicalism of direct democracy, between the grip of the "interests" in boss-ridden states and the enthusiastic and perhaps somewhat visionary idealism of the newer democracy.   One might almost say that the romance, the poetry and even the drama of American politics are deeply embedded in the many state constitutions promulgated since the publication of Paine's Common Sense, the Declaration of Independence, and the Virginia Bill of Rights.   For in them are recorded the growth in the notion of rights, irrespective of race, sex or economic status; the rise of manhood suffrage, its extension to women and modern reactions against the principle of unrestricted voting; and the developing emphasis on morals in provisions about dueling, lotteries, divorce, polygamy and the prohibition of the manufacture and sale of liquor. One may cynically note the earlier belief that legislators were men of "wisdom and virtue," followed by a conviction expressed in most constitutions that they are likely to be corrupt and incompetent and regularly prone to bribery. In the southern constitutions of the *sixties* can be seen the joyous assertion of states' rights and a willingness to appeal to arms, and then the disgrace of recantation at the point of the bayonet, the humiliation of disfranchisement, the bitterness of political subordination to enfranchised slaves and "scalawags," followed in the *seventies* by a return of the whites to power, as shown by the elimination of obnoxious provisions from the reconstruction constitutions. Such and similar changes may be traced in the state constitutions, which unquestionably will in later years be considered as exponents of the conditions and demands of their times, and as among our most valued records of social, political, and constitutional history.

CHAPTER II

ADMISSION OF STATES INTO THE UNION

As is well known, the legal birthday of the United States of America is July fourth, 1776, since on that date delegates of the colonies in the continental congress voted a Declaration of Independence. Yet the colonies had previously by their actions virtually asserted their independence from England, and some had even taken formal action; the state of Rhode Island, for instance, celebrates May fourth as its day of independence. When the colonies asserted their freedom from English control, they became for all domestic purposes free and independent states; although, as the mother country did not admit their right to freedom, the revolutionary war had to be fought and a treaty of peace made before their independence was fully acknowledged internationally.

As new and independent states, each had the right to readjust its form of government as it might deem best, so that the states one by one reorganized the framework of their governments and with later experience made other readjustments so as to meet newer emergencies and changing conditions. This period of self-government and adaptation may loosely be considered as ending with the eighteenth century, by which time the inefficient confederacy of the earlier years had yielded place to a vigorous and effective federation. Under the federation the states were no longer sovereign and independent, though this disputed point was not finally settled until the civil war. Yet, subject to the provisions of the new national constitution, each state had the right to formulate its own local constitution, and to make such modifications in it as from time to time might seem necessary. Changes of some sort became inevitable with the passing of years, so that the methods of procedure developed, and the extent of changes made, naturally form a constitutional study of real importance. Such changes, if few or comparatively insignificant, came to be effected by the process of amendment; if numerous and fundamental, they were made by the process of revision. Amendments as a rule are at present effected by legislatures, revisions by constitutional conventions, ratified in each case with rare exceptions by a popular vote on referendum. Occasionally, legislatures have assumed the right to make or revise constitutions, but this is not in accord with present custom, and should be justified, if at all, on the score of urgent necessity. In a study of state constitutions, therefore, one should keep in mind that constitutions are made, *de novo*, amended and revised; and that legislatures, conventions and electorates are the agencies through which such lawmaking is performed. In Chapter XI attention will be called to commissions as agencies occasionally used for the formulation of amendments or revisions.

If the United States consisted merely of the original thirteen states of the confederation, the study of American state constitutions would be simple and brief. There are at present, however, forty-eight states and, as all know, the newer thirty-five states far exceed the original thirteen in area, wealth, population and importance. Under such conditions it may be well to explain the process whereby so many additions have been made to the list of states in the Union.

STATES ADDED TO THE UNION

At the time of the formation of the national government in 1788 eleven states only composed the United States of America. Within two years the two remaining states[1] of the old confederation ratified the new constitution and were admitted into the Union by formal vote. The thirty-five additions made since that time may be divided loosely into two classes: (1) those made by the partition of existing states, including one by annexation;[2] and (2) the thirty states carved out of the national domain. For completeness' sake, the process whereby these acquired their first constitutions and became states will now briefly be explained.

I. (1) *Vermont*, the first state admitted outside of the original thirteen, was claimed as part of their territory by Massachusetts, New Hampshire, and especially New York. These claims were denied by the settlers of that region who, when the Revolution began, sent delegates to a convention, which January, 1777, declared Vermont to be a free and independent state. The convention after appointing a committee to draft a constitution, then summoned a second convention to pass upon the draft prepared by this committee. This second convention met July second, 1777, and later adopted and put into effect the constitution, without referendum, although there was an adjournment of the convention for five months (July–December) so as to allow the citizens an opportunity to express opinions on the proposed constitution. Under this constitution Vermont fought for its independence, came to terms with its covetous neighbors, ratified the federal constitution

---

[1] North Carolina, Nov. 21, 1789; Rhode Island, May 29, 1790.
[2] Kentucky, Vermont, Maine, Texas, West Virginia.

January tenth, 1791, and some two months later was admitted by congress as the fourteenth state of the Union.

(2) The second request for admission came from the the western frontier counties of Virginia, now known as *Kentucky*. The national constitution provides,[1] that "no new state shall be formed or erected within the jurisdiction of any other state, nor any state be formed by the junction of two or more states or parts of states, without the consent of the legislatures of the states concerned, as well as of the congress." Kentucky therefore in its desire to become a separate state had to secure the consent of Virginia as well as that of congress. After many preliminaries a Kentucky convention met, July twenty-sixth, 1790, which voted a separation in accordance with terms set by Virginia, and then summoned a constitutional convention. Meanwhile in February, 1791, the congress of the United States passed an act giving consent to the formation of the new state. The convention met, April, 1792, prepared a constitution and without referendum ordered it into effect, June first, 1792, on which date the new state became a member of the Union.

(3) In the same manner, at the desire of *Maine*, the legislature of Massachusetts in 1819 gave consent to the formation of the district of Maine into a separate state. A convention was then called in that district, and the constitution thus prepared was later approved at the polls. A petition was then presented to congress, accompanied by a copy of the constitution, asking that Maine be admitted as a state. This petition was granted and a new state thus added to the Union.

(4) The case of *Texas* differs from the preceding in that its territory was not under the American flag but originally

[1] Article IV., Section 3.

formed a part of Mexico. In 1835 Texas declared its independence of Mexico and virtually secured it in March of the following year by the battle of San Jacinto. As an independent state under its own flag it found itself burdened with debt in an attempt to maintain a free existence on scanty resources. It, therefore, opened up negotiations with the United States and by agreement a joint resolution for annexation was passed, first by the congress [1] and then by the legislature of Texas.[2] Under the provisions of an enabling act Texas was authorized to call a convention, which framed a constitution, August, 1845. This was ratified at the polls in October, and some two months later Texas was formally received as a state into the Union.

(5) The case of *West Virginia* was in form like that of Kentucky or Maine. When Virginia seceded from the Union in 1861, the people of the western mountainous part of the state, who were opposed to slavery, refused to join in the movement and organized at Wheeling a loyal government which claimed to be the legal government of Virginia. The legislature of this government then submitted to the voters a referendum asking whether there should be organized a new state to be composed of the forty western counties. The vote being strongly affirmative, a convention was summoned which prepared and submitted a constitution. This was ratified April third, 1862. The legislature then in May gave consent to the formation of the new state and congress was petitioned to allow its admission. This consent was given, December thirty-first, on condition that a change be made in the slavery clause of the proposed constitution. This change was approved by the convention, February twelfth, and by the voters, March twenty-sixth, and on notification of this

[1] Signed by the President, March 1, 1845.   [2] July 4, 1845.

the President of the United States, June nineteenth, proclaimed the admission of West Virginia into the Union.

STATES FORMED FROM THE NATIONAL DOMAIN

II. The remaining thirty states were all formed from the national domain, from lands either ceded by the original states to the Union, or obtained by it from other nations through treaty, war, or purchase. Over these lands congress had jurisdiction and under the constitution might in its discretion organize from time to time suitable portions into republican forms of government,[1] and admit them as states into the Union. This provision has been of profound significance in our constitutional history, since congress following the precedent of the Ordinance of 1787 has definitely insisted on democratic republican forms of government, so that these thirty states were kept at the start from tendencies towards an undue conservatism.[2]

The general practice has been, first, to encourage settlement by generous homestead laws and then to organize portions into territories, each having a form of government not unlike that of a state, except that an act of congress takes the place of a constitution. When a territory is considered by congress to be sufficiently populous, and in other respects also worthy of statehood, an enabling act is passed which provides for the calling of a constitutional convention, sets forth the usual conditions with which the convention must comply,[3] and often dictates special

---

[1] Article IV, Sections 3 and 4. For an explanation of the steps leading up to the Ordinance of 1787, see, Evolution of the American System of Forming and Admitting New States into the Union, by George H. Alden, *Annals*, Vol. XVIII. 3, November, 1901.

[2] The changes demanded by congress in the constitution of New Mexico illustrate this, see, p. 110.

[3] Such as acceptance of boundaries, republican form of government, etc.

conditions by requiring the insertion into the constitution of certain provisions in the form of an "irrevocable compact" between congress and the would-be state.[1] When the constitution made by the convention has been ratified by the voters of the territory, congress may then, if all conditions have been complied with, pass an act admitting the

---

[1] One of the most famous of these is that of Utah, which reads as follows:

ARTICLE III

ORDINANCE

The following ordinance shall be irrevocable without the consent of the United States and the people of this State:

First. Perfect toleration of religious sentiment is guaranteed. No inhabitant of this State shall ever be molested in person or property on account of his or her mode of religious worship; but polygamous or plural marriages are forever prohibited.

Second. The people inhabiting this State do affirm and declare that they forever disclaim all right and title to the unappropriated public lands lying within the boundaries hereof, and to all lands lying within said limits owned or held by any Indian or Indian tribes, and that until the title thereto shall have been extinguished by the United States the same shall be and remain subject to the disposition of the United States, and said Indian lands shall remain under the absolute jurisdiction and control of the Congress of the United States. The lands belonging to citizens of the United States residing without this State shall never be taxed at a higher rate than the lands belonging to residents of this State; nor shall taxes be imposed by this State on lands or property herein belonging to or which may hereafter be purchased by the United States or reserved for its use; but nothing in this ordinance shall preclude this State from taxing, as other lands are taxed, any lands owned or held by any Indian who has severed his tribal relations and has obtained from the United States or from any person, by patent or other grant, a title thereto, save and except such lands as have been or may be granted to any Indian or Indians under any act of Congress containing a provision exempting the land thus granted from taxation, which last-mentioned lands shall be exempt from taxation so long, and to such extent, as is or may be provided in the act of Congress granting the same.

Third. All debts and liabilities of the Territory of Utah, incurred by authority of the legislative assembly thereof, are hereby assumed and shall be paid by this State.

Fourth. The legislature shall make laws for the establishment and maintenance of a system of public schools, which shall be open to all the children of the State and be free from sectarian control.

territory as a state in the Union; or, in case of prospective adjournment before final action in the territory has been taken, it may authorize the president to proclaim the admission of the state, when he is satisfied that all requirements have been fully met.

Some of the territories, unwilling to await the slower action of congress, have endeavored to hasten the process by preparing constitutions on their own responsibility and demanding from congress as their right, recognition as states.[1] Such rights in general have been based on the wording of the Ordinance of 1787, or the constitution itself, or on some treaty provision in the case of lands ceded by France, Spain and Mexico. Whatever basis in right any particular territory might have had, congress admittedly has full discretionary powers and legally need admit no territory as a state except when and how it wills. In the case of some of these territories congress has good-naturedly admitted them on request, when accompanied by a proper constitution, but in other cases conflicting interests or reasons of policy dictated a refusal and compelled delay.[2]

FIVE PERIODS OF DEVELOPMENT

In concluding these explanations preliminary to the study of the growth of state constitutions from 1776, it may be said that there are five natural periods of constitutional development, each of which will now briefly be described and then elaborated more in detail in later chapters.

(1) In the first or revolutionary period, ending with the election of Jefferson in 1800, the thirteen colonies declared

---

[1] For example: Tennessee, Arkansas, Michigan, Florida, Iowa, Wisconsin, California, Oregon, Kansas, Nevada, Nebraska, Colorado.

[2] Typical illustrations of the details of such actions may be found summarized in Jameson's Constitutional Conventions, pp. 175–208.

their independence, began to practice the art of government unhampered by an English colonial policy, sought to develop a spirit of coöperation in war and diplomacy, and experimented in the making of state and national constitutions. To the original states three others were added in accordance with the provisions of the national constitution. (2) The period from 1801 to 1830 was in general characterized by a slow growth in nationality. The Louisiana Purchase from France and the Florida accessions from Spain permitted an expansion of population into national territory as against state growth; the war of 1812 helped to fix the place of the nation among other nations, though at a heavy cost; the freedom of economic intercourse irrespective of state lines, and the rapid expansion of manufactures in the north and of the production of cotton in the south, helped to smooth out petty differences by a general prosperity; and the decisions of the supreme court under John Marshall were steadily recording the growth of a national unity soon to be eloquently voiced by Daniel Webster in his famous debate with Hayne. During this period the last of the eastern states, Maine, and seven others west and south were added to the Union.

(3) The third period, from 1831 to 1860, was one of much constitutional turmoil. The wave of Jacksonian democracy had reached its height; the glorification of American institutions had begun, as illustrated by De Tocqueville's Democracy in America[1]; and the war with Mexico and the Oregon controversy with England had resulted in the rounding out of the national domains on the Gulf and on the Pacific. On the other hand sectional discord and racial dissension had become burning questions, through slavery and an influx of immigration largely made up of

[1] Issued 1835. See, also, Jacksonian Democracy, by William MacDonald.

those "alien to our national institutions." During this period ten new states south and west were admitted to the Union after much controversy and compromise. (4) The fourth period, from 1861 to 1885, the beginning of Cleveland's administration, is dominated by the constitutional changes involved in the secession and reconstruction of eleven southern states. West Virginia and three states of the middle west were added to the Union, and Alaska acquired by purchase.

(5) The last period, from 1886 to 1914, is distinguished by a national expansion in area and prestige. The national domains were broadened by the acquisition of possessions in the West Indies (Porto Rico), the Pacific (Hawaii and the Philippines), and of rights over the Panama Canal Zone. Within the Union may be noted several well-marked features : (a) Ten new states have been added to the Union, created from the agricultural and mining lands of the west, and completing the statehood of all territorial lands held by the United States before 1860. (b) The rapid economic expansion of the United States since the civil war finds its expression in the state constitutions in new and enlarged articles in regulation of corporations, trusts, and industrial conditions. (c) The question of suffrage becomes prominent, finding its chief expression in the suppression of the negro vote in the south, the extension of women's suffrage in the west, and in the limitation of suffrage through systems of registration and educational qualifications. (d) A wave of radicalism voicing itself in the *nineties* through the populistic movement and the free silver agitation, has in this century taken the form of a denunciation of governmental incompetence, and a demand for administrative and legislative reorganization, through the introduction of a more direct participation of

the electorates in government, through such devices as the initiative, the referendum and the recall. At the close of this period problems of state government are definitely to the front, and indications point to a more constructive attitude towards state constitutions.

The constitutional and governmental developments and changes of each of these periods will now be taken up in order.

CHAPTER III

THE FIRST STATE CONSTITUTIONS

In this period, from 1776 to 1800, the original colonies became independent states, organized their governments, experimented with a weak national confederation, and finally, somewhat unwillingly, united into a federal Union. Excellent accounts already exist showing how the constitutions of the several states[1] and of the federal government came into existence. In general it may be said that these in their provisions shunned radical experiments and embodied into brief articles the familiar features of English and colonial experience. The theater of events was from a world standpoint relatively insignificant, since those transactions took place in a then remote corner of the earth, in a backwoods civilization, among a population numbering scarcely three millions of people. Yet these experimentations in the application of the principles of democracy under written constitutions and a federation have become world-wide in their influence and have made permanent and fundamental contributions to the politics and political theory of civilization.

THE EARLY CONSTITUTIONS

In the first place it may be noted that the written constitution had become accepted as the proper means through

[1] Note especially articles in *Annals* by William C. Morey, First State Constitutions, Vol. IV. 2. September, 1893; and by William C. Webster, State Constitutions of the American Revolution, Vol. IX. 3. May, 1897. Also, Dodd's Revision and Amendment of State Constitutions, chap. i.

which a fundamental law should be formulated. The confederation of 1776 was under an unwritten constitution up to 1781, when the last state ratified the written constitution submitted in 1777, although the governmental organization actually employed by the confederation was in fact that set forth in the proposed constitution. Almost from the beginning written constitutions were adopted by all the states, except Connecticut and Rhode Island; these used their written charters as constitutions, substituting the authority of the people for the authority of the king, and retaining them as fundamental law until formal constitutions were adopted in conventions held in the years 1818 and 1842 respectively.

In the formulation of the several state constitutions of this period it may be noted that there was a sort of uniformity in procedure, though wide variations in detail. During the interim between colonial government and independent statehood, there was formed whenever necessary in any colony, a unicameral congress or revolutionary convention, acting through executive committees authorized to remain in session after the adjournment of the congresses or conventions. As the necessity for more stable forms of government became evident, and the possibility of independence more immediate, the continental congress on a request for advice from certain colonies, suggested in June, 1775, again in November of the same year, and finally on May fifteenth, 1776, that each colony summon a body of representatives to form a more permanent government. Acting on this advice the several colonies proceeded to organize frameworks of government, each using its discretion as to the methods employed. The colonies had few precedents by which to guide themselves outside of their own revolutionary conventions, or the English conventions of 1660 and 1689, and the Lockean notion of a social compact made by an assembly of the people. Yet there was an urgent necessity for some immediate action, coupled with the thought that nothing really permanent needed to be formulated, since reconciliation with England was a likely possibility. The earlier action, therefore, taken by the colonies was rather temporary in nature and in most cases was soon followed by a more carefully prepared organization, when independence seemed assured and experience taught the necessity of a thoughtfully prepared framework of government, based on republican principles. For this reason it may be well to explain briefly the methods adopted in each of the states during this revolutionary period, since these became the basis from which developed the constitutional system of the nineteenth century.

(1) *Massachusetts*, 1775–6, summoned delegates from the towns and reorganized its government substantially in accord with the provisions of its former charter. This was considered to be a provisional arrangement and, after some delay the general assembly sat as a convention, 1777–8, and prepared a constitution, which was referred to the town-meetings but rejected by a heavy majority. In the following year the voters on referendum demanded a constitutional convention, to be made up of delegates chosen for that purpose only. This convention met, September first, 1779, and on the following March second, recommended to the voters a bill of rights and a constitution. These were approved at the polls by more than a two-thirds vote and the convention, reassembling in June, announced the result and set a date when the new constitution should go into effect. By constitution a referendum was required in 1795 on the calling of another convention. The convention, however, was not demanded until 1820.

(2) In *New Hampshire* the provincial congress in November, 1775, provided for the election of a convention which met December twenty-first and by January fifth, 1776, had framed a brief constitution. This was at once put into effect without referendum, the convention continuing to serve as a legislature. In 1778 a special convention was elected, which prepared a constitution and submitted it to the voters in the town-meetings of 1779, who promptly rejected it because of its inadequate provisions. A new convention was chosen which met June, 1781, and after two failures succeeded in submitting a constitution which met with approval and went into operation, June second, 1784. Another convention summoned in 1791 revised this constitution, and the revision meeting with approval at the polls was declared to be in operation, September fifth, 1792, by the convention, which reassembled for that purpose. This constitution proved so satisfactory that no further change was made in it for the next fifty-eight years.

(3) In *South Carolina* the revolutionary convention itself framed and promulgated a constitution, March, 1776, without a referendum or the use of a specially elected convention. This proving unsatisfactory, the legislature of 1777 prepared a new constitution, which was printed and action deferred until the following year when it was put into effect without referendum, being passed as an act of the assembly. Finally the assembly in 1790 on its own authority summoned a constitutional convention, which prepared a constitution and put it into effect June third, 1790, without the use of a referendum; this remained as the fundamental law of the state down to the secession movement of 1861.

(4) *Delaware* through its assembly summoned a constitutional convention, which on election met, August twenty-seventh, 1776, and adopted a constitution, September

twenty-first, which went into effect without referendum. The amending clause of this constitution was so stringent that no changes could be made; the assembly therefore, voicing a popular demand, on its own authority and against the express provisions of the constitution, provided in 1791 for the election of a constitutional convention. This body met in June, 1792, and prepared a constitution which went into effect without referendum and lasted without further revision for forty years.

(5) In *Virginia* the revolutionary convention elected April, 1776, for general purposes, met on May sixth as a constitutional convention and adopted, June twenty-ninth, a constitution without referendum. This remained as the constitution of the state for over fifty years.

(6) In *New Jersey* a new revolutionary congress was elected, May fourth, 1776. In addition to its general duties this body also formulated a constitution for the state, which, July second, without referendum became the fundamental law, lasting without revision for nearly seventy years.

(7) In *Pennsylvania* a revolutionary convention was not organized until July, 1776. Among other duties it prepared a constitution which without referendum was put into effect, September twenty-eighth of the same year. This constitution provided that every seventh year a council of censors[1] should be elected, which in addition to other tasks should, if deemed advisable by a two-thirds vote, summon a convention to amend the constitution. This council, when chosen in 1783, failing to agree adjourned without action, September twenty-fifth, 1784. In March, 1789, the general assembly requested the voters to express their desire at the next general election for or against the calling of a constitutional convention. The vote being satisfactory, the

[1] See, Haines, Judicial Supremacy, chap. vi.

assembly, disregarding the provisions of the constitution, summoned a convention for November, 1789, which completed a constitution by February twenty-sixth, 1790, and, after an adjournment so as to secure public opinion, but without referendum, again met August ninth, and finally proclaimed the new constitution, September second, 1790. This document endured as the fundamental law for nearly fifty years.

(8) In *Maryland* the revolutionary congress resolved July third, 1776, to summon a convention. This body when organized, August twelfth, exercised general powers and in addition made a constitution, which was adopted, November eighth, and went into effect without referendum, lasting for seventy-five years without revision.

(9) In *North Carolina* the revolutionary convention through its council of safety advised the election of a congress. This body met November twelfth, exercising general powers as well as preparing a constitution, which was completed December eighteenth. This went into effect without referendum, lasting without revision for nearly sixty years.

(10) In *Georgia* the revolutionary congress reorganized itself temporarily, early in April, 1776, and in July ordered an election for delegates to a convention. This met in October, at once assumed general powers and began the preparation of a constitution. This was completed and ratified, February fifth, 1777, but without referendum. In 1788 the legislature nominated and appointed the members of a convention (or commission) summoned to meet November fourth, who adopted a constitution on the twenty-fourth, but referred it for approval to a convention of elected delegates, who met January fourth, 1789. This body recommended certain changes so that the whole matter was

referred to a third convention, which met May fourth, made selections from the recommendations submitted to it, and passed these two days later as the constitution of the state without referendum. In 1795 another convention met and May sixteenth, passed certain amendments to the constitution which went into effect without referendum. Again in 1798 a constitutional convention was called which after a short session passed a revised constitution, May thirtieth, which was put into effect without referendum and lasted without further revision for almost forty years.

(11) In *New York* the revolutionary congress advised the election of a convention, which on election met July ninth, 1776. This body was too busily engaged in the exercise of its general powers to spend much time in the preparation of a constitution, but March twelfth, 1777, a preliminary draft was presented and discussed until April twentieth, when a constitution was adopted but without referendum. No further change was made in it until 1801.

(12) *Vermont*, which was practically a fourteenth colony in the Revolution, proclaimed itself an independent state in 1777. Its revolutionary convention in June of the same year appointed a committee (or commission) to draft a constitution and summoned a constitutional convention to meet July second, which passed on the recommendations of the committee. The convention adjourned July eighth, having adopted and put the constitution into operation, but without a formal referendum. This constitution in imitation of that of Pennsylvania,[1] provided that an elected council of censors be summoned every seven years, authorized among other duties to recommend amendments, if such seemed necessary, to a convention which it was

[1] For the relationship between the Vermont and Pennsylvania constitutions see, Thorpe's Constitutions, Vol. VI. pp. 3778–80.

empowered to call. The council met in 1785-6, and again in 1792,[1] in each case summoning a convention to pass on proposed amendments. The action of these conventions was favorable, so that Vermont had its constitution revised in 1786 and again in 1793. The council of the next period (1799) summoned no convention, and in fact the constitution of 1793 remained unchanged for the next thirty-five years.[2]

(13) *Kentucky* from 1784 to 1790 was busily engaged in seeking by negotiation to separate itself from Virginia and to be admitted as a state. An amicable arrangement was finally made with Virginia, July twenty-sixth, 1790, by a Kentucky convention called to consider the matter, and this same convention provided for the election of delegates to a constitutional convention summoned for April, 1792. This body completed its work and arranged that the constitution go into effect June first, 1792, without referendum, since the national congress had already agreed that Kentucky be admitted as a state on that day. In accordance with Article XI of this constitution, the citizens having voted that a convention be called, a convention was held in 1799 which revised the constitution and promulgated the revision without referendum.

(14) The territory later known as *Tennessee* was originally part of North Carolina. The eastern part, even as early as 1772 under the name of Watauga had adopted a sort of constitution and attempted to free itself from its mother colony. Later, in 1784-5, as the "state of Franklin" (Frankland), it again adopted a constitution.[3] North Carolina in 1790 ceded her claims to the nation and the entire ceded district including "Cumberland" was organized

---

[1] Vermont was admitted as a state in the Union in 1791.
[2] See, Meader's The Council of Censors.
[3] Ramsay's History of Tennessee, chaps. ii. and iv.

into a territory. The inhabitants weary of waiting for statehood took matters into their own hands and through their territorial assembly summoned a constitutional convention. This body met January eleventh, 1796, completed the constitution February sixth, 1796, without referendum, and requested admission to the Union. Congress after some hesitation passed the act required and Tennessee became a state June first, 1796. No .further revision was made in this constitution for nearly forty years.

These fourteen states with the two charter states of *Connecticut* and *Rhode Island* make up the number within the Union at the close of the eighteenth century. It may be noted that eight of these were using as fundamental law constitutions and charters made before 1780 and that the other eight were all made or revised after the formation of the Union in 1789. In general it may be said that there was not much difference between the two sets of fundamental law, though in the latter set may be observed a steady trend in the direction of more democratic control of the machinery of governmental systems. These constitutions as a whole will now be considered and their general provisions summarized.

Chief Provisions of These Constitutions

It is worth noting that five[1] of the constitutions contained no express provisions providing for their amendment. This of course did not bar changes, since it was assumed that the people had the inherent right to change their form of government through their elected representatives in

---

[1] New-York, Virginia, North Carolina, Pennsylvania (1790), New Jersey. Also the early constitutions of New Hampshire (1776), and South Carolina (1776). New Jersey, however, assumed the right of the assembly to change the constitution, by expressly forbidding the alteration of certain sections (Section XXIII).

legislature or convention. This right was apparently superior even to set methods of change contained in the constitutions, for both Delaware and Pennsylvania (in 1789) calmly disregarded the methods of change laid down in their constitutions when these proved unworkable. The modern distinction between amending and revising was not clearly made in the eighteenth century,[1] but Delaware and South Carolina had each a special procedure for amendments and another for conventions.

In two states[2] changes in the constitution were expressly authorized through the assembly only, though two superseded constitutions had had the same method.[3] The constitutions of Delaware and South Carolina provided for amendment indifferently either through assembly or convention but the constitutions of Kentucky, Tennessee, Massachusetts and New Hampshire through convention only, and Vermont through the joint action of censors and convention. So as to insure the possibility of amendment in case an assembly should prove to be unwilling to make changes, a definite period was set in several constitutions, such as the seven-year period of New Hampshire and the seven-year censorial councils of Pennsylvania and Vermont.[4] Delaware allowed the question to be raised at any general election. On the other hand three states authorized their assemblies to call a convention at discretion[5] and three[6] others at discretion to refer the question

[1] That amendments arise in the legislature and revisions be made by a convention.
[2] Georgia and Maryland.
[3] Delaware (1776), South Carolina (1778).
[4] Kentucky in its constitution of 1792 ordered a referendum in 1799 on the calling of a convention, and Massachusetts in its constitution of 1780 ordered a similar referendum for 1795.
[5] Maryland, South Carolina and Georgia.
[6] Delaware, Tennessee and Kentucky.

to the voters for decision. The referendum however on
amendments or revisions was not employed except in New
Hampshire and Massachusetts. An approximation to it
was found in those states where a convention, after completing its work, adjourned for several months so as to
secure an informal public opinion before final ratification.[1]

As a guaranty against too hasty changes, the passing of
amendments required in some cases special procedure:
the action of two assemblies was required by four states;[2]
or a larger fraction than a majority was required, preferably
two-thirds.[3] Massachusetts and Delaware sought to secure
the representative character of their conventions by providing for their composition; the former using the house
as the basis and the latter, the legislature.

In further summarizing these several methods of forming,
adopting and amending constitutions, it may be said that
in a time of revolution the easiest and quickest way is preferable and safeguards develop later through experience and
reflection. Hence in the exigency of the first few years
it is not strange that the revolutionary convention or a
hastily summoned legislature should exercise arbitrary
powers and prepare and promulgate constitutions on their
own authority. At a later stage the assembly on its own
authority may summon a convention for the one purpose

---

[1] E.g., in Pennsylvania 1790, South Carolina 1777.

[2] Delaware, Maryland, South Carolina, Georgia. In Delaware the
governor had to concur with the action of the first assembly.

[3] A two-thirds popular vote was required by Massachusetts and New
Hampshire in voting on amendments. South Carolina and Georgia required
a two-thirds vote from each house in submitting amendments; Delaware
required a two-thirds in the first and three-fourths in the second assembly;
the censors in Pennsylvania and Vermont summoned conventions by a two-
thirds vote. In taking a popular vote as to whether a convention should
be called, Tennessee demanded a majority of those voting for representatives, and Delaware and Kentucky a majority of those citizens qualified to
vote for representatives.

of preparing a constitution, or voters at the polls may express their desire that a convention be called, or an existing constitution may specify provisions for amendments and conventions under certain contingencies and special procedure. The change from a convention with autocratic powers to a convention bound by law to refer its work to the voters is seen in the procedure of New Hampshire and Massachusetts.[1] Among variations in methods of amending should be emphasized the censorial councils of Pennsylvania and Vermont,[2] and the appointed conventions (or commissions) authorized to prepare constitutions for submission to a following elected convention, as mentioned on pages 29, 30.

So far as other provisions of the fourteen constitutions are concerned it is unnecessary at this day to rehearse ·them in detail. In the constitutions by the end of the eighteenth century may be found the preamble, the ratifying clause, the schedule made up of provisions for the period of transition, and a formal bill or declaration of rights, rights both "natural" and customary. Not all of the earliest constitutions contained bills of rights, but the example set by such states as Virginia, Pennsylvania, and Massachusetts determined the trend for future constitutions. The provisions of these famous bills may be traced from *Magna Carta*, the English Declarations of the seventeenth century,

---

[1] When a convention promulgates a constitution on its own authority, it assumes that it has by delegation the sovereign powers of the people and hence is for the time being itself the sovereign, voicing the people's will. Under the Massachusetts theory, however, the convention is a body appointed for one purpose only, works under instructions of constitution or legislature, and must submit the results of its deliberations to the electorate for approval or rejection.

[2] These councils had censorial duties as well as the discretionary power of submitting amendments. Pennsylvania dropped its council from the constitution of 1790 and Vermont in 1870.

and the colonial Bills of Rights in 1765 and 1774, as well as the Declaration of Independence. Although the earliest constitutions did not for the most part formally provide for the separation of powers, yet the states emphasized the virtual independence of the judiciary, as the governmental agency through which the rights of men and of citizens were to be safeguarded.

It must be admitted, however, that the principle of religious freedom was not fully established in the constitutions, for practically all of them discriminated in favor of Christians or Protestants, and several demanded the acceptance of doctrinal beliefs for officeholding and voting. Thus in Pennsylvania the constitution of 1776 required each member of the assembly to subscribe to the following declaration:

"I do believe in one God, the creator and governor of the universe, the rewarder of the good and the punisher of the wicked. And I do acknowledge the scriptures of the Old and New Testament to be given by divine inspiration."

Similarly, the constitution of South Carolina, 1778, states:

"The qualification of electors shall be, that every free white man, and no other person, who acknowledges the being of a God and believes in a future state of rewards and punishments . . . shall be deemed a person qualified to vote."[1]

The governor, who had in general been the representative of the king in the colonies, was deprived of most of his former powers, made elective in eight states, and was appointed by the legislature in the remaining six.   Seven states granted a one-year term only, three allowed three years, three had a two-year term and one (Kentucky) gave four years.   The

---

[1] For a more complete statement see, Webster's article in *Annals*, May, 1897, pp. 87–9.

council of the colonial governor had split into two bodies, an executive council and an upper legislative house.   In the earlier eleven constitutions the executive council appeared in all but two of them (New York, New Jersey) ; its members were either elected by popular vote or by the legislature. But by the end of the century four states [1] had dropped the provision from their revised constitutions, and only one of the three new states (Vermont) had adopted it. As neither Connecticut nor Rhode Island had councils of that nature, six states only [2] had a governor's council at the beginning of the nineteenth century. The governor's veto was permitted in one state only (Massachusetts) in the earlier constitutions,[3] but by the end of the century four other states had adopted the governor's veto [4] and Vermont had granted the power to governor and council.

In the colonies the legislature had been bicameral except in Georgia and Pennsylvania. These in their first constitutions continued their unicameral organizations but in their later constitutions of 1789, 1790 respectively, changed to the bicameral system.[5] Vermont, however, entered the Union with a single chambered legislature retaining it up to the year 1836. The colonial governor's council in becoming a senate became elective, and its members were chosen either from existing or artificial districts, representing

[1] Delaware, Pennsylvania, South Carolina, Georgia.

[2] Massachusetts, New Hampshire, Vermont, Maryland, Virginia, North Carolina. The constitution of Maine (1820) provided for a governor's council. On the other hand Vermont in 1836 substituted a senate for its council; Maryland in 1837 and Virginia in 1850 dropped their councils; in 1868 the council in North Carolina was made to consist of members *ex officio*, instead of members elected by the legislature.

[3] In New York the governor and a special *ex officio* council had veto powers over legislation.

[4] New Hampshire, Georgia, Kentucky, Pennsylvania.

[5] See, Johns Hopkins Studies, Rise and Development of the Bicameral System in America, by T. F. Moran, Series XIII.

either population, or the district as such. The membership of the senate, which in general was supposed to represent propertied interests, varied from nine in Delaware
to forty in Massachusetts. Senators were elected annually
in seven of the states including the "Assistants" of Connecticut and Rhode Island. Five states had a four-year
term and three states respectively had terms of two, three
and five years. Six of the states elected their senators on
the class or rotation system. Only one state (Maryland) [1]
used an indirect form of election, all the others elected
senators by direct vote. The lower house was continued
practically as it had been under colonial organization. It
aimed to represent the people as such and hence membership was roughly apportioned among the districts according
to the number of citizens, or tax-paying inhabitants, who
in general formed the electorates in their several states.
Elections were annual except in South Carolina and Tennessee where biennial elections were held.

The judicial system also in general remained unchanged,
except that judges formerly named by the Crown were
either chosen by the legislature or by the governor and
council. Judges of the higher courts were elected by the
legislatures in six states,[2] appointed by the governor either
with or without the aid of council or senate in six states,[3]
in New York appointed by a committee of four senators, and in Georgia elected by the voters for a three-year
term.

[1] In the assembly of Maryland the deputies were to be "the most wise,
sensible and discreet" of the people, and the senators to be "men of the
most wisdom, experience and virtue."

[2] New Jersey, Virginia, North Carolina, South Carolina, Tennessee,
Vermont.

[3] By the governor, Pennsylvania, Delaware; by the governor and
senate, Kentucky; by governor and council, New Hampshire, Massachusetts, Maryland.

The constitutions themselves were terse and contained few details. The earliest, being temporary, were short, but they lengthened at each revision. By the end of the century the shortest constitution (New Jersey) contained about twenty-five hundred words, and the longest (Massachusetts) about twelve thousand.

As for the charters of Connecticut (1662) and Rhode Island (1663), they were substantially identical [1] in phraseology and in their form of government. Each provided for an elected governor, deputy-governor, and body of assistants, forming an upper house of a general assembly; the lower house was made up of delegates from the several towns, varying in number with population. The assembly had general powers of oversight and administration under the charter and annually elected the judges of the courts, itself also having certain judicial functions. The usual rights of Englishmen were guarantied and in Rhode Island religious liberty also. Elections were annual, and as in the other states a property or taxpaying qualification was necessary for the privilege of voting. There was of course no provision for the amending of the charters, so that when these colonies in 1776 became states the general assemblies were the repositories of the powers of their respective states and legally autocratic.

[1] *Verbis mutatis mutandis.*

CHAPTER IV

GROWTH OF STATE CONSTITUTIONS FOR THIRTY YEARS

In the second period, from 1801–30, the trend of constitutional development can best be indicated by noting (1) the changes made in the sixteen older constitutions, and (2) by summarizing the chief provisions of the constitutions of eight new states; Maine in the east, Missouri, the first of the trans-Mississippi states, three [1] from the northwest territory and three in the south. [2]

Changes in the Older Constitutions

Of the older states six only made use of the convention, the remaining ten either made no alterations in their constitutions or were satisfied with such changes as could be accomplished by the ordinary processes of amendment. The amendments for the most part were of small consequence but the changes in three states deserve mention. Maryland abolished the property qualification for suffrage and for officeholding and reorganized its judicial system; Georgia also reorganized its judicial system and provided that the governor be elected by the voters instead of by the assembly, and South Carolina in 1808 rearranged its representation in the house, trying the experiment of basing one half the representation on white population and the other half on the proportion of "taxes raised by the

[1] Ohio 1802, Indiana 1816, Illinois 1818.
[2] Louisiana 1812, Mississippi 1817, Alabama 1819.

legislature of the state." The population basis for representation was not adopted until 1868.

The significant changes or attempts at change made by the six states making use of the convention, will now be specified briefly:

(1) The *New York* constitution of 1777 had made no provision for its amendment, but in 1801 the state legislature under its general powers summoned an elected convention to consider certain specified parts of the constitution. The body met October thirteenth and adjourned two weeks later, having confined itself strictly to the business set for it by the legislature. Its chief task was to reorganize and reapportion the membership of the legislature, and it promulgated its five amendments without referendum. In 1821 a convention was again summoned which met August twenty-eighth, and after revising the entire constitution adjourned November tenth. In February the revised constitution was submitted to the voters on referendum and adopted. The chief changes involved slight alterations in the apportionment of membership in the legislature, whose per diem incidentally was fixed at three dollars; the governor was given the veto power, and he with the senate was authorized to appoint judges. His term was made two instead of three years. A good behavior tenure was set for the justices, with retirement at sixty years. Eight sections of Article VII were devoted to guaranties of rights and a special article set forth a method of amendment. This provided for the action of two legislatures, the first by a majority and the second by a two-thirds vote, followed by a referendum. No provision was made for the calling of a convention. In 1826 an amendment was passed abolishing the property qualification for the suffrage.

(2) The council of censors in *Vermont* proposed no amendments in 1806 but in 1813, and again in 1821, amendments were referred to conventions, which however rejected them all. Three were submitted in 1828 but one only was passed, restricting suffrage to native-born Americans or to naturalized citizens. (3) The legislature of *Connecticut* in 1818, under its general powers, summoned a convention, which substituted for the ancient charter of the state a constitution which to a quite large extent reproduced the charter organization of government. The constitution was referred to the freemen of the towns, adopted October fifth, and proclaimed by the governor on the twelfth. It contained a preamble, a declaration of rights in twenty-one sections, and provided in form for the separation of powers. The lower house remained without change, the upper house as a senate of twelve members was made to represent census population and elected at large.[1] The annual election was retained, the governor given the veto power, and judges were to be elected by the assembly, holding office during good behavior. Provision was made for amendments through the action of two assemblies and a referendum to the voters. (4) In *Rhode Island* agitation for readjustment of representation resulted (1824) in the call of a convention by the legislature under its general powers, but the constitution submitted was rejected at the polls. (5) In *Massachusetts* the general court (the legislature) under its general powers summoned a convention which met November fifteenth, 1820, to January ninth, 1821, and submitted nine articles of amendment, which on referendum were adopted April ninth, 1821. Of these Article II asserted the authority of the general court to constitute and

---

[1] In 1828 an amendment increased the membership of the senate and provided for election by districts.

to regulate municipal governments in the towns at discretion, and Article IX provided for a method of amendment through the action of two successive legislatures and a popular referendum, approving by a majority of those voting thereon. (6) The *Virginia* assembly under its general powers summoned a constitutional convention which met October fifth, 1829, to January fourteenth, 1830, and submitted to the voters a revised constitution which was approved April, 1830. The chief change made was a reapportionment of representation in the assembly. The assembly continued to elect governor, council and judges, but the governor was given a three-year instead of a one-year term and the council was reduced to a body of three members instead of eight.

CONSTITUTIONS OF THE NEW STATES

Maine, among the new states, being an offshoot of Massachusetts, tended to follow the form of the parent constitution to some extent, but in its fundamental law departed somewhat from the conservative New England type, and inclined to the democratic radicalism of the newer western states. The convention sat, October 11–29, 1819, and its constitution was on referendum approved December sixth, and the state admitted into the Union March third, 1820. The constitution contained a preamble, a declaration of rights in twenty-four sections, and an article making a formal distribution of powers. It provided for a bicameral legislature, in general based on population, but with provisions for the representation of the towns in the house. The governor was given the veto power, the appointment of the most important judicial officers, and was to be assisted by a council of seven, elected by the legislature. Elections were annual and manhood suffrage without property qualifications was provided. The legislature by a two-thirds vote might submit amendments on referendum, which went into effect if indorsed by a majority of those voting thereon.

The seven other states admitted into the Union from 1801–30 plainly represented in their constitutions a common type, having its basis in the Ordinance of 1787, and including those features of rights, popular representation, and democracy characteristic of the great middle west of that period. These states had been created out of the national domain and except in the case of Ohio followed a procedure set by congress which determined the precedents for the admission of territories as states. It included the enabling act permitting the calling of a convention, and it lay down conditions which were to be embodied in an ordinance, usually in the form of an "irrevocable compact"[1] between the territory and the congress. Ohio formed a constitution on its own initiative without an enabling act but the other six states were admitted under conditions or "compacts." In the case of Missouri also it was further stipulated that the state should not be admitted until the legislature by formal vote should disown a possible unconstitutional interpretation of the fourth clause of Article III, Section 26, a slavery provision. The legislature assented to this, June twenty-sixth, and the state was proclaimed August tenth, 1821.

These seven constitutions were not submitted to popular referendum except in the case of Mississippi. A later precedent of congressional enabling acts, starting with the enabling act for Minnesota in 1857, made a referendum obligatory. The length of the constitutions was slightly increasing, ranging from seven thousand to eleven thousand

[1] See, p. 19.

words, averaging just about nine thousand words. The additional length was due to a greater elaboration of details and the insertion of new subjects of regulation. There were many provisions fixing compensation, regulating office-holding, determining legislative procedure, and making provisions for education, in regulation of banks and slavery,[1] and against bribery. A lengthy bill of rights, varying from twenty-two to thirty sections, was inserted in each, except in the case of Louisiana, which however contained a few guaranties under General Provisions.[2] In all cases the three departments were in form separated. The legislature was bicameral and in general each house was based on voting population, "free white males," or inhabitants. Annual elections were favored in four states and biennial in the remaining three. The senate was divided into classes with two, three or four year terms. The governor was elected by popular vote, had veto powers,[3] except in Ohio, and held office for varying terms of two, three or four years. Judges of the supreme court were appointed by the assembly in four, and by the governor and senate in three states, holding office for terms varying from seven years to a life tenure during good behavior. Suffrage was manhood (free white) except in three states[4] which required payment of a tax to either state or county.

Each of the constitutions provided a method of amendment, and most made possible the calling of a convention for the purpose of revision. The widely variant requirements

[1] See, e.g., the three hundred-word provision of Missouri; Article III, Sections 26–8.

[2] Louisiana inserted its first formal bill of rights in the constitution of 1868.

[3] In Illinois the veto power was exercised by the governor and the judges of the supreme court.

[4] Ohio, Louisiana, Mississippi.

showed the lack of settled practice among the states. Missouri made amendments through the action of two successive assemblies voting by two-thirds vote, without a referendum; Alabama referred amendments by a two-thirds vote, and then if the referendum were affirmative, required a further ratification by the next assembly. Three states[1] by a two-thirds vote of their legislatures might submit a referendum asking whether or not a convention should be called to revise the constitution; Indiana authorized a referendum every twelve years for the same purpose, but in Louisiana the assembly by a majority vote was required to submit the question for two successive years. The referendum when submitted, required in four states[2] a majority of those voting for representatives, Louisiana made it harder by demanding a majority of those entitled to vote for representatives, and Indiana insisted on a majority of all votes cast at a general election. Four states also provided that the convention, if called, should be based on the same representation as was had in their respective assemblies.

[1] Ohio, Illinois, Mississippi.
[2] Ohio, Illinois, Mississippi, Alabama.

CHAPTER V

THE PERIOD OF DEVELOPING DEMOCRACY

THIS period, 1831–60, is the high water mark for the making of constitutions among the states. By the year 1830 there were twenty-four states in the Union, and during the next thirty years ten[1] new ones formed their first constitutions, two of them so unsatisfactorily that they found it necessary to revise them within this same period. Of the twenty-four older states, eighteen[2] of them revised their constitutions through conventions, two[3] of these even making

[1] Arkansas, 1836; Michigan, 1835, 1850; Florida, 1845; Texas, 1845; Iowa, 1846, 1857; Wisconsin, 1848; California, 1850; Minnesota, 1858; Oregon, 1859; Kansas, 1859.

Iowa had tried to adopt a constitution in 1844 but the convention's work was rejected. Wisconsin had the same experience in 1846. The Kansas troubles had given birth to three conventions with their constitutions, (1855, 1857, 1858) before the territory succeeded in making another constitution acceptable both to the voters and to the congress. Though this constitution was made in 1859, the state itself was not admitted into the Union until January 29, 1861, after the withdrawal of southern congressmen had made this possible.

[2] Delaware, 1831 (1852); Mississippi, 1832; Georgia (1833), 1839; Tennessee, 1834; North Carolina, 1835; Vermont, 1835, (1842), 1849, (1856); Pennsylvania, 1837; Rhode Island, 1842; New Jersey, 1844; Louisiana, 1844, 1852; New York, 1846; Illinois, 1847; Kentucky, 1849; New Hampshire, Maryland, Virginia, Ohio, Indiana, all in 1850.

[3] Louisiana and Vermont. In Vermont it will be remembered that according to the provisions of the constitution, boards of censors met at seven year intervals. The boards of 1835, 1842, 1849 and 1856 in each case summoned a convention for the year following to consider amendments prepared by the board. No amendments were adopted by the conventions of 1843 and 1857 but the convention of 1836 adopted twelve, and that of 1850 ten amendments.

47

two revisions. Georgia had a revision rejected in 1833 but was more successful in 1839. Delaware revised in 1831 but a second attempt in 1852 met with defeat at the polls. Yet the eighteen states can hardly be accused of undue haste in revision. The average age of their constitutions was forty-one years, six were over fifty years old,[1] and, aside from Vermont, the constitution of Mississippi was the only one less than twenty years old. The constitution of Maryland had lasted for seventy-four years at the time of its revision.[2] Some of these revised constitutions had been amended by separate amendments before revision but these were few in number and comparatively unimportant. All constitutions of this period, whether new or revised, were regularly referred to the voters for approval or rejection.[3]

Of the six states that preferred amending to revising,[4] Maine adopted nine amendments, Massachusetts sixteen, Connecticut eight, Missouri seven, Alabama three and South Carolina two.[5] Some of these were really important and the set as a whole was regularly democratic in tendency. Of the eighteen states calling conventions, eight [6] summoned

[1] Rhode Island, North Carolina, New Jersey, Kentucky, Maryland, New Hampshire.

[2] In 1837 however owing to popular agitation it had made extensive amendments, totaling nearly four thousand words in length. The procedure set by the constitution was not strictly followed in calling the convention, and the same is true of the conventions of 1864 and 1867.

[3] The exceptions were, Delaware, Arkansas and Mississippi, and remembering that in Vermont the referendum was from the board of censors to a convention.

[4] Yet two of these had endeavored to revise their constitutions through conventions, but the revised constitutions had been rejected at the polls; Missouri, through its convention of 1845-6, and Massachusetts in 1853.

[5] The amendment of 1834 emphasized allegiance to the state in the oath to be taken by officials, an echo of the nullification agitation.

[6] Vermont, New Hampshire, Delaware, Tennessee, Kentucky, Mississippi, Ohio, Illinois.

them in accordance with provisions in their constitutions. In nine[1] others the legislatures called them under their general legislative powers.[2] Louisiana in 1844 called a convention in accord with its constitution but as the revised constitution, which was adopted, contained no provision for a convention, the convention of 1852 was called under the general powers of the assembly.

In respect to the nine states using their general legislative powers it may be noted that Maryland's convention of 1850, and Georgia's of 1833, 1839, were not only called under the general powers of their assemblies but in direct opposition to the provisions of their constitutions, which expressly required all changes to be made through assembly action only. In Maryland[3] a condition of discord similar to that of Rhode Island ten years before had arisen, which the assembly settled by calling a convention after a referendum to the voters. The situation in Rhode Island may be briefly mentioned as an excellent illustration of democratic struggles against adverse conditions. This state, it will be remembered, had retained, with verbal changes, its old colonial charter as its fundamental law. Many of its provisions, especially in respect to suffrage and representation, had become antiquated, more especially through the rise of a commercial manufacturing population, which demanded political rights from the landholders in whom political power was vested by charter. A convention was summoned in 1834 by the assembly under its general powers, but it adjourned without definite action. In 1841 the

---

[1] Rhode Island, Pennsylvania, Virginia, North Carolina, Indiana, New Jersey, New York, Georgia, Maryland. To this list should be added Massachusetts and Missouri already mentioned in note 4 on preceding page.

[2] For a discussion of such general powers see, Jameson, pp. 601–15 and Appendix E.

[3] See, Jameson, Sections 224–5.

assembly summoned another convention which submitted a constitution to the legal voters, who promptly rejected it. Meanwhile in the summer of 1841 mass meetings were organized which summoned a constitutional convention. The constitution of this convention was submitted to the male adults of the state in December and declared adopted January thirteenth, 1842. The attempt to organize this popular government resulted in the Dorr Rebellion, which was promptly suppressed. In view of the tense situation the assembly summoned for September another convention whose constitution was ratified in November and went into effect May, 1843. This constitution for the most part merely continued the fundamentals of the old charter but made some concessions in respect to suffrage and representation. An excellent bill of rights was added, the departments were separated in form if not in fact, and provision made for the passage of amendments but by a rather difficult process.

In respect to the ten new states, only one of them, (Minnesota), entered the Union by the ordinary procedure, viz., through an enabling act. Texas entered the Union by annexation, through a joint resolution of congress and mutual formal consent. In the remaining eight territories, the inhabitants, in their eagerness for statehood, called conventions on their own account and then petitioned congress for admission.[1] Congress complied in each case but insisted on an "irrevocable compact" ordinance or conditions tantamount thereto, except from Texas, whose status was that of a sovereign state, not of a dependent territory.

---

[1] But in the case of Wisconsin, this applies only to the constitution of 1848, the rejected constitution of 1846 was in harmony with an enabling act of congress.

By the admission of Florida, Michigan and Wisconsin, all of the national territory east of the Mississippi, except the District of Columbia, had assumed statehood. The entrance into the Union of Minnesota, Iowa and Arkansas had completed the first tier of states across the Mississippi, and the admission of Texas had rounded out the Gulf states. California and Oregon fronted on the Pacific coast, looking westward towards the Far East; and Kansas was the first of fourteen states destined to be formed from the farming and mining lands of the great west. It was the era of western expansion, of boundless faith in "manifest destiny" and democratic principles, shadowed only by an "impending crisis" due to the existence of slavery in the south.

It would be tedious and is unnecessary to enumerate in any detail the substance of these new and revised constitutions and the amendments of those not revised in convention. The mass of detail would prove confusing and the advantages gained from it if set forth are not obvious. Then, too, it was a period when the processes of assimilation and conscious selection were prominent, not differentiation except in incidentals, so that resemblances rather than differences need to be emphasized. Throughout this period about fifty constitutional conventions had been held in the land, from the Atlantic to the Pacific and from the Gulf to the Canadian border. Interest in state constitutions had been aroused and debates in conventions in the discussion of constitutional points at times rivaled the writers of the *Federalist* in their clear enunciation of fundamental principles.[1] The railroad and the telegraph had come into use as well as improved postal facilities, so that all sections of the country through more frequent intercourse had begun

[1] Like, for instance, the debates of the Massachusetts convention of 1853.

to exchange ideas, to move towards common fundamentals in governmental organization, and towards a sort of type or standard for a state constitution. This was not modeled after those of New England or the older constitutions of the eighteenth century, but found its best patterns in the states of the Mississippi valley, where more democratic conditions were supposed to exist. The older states of course revised conservatively, and the south in its constitutions had to keep in mind "its peculiar institution" (slavery); sectional interests caused a varied emphasis on such subjects, for instance, as corporations, finance, and public debts in the north; or land, homesteads, and educational systems in the west. Naturally, the trend towards democracy might best be observed in the constitutions of the ten new states, unhampered by traditions that extended beyond the memory of living men.

The Older Constitutions

The twenty-four older states, in their revisions, had of course to remember their past, the strong prejudice in favor of *status quo*, and the natural indisposition of their citizens to try the seemingly rash experiments demanded by the growth in democratic conditions. The changes effected therefore in these older constitutions may be summarized as: readjustments in the memberships of legislatures, so as to have them conform more closely to changes in population; property qualifications for office-holding and for suffrage for the most part disappeared, and two states added an electional qualification for suffrage;[1] popular elections for administrative and judicial officers, especially in the case of local officials, sheriffs, and judges, largely

---

[1] Connecticut, 1855; Massachusetts, 1857.

superseded the former system of executive appointment or legislative election. Limitations on the powers of legislatures became prominent, especially in finance matters and through the addition of articles regulating important interests. The governor's office definitely became elective, the veto power bestowed on him largely added to his prestige,[1] and two states[2] dropped from their constitutions the old fashioned governor's council. The well known democratic fondness for justice in litigation found expression in repeated attempts to make satisfactory, unsatisfactory judicial systems,[3] and in numerous changes from life tenure judgeships in the higher courts to fixed terms and popular elections. Biennial elections and to a less extent biennial sessions succeeded to the ancient annual election and session; a plurality requirement for election superseded the requirement of a majority, limitations on state taxes and debts multiplied, and religious restrictions of all sorts began to drop from constitutions and to be followed by prohibitions of the use of public moneys for sectarian purposes.

THE NEW CONSTITUTIONS

The ten new constitutions were much longer when compared with the constitutions of the earlier period. They averaged about eleven thousand words in length, varying from nine thousand to fourteen thousand words. This increase is due to the insertion of additional articles on subjects ignored in the earlier constitutions. The headings Banks, Corporations, Local Government occupied

[1] The *item* veto appears first in the Kansas constitution of 1859.

[2] Vermont, Maryland.

[3] Maryland, for example, devoted nearly five thousand words to its judicial system, in addition to about two thousand words to its administrative officials and departments.

more space, Education concerned itself with school lands generously bestowed from the public lands of the Union, and the vexed Judicial Department evidently was a source of anxiety. Legislatures were no longer honored bodies but were repressed by limitations on their powers, especially in respect to taxation and finance and the passing of local and private legislation; there were also prohibitions against the incurring of public debts beyond a fixed maximum, while numerous provisions against bribery seemed to cast doubt on the integrity of legislators and administrative officials.

The constitutions had a combined preamble and enacting clause, and bills of rights, except that Michigan scattered its provisions throughout the constitution instead of collecting them into a formal bill. Free white male citizens formed the electorate, except that four states allowed aliens to vote who had declared their intention of becoming citizens of the United States. Property qualifications did not exist, and representation in the legislatures, with minor exceptions, was based in both houses on census population. There was a decided emphasis in favor of the biennial election and legislation session, and the lengthening of terms of administrative officers. In each state the governor was elected and had the veto power; administrative officers and judgeships of all grades were almost entirely elective or became so through later amendments.

In respect to amendment and revision there was still wide variation. The processes of change were simpler, more democratic, and were approximating towards the present system. But there were still differences; as illustrated, for example, by the variations in the vote required for a referendum : — "a majority of those voting thereon," "a majority of the electors," "a majority of those qualified to vote," "a majority of those voting at an [general] election." Modern experience is roundly against the last three of these requirements.

A comparison of these two sets, the new and the revised constitutions, shows that they were not so far apart. The real difference would be found in what the older constitutions retained without change. The changes they actually made were in quite full agreement with the provisions of the newer constitutions. The period of change seemed to reach its climax in 1850 when seven constitutional conventions met in as many different states. After that date questions of slavery and secession began to absorb the attention of the states, so that national interests came to the front and held the stage for over forty years. The period of reconstruction at the close of the war, aroused interest in the constitutions of the southern states, and the many-sided development of the last twenty-five years in the United States has once again given an impetus towards the study of all state constitutions.

CHAPTER VI

SECESSION, RECONSTRUCTION AND READJUSTMENT

IN this period, from 1861 to 1886, occurred the civil war and the period of reconstruction, both deeply significant in American history and indirectly of great importance in the development of state constitutions. The influence exerted by these events on constitution-making can best be seen after an explanation of the changes necessitated by them in the southern states, so that the constitutional modifications brought about by secession and reconstruction will now be set forth. This will be done in detail so as to make clear the state constitutional history of the period, presenting it from the standpoint of state constitutions.

The twenty-five years of this fourth period present three sets of constitutions for consideration : — (1) the constitutions of the southern states; (2) the efforts, more or less successful, of eleven other states to revise their constitutions; and (3) the constitutions of the four new states admitted into the Union. The first set will be explained under two headings; viz., Secession, and Reconstruction.

I. THE STATE CONSTITUTIONS OF THE SOUTH

Secession. The secession movement of the south, with the resultant civil war and the inevitable period of reconstruction and readjustment, presents one of the most striking chapters in state constitution-making. An empire of agricultural states, wealthy and populous, dominated

by an aristocratic class of great landowners, found itself
rather unexpectedly plunged into a fierce war lasting nearly
four years.   From this it at last emerged, beaten, decimated
in battle and poverty-stricken; no longer a band of sovereign states or equal states in the Union, but merely a series
of conquered provinces.   In its humiliation it saw its former
slaves made into free and equal citizens, and for a time even
superior before the law.   Finally, when weighed down by
the sting of defeat and the grief of bereavement, it was
compelled to readjust its civilization, its institutions,
and its ideals to the newer conditions environing it, and to
work out new systems of economic, political and social
standards, suited to the situation thrust upon it.   Naturally
such readjustments required time and in their broadening
ramifications can hardly be said to be fully accomplished
even yet, though fifty years have elapsed since the close of
the war.

The history of this period has been quite thoroughly
covered by many excellent general and special works [1] and
is doubtless familiar to the reader, so that that part only
demands attention, which is needed in explanation of
changes in the constitutions of the southern states.

As is well known, the presidential election of 1860,
which resulted in the choice of Abraham Lincoln, was the
turning point in the march of events.   The legislature of
South Carolina which was in session when the results of
the election were announced, on November tenth summoned
a convention to meet December seventeenth, for the purpose of considering the relations of the commonwealth
"with the Northern States and the Government of the
United States."   On December twentieth, this convention
unanimously passed an ordinance of secession and soon

[1] See references at end of chap. vii.

afterwards issued a "Declaration of Causes," and an "Address to the People of South Carolina and to the People of the Slave-holding States," in which these were urged to unite in forming a Southern Confederacy. This method of action was in general followed by the other seceding states. By the first of February, 1861, the six [1] other cotton producing states had seceded, conventions being summoned by the legislatures for this purpose. On February fourth delegates from six of the states [2] met in Montgomery, Alabama, and organized a temporary government, electing Jefferson Davis and Alexander H. Stephens respectively as President and Vice President, under the terms of a provisional constitution. On March eleventh a permanent constitution was adopted by the congress and was ratified by the last (Florida) of the seven state conventions, April twenty-second. It was practically the national constitution with variations in favor of state sovereignty, slavery, and against a tariff for protective purposes. On April eleventh Fort Sumter was bombarded and war had begun. It was necessary that the other southern states [3] should make their decisions at once, since each state in the Union was summoned by Lincoln to send its militia to aid in the suppression of the rebellion. *Virginia* in convention voted to secede, April seventeenth, and fixed on the fourth Thursday of May as the date for a referendum. This when taken was strongly affirmative for secession. The convention of *North Carolina* in its first session had refused to pass an ordinance of secession, but May first the

[1] Mississippi, Florida, Alabama, Georgia, Louisiana, Texas.

[2] Texas sent its delegates a few days late, as it was awaiting the result of a referendum (February twenty-third) on secession.

[3] There were seven other states fully or partly in sympathy with the South : Virginia, North Carolina, Arkansas, Tennessee, Kentucky, Missouri, Maryland.

legislature summoned for the twentieth of the month a convention, which promptly on assembling voted to secede. The legislature of *Arkansas*, January fifteenth, summoned a convention which met March eleventh and adjourned on the twenty-first without acting on the question of secession. On May sixth it reassembled and at once passed an ordinance of secession. *Tennessee* on referendum had refused to call a convention, but May sixth–seventh, the legislature identified the state with the fortunes of the south by seceding and ratifying the confederate constitution. This action was endorsed on referendum, June eighth. The governor of *Kentucky*, who favored secession, summoned the legislature of the state to meet in special session, May sixth. This body refused to take sides and sought to maintain a policy of neutrality. In August a new election was held, resulting in a strong Union legislature, which henceforth coöperated with the north. The convention of *Missouri* meeting February twenty-eighth had even in March declared strongly against secession. When war broke out the question again became an issue and culminated, July thirtieth, when the convention on reassembling definitely sided with the north by deposing Governor Jackson, a southern sympathizer, and then reorganized the state administration so as to favor the Union cause. Lastly, the legislature of *Maryland* refused to call a convention or to pass an ordinance of secession, so that the state legally and officially remained within the Union. As the result therefore of the secession movement, eleven of the fourteen slave-holding states withdrew from the Union, becoming members of the Southern Confederacy, but the other three, Kentucky, Missouri and Maryland, by preference threw in their lot with the north.

It will be noted that in the secession movement a special

convention was the agency through which action was taken. When secession was voted, the convention then made alterations in the constitution so as to have it conform to the new order of things. Still further, the conventions in most cases assumed charge of government, passed ordinances, appropriated moneys from the state treasuries, raised troops, secured war supplies, and served as ratification conventions for the new constitution of the confederacy. Obviously these conventions were only incidentally constitutional conventions, they were rather revolutionary conventions exercising the sovereign powers of their states in a time of crisis, on the assumption that for the time at least they were voicing the wish and will of their respective states.

Reconstruction. As the civil war approached its termination, it became necessary to decide on the method whereby the conquered states might be restored to their former place in the Union. To this end, three policies developed, one after the other, viz., the policies of Presidents Lincoln, Johnson, and of congress. (1) Lincoln's policy was voiced in his Amnesty Proclamation of December eighth, 1863, in which he invited the citizens of ten of the rebellious states (excepting Virginia[1]) to resume their allegiance and

---

[1] Virginia was excepted because Lincoln's policy was already working out in that state. A loyal legislature, purporting to be the legislature of Virginia, had already given sanction to the separation of West Virginia. The remnant, after the withdrawal of the West Virginia delegates, made up of delegates from that small part of the present Virginia then in the Union lines, on December twenty-first, 1863, summoned a convention to amend the constitution. This convention consisting of about twenty members, met February thirteenth, 1864, and on April seventh adopted a constitution, which was submitted to the voters for approval or rejection and in June endorsed by a total vote of about five hundred. This constitution of 1864 was practically a sort of provisional constitution, and the government organized under it, the "Pierpont Government," met with some recognition from the executive department of the national government.

to organize loyal governments within their respective states. The proclamation, furthermore, suggested the methods that should be followed, in order to construct governments that would be satisfactory to the federal government. Three states only of the ten, availed themselves of this opportunity ; Arkansas, Louisiana and Tennessee.

In *Arkansas* a loyal convention claiming to represent twenty-two out of the fifty-four counties of the state, met January eighth, 1864, at Little Rock, and later in the month submitted to the loyal voters a constitution, which, March eighteenth, was almost unanimously ratified, so that a government under its provisions was organized by April eleventh.   In *Louisiana* at the suggestion of General Banks then in command, a convention met at New Orleans April sixth, 1864, and completed by August, a constitution, practically that of 1852 with necessary additions and changes, which was submitted to a small body of voters September fifth and ratified.   In accordance with the provisions of this constitution a loyal government was organized.   In *Tennessee*, Andrew Johnson, then military governor, urged its loyal citizens to prepare a constitution. After much preliminary discussion a convention met at Nashville January ninth, 1865, which added to the constitution of 1834 an amendment abolishing slavery and property rights in human beings, and passed a schedule repealing the secession legislation and providing for the readjustment of relations with the Union.   These were submitted to the loyal voters of the state on February twenty-second and ratified almost unanimously.

Congress, however, was not altogether in agreement with the president as to the methods of readmission.   It refused to receive congressmen from the four reconstructed states or to recognize the states as reconstructed.   President

Lincoln, nevertheless, continued to treat with them as proper governments, though inasmuch as they were practically under military control their constitutions can hardly be considered as really and legally in effect.

(2) On April fourteenth, 1865, President Lincoln was assassinated, dying next day, and Vice President Johnson became president. His policy of reconstruction, virtually an extension of Lincoln's, went on the assumption that the executive department as the military authority had jurisdiction. On May twenty-ninth he issued a proclamation of amnesty and began reconstruction by appointing provisional governors for the seven states not yet reconstructed. ˙These governors organized temporary governments and summoned constitutional conventions. Each convention, under the instructions given by the president, was to provide for a new state government based on the constitution and laws as they were in 1861, but without slavery; to abolish slavery, to ratify the thirteenth amendment, to repudiate debts in aid of the rebellion, and to declare the ordinance of secession null and void. Elections were then to be held for local, state and congressional officers, and when completed, the provisional governments were to be withdrawn and the rebellious states restored to their former relationship within the Union.

In harmony with this plan conventions were held in the seven states, constitutions adopted, referred in three cases[1] to the voters and ratified, and governments organized. The first convention met August fourteenth in Mississippi, and in order followed South Carolina, Alabama, North Carolina, Georgia, Florida, and Texas, whose convention adjourned April second, 1866. A referendum, voting affirmatively, was taken in Texas, June twenty-fifth, so that by that

---

[1] North Carolina, Georgia, Texas.

date the eleven states had apparently been reconstructed. The president in his message to congress, December fourth, and December eighteenth, in his special message to the senate, called attention to the rapid progress of reconstruction and expressed the hope that there would soon be established "a harmonious restoration of the relations of the states to the national Union." On December eighteenth, also, the secretary of state proclaimed the ratification of the thirteenth amendment by the consent of twenty-seven out of the thirty-six states, the interesting point being that eight of the twenty-seven were secession states, states in the Union according to the executive, but not so in the later opinion of the congress. For, powerful though the president is, with his enormous prestige and his headship of the army and navy, his power, after all, depends on the willingness of congress to coöperate with him by submitting to his leadership. Should congress object and force the issue, neither the president, nor the supreme court, singly or combined, can resist the final authority that comes through the possession of the power of legislation. Such an issue had arisen between President Johnson and the congress, which finally definitely rejected his policy of reconstruction and itself took up the task.

(3) In December, 1865, it appointed a joint Committee on Reconstruction to report on the situation and its several recommendations formed the basis for later action. Meanwhile it refused to receive into either house members from "any of the said so-called confederate states." On July twenty-fourth, however, an exception was made in the case of Tennessee and that state was readmitted, but with the distinct assertion that "said state government can only be restored to its former political relations in the Union by the consent of the lawmaking power of the United

States." The gist of the congressional objection to read-mission lay in the fact that the reconstructed states were denying rights and suffrage to the enfranchised blacks. This meant that if the states were readmitted into the Union negroes would be permanently subordinated to the whites, and furthermore, that the southern states, since each freed person henceforth would count as one instead of three-fifths for purposes of representation in the house,[1] would increase their proportion of representation and that this would be controlled by the democratic white citizens. As a legal check on these possibilities, the fourteenth amendment was passed by the congress, June thirteenth, and then referred to the states for approval or rejection. As the vote of the southern states against this amendment would surely defeat it, it was doubly important that they should not be considered by congress as readmitted.

The congressional plan proper began with the first reconstruction act of March second, 1867. This divided the ten southern states (excepting Tennessee) into five military districts and arranged that conventions should be called to reorganize state governments, but with the proviso that the voting body should include all domiciled male adults of whatever race, color, or previous condition, except those disfranchised for participating in the rebellion. In other words, the electorates would be made up largely of negroes, northerners resident in the south (locally known as carpet-baggers), and native southerners unionists in sympathy (known as scalawags). Furthermore, each state, through its legislature when organized under the new constitution, was required to ratify the fourteenth amendment as a requisite for admission. On March twenty-third, a supplementary act was passed, authorizing the commanding

---

[1] Constitution of United States. Article I. Section 2, clause 3.

general in each district to see to it that voters were properly registered and conventions called. A third act, July nineteenth, made clear the point that the provisional governments[1] in the ten states were not to be recognized as legal governments, and during their continuance, were to be in all respects subject to the military commanders of the respective districts and to congress. All three of these acts were vetoed by the president but were repassed over his veto.[2] Finally, congress, in order to strengthen its position still further, forbade the supreme court[3] to exercise jurisdiction over *habeas corpus* cases arising under the reconstruction laws of congress.

In pursuance of these acts the military commanders in their several districts saw to it that voters were listed, conventions called, constitutions submitted, and governments organized under the adopted constitutions. The first conventions began their sessions in November, 1867, and by the end of the following June several states were ready for readmission. Arkansas was the first readmitted, June twenty-second, it having endorsed the fourteenth amendment. Three days later North Carolina, South Carolina, Louisiana, Alabama and Florida were by act informed that they would be readmitted, as soon as their legislatures had endorsed the fourteenth amendment; Georgia received the same promise but with a further condition in respect to certain clauses in its constitution which discriminated against loyalists. These six states by July twenty-first having complied with all conditions were, therefore, readmitted. These ratifications completed the

---

[1] Organized under Presidents Lincoln and Johnson.

[2] A fourth act was passed March eleventh, 1868, modifying and supplementing the previous acts.

[3] Act March twenty-seventh, 1868. See, *Ex parte* Wm. H. McCardle, 7 Wallace, 506–15.

number necessary for the passage of the fourteenth amendment and it was proclaimed July twenty-eighth, 1868.

In the case of the three remaining states,[1] where complications had arisen, congress on April tenth, 1869, by act made some modifications in its requirements for their admission but demanded that their legislatures, when organized, should ratify the fifteenth amendment, which had been passed February twenty-seventh and referred to the states. Finally these three states complied with the requirements, and in 1870 were readmitted, Virginia on January twenty-sixth, Mississippi on February twenty-third, and Texas on March thirtieth, on which date the passage of the fifteenth amendment was proclaimed.

Summary of Changes

In summarizing the changes made in the southern constitutions, it may be said that the secession changes merely made the needed readjustments to the new system. Under the Lincoln policy of reconstruction, emphasis was placed on the fact that the new governments should be loyal and should therefore repeal the ordinance of secession, repudiate debts incurred in aid of the rebellion and preferably should abolish slavery. These changes involved questions of civil rights and suffrage, since the status of slaves made free needed to be defined. The points discussed in the conventions therefore were; should the suffrage (and office holding) be confined to loyal whites, or thrown open to negroes also? Furthermore, should negroes be enrolled in the militia of the state, and should the public schools of the state be thrown open to children without regard to race or previous condition of servitude? The four states [2]

---

[1] Virginia, Mississippi, Texas.
[2] Virginia, Arkansas, Louisiana, Tennessee.

concerned, through their conventions, met these problems
in varying fashion in the constitutions they devised, but as
the conventions represented small minorities only of their
populations, and as congress refused to readmit three of the
states under these constitutions, they may well be omitted
from the discussion. In the same manner the seven states
reconstructed by President Johnson had practically the same
situation, complicated only by the necessity of acting also
on the thirteenth and fourteenth amendments. There
was virtual unanimity in respect to the repeal of the secession ordinance, the repudiation of war debts, and the
abolition of slavery, but wide differences of opinion in
respect to the extension of suffrage and office holding rights,
and little or no desire to go far in the extension of political
rights or effective civil rights to the enfranchised blacks.
Nor, finally, was the fourteenth amendment at all favored,
because of the character of its sweeping changes in enlarging federal powers.

In consequence of this situation, and in view of the
turmoil and disorder prevalent in the South, congress took
the entire matter into its own hands, placed the ten states
(excepting Tennessee) under military rule, laid down conditions, and insisted that action be promptly taken. Conventions were thus organized made up almost entirely of
colored and loyalist delegates, who prepared constitutions,
which in many instances reproduced provisions from
Northern constitutions, and which were later submitted to
voting bodies made up of domiciled adult males of both
races, who were not disqualified for rebellion. Pressure
was then brought so as to ensure prompt action and satisfactory results. Technicalities were not allowed to stand in
the way : Alabama's constitution which did not receive the
proper majority was yet accepted ; Virginia, Mississippi

and Texas were allowed to separate obnoxious clauses for separate votes, in order that the main constitutions might be endorsed; Georgia after readmission was again put under military control and reconstructed; but finally in about three years after the passage of the first act, the eleven states were restored to the Union and a "Roman peace" prevailed throughout the south. Then, as a sort of climax to the whole matter came the decision of the supreme court in the .case of Texas *vs.* White (1868), in which it was declared that the United States is "an indestructible Union, composed of indestructible States." Hence, the eleven states had never legally seceded, each had remained a state in the Union but with suspended rights on account of rebellion. Congress therefore had performed its duty in restoring the southern states once again into harmonious relationship with their sister states in the Union.

From another standpoint the essence of the changes made in reconstruction might best be summarized as follows; the secession ordinances were declared illegal and the "paramount authority of the federal government" asserted. War debts in aid of the rebellion were repudiated, and the three war amendments to the national constitution were forced through as conditions for admission. This involved the abolishment of slavery and the admission of the colored to suffrage and office-holding privileges on the same terms as the whites. The right to serve in the militia and to secure similar educational privileges as the whites were also secured to the blacks by the terms of the fourteenth amendment, though not expressly stated in the constitutions. The real struggle in the conventions was as to how far discrimination should be made against those who had fought in the rebellion. The exceptions made by congress in favor of Virginia and Mississippi, for instance, lay in permitting these to vote separately on test oath and disfranchisement clauses, which the voters then joyously voted down.   In general, however, throughout the south the leading whites were disfranchised and the negro voters with their friends were in power — the so called "carpet-bag governments."

In all these changes real revisions of the constitutions were not made.   There was one definite issue before the conventions — readmission to the Union by accepting the terms set by congress — and other matters were neglected. Later, when excitement had died down, and war and reconstruction were really over, questions of revision came to the front and occupied the attention of the states.

CHAPTER VII

SECESSION, RECONSTRUCTION AND
READJUSTMENT (*Continued*)

In the congressional acts for the readmission of the ten rebellious states it was made a fundamental condition that the constitutions should never be so altered "as to deprive any citizen or class of citizens of the United States of the right to vote, who are entitled to vote by the constitution herein recognized." Under the theory of the constitution the states within the Union are equal one to another. Congress may dictate terms to territorial governments, and to provisional governments in states, and place upon them conditions, or insist on "irrevocable compacts," but once the state becomes a full fledged member of the Union, such conditions and compacts may remain as moral obligations but would hardly be enforcible at law. Presumably congress, if it took the matter seriously, might exert pressure on the recalcitrant state, but such a possibility is hardly conceivable. In the main such conditions are in themselves reasonable and are endorsed by the public opinion within the states, but should this not prove to be true, then the states might feel inclined to disregard what may come to be considered as unjust restrictions, and by constitutional amendment may rearrange their fundamental law in accord with what seems right under the conditions.

Such a process of readjustment has been going on in the south since reconstruction. On the part of congress successive acts have been passed removing the disabilities formerly placed on those who participated in the rebellion. Within the states themselves there came a revulsion of feeling against the misrule and corruption of reconstructed "carpet-bag" governments, so that one after the other the states of the rebellion overthrew the organizations of the republican party in control of their governments, established by fair or unfair methods white supremacy, and by amendments and revisions to their constitutions readjusted these documents to their own liking and virtually deprived the mass of negroes of suffrage. Suffrage restrictions of a constitutional sort did not begin until 1890, with the constitution of Mississippi, but in other respects readjustments began almost immediately, so that within the first decade seven of the states [1] revised their constitutions through conventions, one [2] in the decade following, two [3] others in the last decade of the century, and Virginia last of all in 1902. Omitting for the present the last three, attention will now be given to the chief changes wrought in the constitutions of the southern states, taking up (1) the three reconstruction constitutions of Mississippi, South Carolina and Virginia and (2) the revisions made in the reconstruction constitutions of the other eight states.

THE RECONSTRUCTION CONSTITUTIONS

Mississippi in its reconstruction constitution of 1868 put forth a moderate document in length about eleven thousand words. In its earlier form it was rejected at the polls but was endorsed when by exception its disability

---

[1] Tennessee, 1870; Arkansas, 1874; Alabama, North Carolina and Texas, 1875; Georgia, 1877; Louisiana, 1879.

[2] Florida, 1885.

[3] Mississippi, 1890; South Carolina, 1895.

and test oath clauses were allowed to be voted on separately and voted down. Consequently, as in the similar case of Virginia, there was no immediate necessity for change in the *seventies*. The constitution included the "paramount allegiance" clause and a declaration against secession and slavery. It forbade up to 1885 a property or educational qualification for voting; though elections were biennial there was to be an annual session of the legislature,[1] but this was changed by amendment in 1878. The governor had a four year term and the veto, the important judges were appointed by governor and senate, free schools were provided for, and in the amending clause no provision was made for a convention, it being assumed that the legislature had that general power.

South Carolina had also in its reconstruction constitution the usual declarations against slavery, secession and in assertion of the "paramount authority" of the Union. Its constitution numbered about twelve thousand words and was fair in its attitude towards its white citizens. Its disqualification clause followed in the main the attitude taken in the fourteenth amendment, suffrage was thrown open to male citizens, and provisions made for free public schools open to all without regard to race or color. The election of presidential electors passed from the legislature to the citizens, readjustments were made in legislative representation, the governor had a two year term with the veto, and important judges were to be elected by the assembly. In addition to other matters provisions were inserted for the revision of laws, and the better regulation and control of corporations and penal and charitable institutions. Amendments needed the action of two assemblies and a provision was inserted providing for the calling

[1] A usual provision in the congressional reconstruction constitutions.

of a convention. In 1873 by amendment a maximum debt provision was inserted with a referendum requirement in the case of a debt proposed in excess of the maximum. *Virginia*, like Mississippi, was favored by being allowed to vote separately (of course adversely) on its test and disfranchisement clauses, so that there was no special need for a speedy revision. Its reconstruction constitution was lengthy, over fifteen thousand words, and had the usual provisions against slavery and secession and in favor of general education and a paramount allegiance. It provided for biennial elections with annual sessions,[1] limited to a ninety-day session, a specified reapportionment for the legislative branches, a governor's term of four years and the veto, with a judiciary elected by the assembly. Provision in respect to local government occupied much space and provision was made for free schools throughout the state. The suffrage requirement of male citizenship was in 1876 altered by excluding those guilty of "petit larceny," and by demanding a prepaid poll tax, though this latter provision was dropped by amendment in 1882. An article provided for amendments but not for a convention.

REVISION OF RECONSTRUCTION CONSTITUTIONS

Turning now to the eight reconstruction constitutions which were revised in the next fifteen years, it may be noted that the changes were chiefly directed towards the removal of the disqualification and compulsory clauses of the reconstruction period. Furthermore, may be noted a readjustment necessitated by the three war amendments to the national constitution; a partial return to the constitutional system prevailing before the war, and somewhat

[1] Changed to biennial in 1876 by amendment.

awkward attempts to meet new economic conditions arising in the south.

Tennessee began by calling a convention in 1870 which referred its constitution to popular vote. The constitution was largely a return to its earlier constitution, eliminating its severe disfranchisement clauses and by contrast requiring a prepaid poll tax for suffrage, separate schools for black and white and forbidding miscegenation. The amending article provided also for the calling of a convention, if a referendum so demanded.

In *Arkansas* the fourteen thousand word reconstruction constitution was increased by over seven thousand words when a convention met in 1874 and submitted a constitution to the voters. One might assume that there was something besides religious fervor in the hearts of the members when they added to the preamble, "grateful to Almighty God for the privilege of choosing our own form of government." From the new constitution were dropped the secession, paramount allegiance, test oath and disfranchisement clauses. Biennial elections[1] and the governor's veto over items in appropriation bills appear along with a reapportionment of the legislators. Much attention was given in lengthy sections to the reorganization of the judiciary and the courts of the State.

The *Alabama* constitution of 1875, approved on referendum, was about four thousand words longer than the reconstruction constitution of 1867. The oath and disqualification clauses disappear, a specified reapportionment in the legislature is given, the annual session yields to the biennial, and the governor gains the power to veto items of appropriation bills. Separate racial public schools are required and Taxation enlarges from seven printed lines

[1] Added by amendment in 1873.

to a page and a quarter. An awkward and cumbersome method of amending was provided, and a simple procedure for the calling of a convention.

North Carolina made few changes of significance in its revision of 1876, which was ratified at the polls. The constitution in size remained about the same, and the secession and paramount allegiance clauses were not dropped. "Carpet bag" government debts as well as war debts were repudiated, separate schools provided, miscegenation forbidden, and voters required to register. The governor had a four year term but no veto, and judges were to be elected. Provision was made for amendment and revision by simpler methods than those of the earlier constitution.

Texas in revising its constitution, which was prepared in 1875 and ratified in 1876, increased its length by over six thousand words, a total of about twenty-three thousand. The usual clauses disappear : secession, national supremacy, disqualifications, as well as a provision against peonage. Annual sessions yielded to biennial, judges were elected instead of appointed by governor and senate, and the governor received the right to veto items of appropriation bills. Separate racial schools were demanded and many restrictions placed on the powers of the legislature. The cumbersome two legislature system of amending yielded to the simple method of joint action through one legislature and the electorate.

Georgia in its constitution, made and ratified in 1877, lengthened its fundamental law from about eleven thousand to eighteen thousand words. The reconstruction constitution contained no test oath nor severe disfranchisement clauses but the new constitution dropped the paramount allegiance clause and provided for separate racial schools. Legislative apportionment was detailed in the constitution and biennial took the place of annual sessions. The governor received the right to veto items but judges of the supreme court were elected by the assembly. Insurance companies were regulated rather fully and provisions inserted for a convention as well as for amendments.

Louisiana in 1879 formulated and ratified a new constitution which in length jumped from eleven thousand to over twenty thousand words, vying with that of Maryland (1867), the longest of its day. As usual, from its revised constitution were dropped the sections in respect to test oaths, disfranchisement, secession, and paramount allegiance, as well as a prohibition against separate racial schools. Annual sessions yielded to biennial, legislative apportionment was detailed and numerous restrictions were inserted on legislative authority. The governor's veto was strengthened by the power to veto items but the supreme court was appointed by governor and senate. The three page judiciary article of the earlier constitution lengthened to fourteen pages, provisions against bribery were inserted, the charter of the Louisiana Lottery was ordered canceled in 1895, and lengthy articles on Local Government, Corporations, Taxation and Indebtedness, occupied much space. No provision was made for a convention, but the amending process was made simpler.

Florida had not inserted in its reconstruction constitution stringent test oaths and disfranchisement clauses, so that there was no urgent need for revision. Its convention met in 1885 and the constitution was ratified the following year, lengthening in size only by about a thousand words. The secession section was dropped but the paramount allegiance clause retained. Separate schools were required and miscegenation forbidden. The annual session yielded to the biennial, the governor was allowed to veto items and judges were in part elected and in part appointed. A legislative reapportionment was made, much attention given to administrative officers and a special article given to Public Health. The complex and difficult methods of amendment in the earlier constitution were superseded by simple provisions for both amendment and revision.

OTHER STATE CONSTITUTIONS REVISED OR AMENDED

During this same fourth period, in addition to the eleven seceding states of the south, twelve other states sought through convention or commission to effect some changes in their fundamental law. Of these Missouri and Maryland demand special attention since they were largely southern in sympathy.

(1) *Missouri*. When the secession movement broke out the governor of Missouri sought to draw his state into secession. But on February twenty-eighth, 1861, a convention met which strongly favored the Union. It promptly assumed direction of affairs, deposed the existing administration, cancelled its obnoxious laws, and reorganized the government. The convention remained in existence until July first, 1863, acting as a sort of revolutionary convention, serving both as a legislature and as a constitutional convention. It provided for the organization of the state militia, defined the qualifications of voters, and demanded a test oath from civil officers, so as to eliminate sympathizers with the south. On July first, 1863, it abolished slavery in Missouri after July fourth, 1870, declaring free all slaves henceforth brought into the state.

On January sixth, 1865, a constitutional convention met which submitted, April tenth, a revised constitution to the voters who ratified it, June sixth. It was essentially a "reconstruction" constitution, since it denied the right of secession, asserted the paramount authority of the United States, disfranchised rebels, required a test oath, and declared against slavery or quasi-slavery in the form of apprenticeship. It at the same time made a legislative reapportionment, but confined the suffrage to white males, and permitted an educational qualification after January first, 1876. The amending article provided a simple and easy method both for amendment and revision. In 1870 the test oath, the disqualification section, and the word " white " were dropped by amendment from the suffrage article of the constitution. In 1875 a convention was called and the constitution it submitted was ratified at the polls. This constitution was about twenty-four thousand words long, exceeding its predecessor by nine thousand words. From it was dropped the paramount allegiance clause and in place of it came an emphasis on local rights and autonomy.[1] Suffrage became the usual manhood form and the provision of the previous constitution that there "may be" separate racial schools became a "shall be" at this time. In many respects the two constitutions were alike, but in the newer document the governor had the item veto and a four year term (instead of two) ; three and one half pages of limitations were placed on the legislature, as well as numerous regulations of procedure. The judicial system made use of about twenty-five hundred words, and local government, especially that of St. Louis, received lengthy

[1] It read as follows :

"That Missouri is a free and independent State, subject only to the Constitution of the United States; and as the preservation of the States and the maintenance of their governments are necessary to an indestructible Union, and were intended to coexist with it, the Legislature is not authorized to adopt, nor will the people of this State ever assent to, any amendment or change of the Constitution of the United States which may in anywise impair the right of local self-government belonging to the people of this State." Article II. section 3.

attention. The amending process was continued without change.

(2) *Maryland.* The abortive movement towards secession in this State was easily suppressed and it remained definitely within the Union. On April twenty-seventh, 1864, a convention under Unionist auspices met which by September had prepared a new constitution. This was ratified by popular vote, October thirteenth. Three years later a second convention met and its constitution when submitted was also ratified. Maryland is a small state, not in need, one would suppose, of a lengthy constitution. The constitution of 1851 contained sixteen thousand words; that of 1864, twenty-one thousand; and that of 1867, over twenty-five thousand; showing the steady increase in length characteristic of state constitutions.

The constitution of 1864 was of the "reconstruction" type. It included a test oath, the disfranchisement of rebels, a declaration against slavery and an assertion of paramount allegiance to the United States. Suffrage was restricted to white males and the bill of rights included forty-five sections, about twice the usual number. The executive had no veto but judges were elected, nearly five thousand words were needed for the judicial system, and biennial sessions were demanded with a payment limited to a session of eighty days.

From the constitution of 1867, prepared under Democratic influence, as might be expected, were dropped the test oath, disfranchisement clause, and the section on paramount allegiance, and by contrast Article 24 of the bill of rights demanded compensation from the United States for enfranchised slaves. The governor had the veto power given to him, and the eighty day limit for the legislature was made ninety.

(3) *Vermont.* In this State, it will be remembered, the board of censors was to meet every seven years to propose amendments. No action was taken in 1862 but in 1869 the board recommended a change from an annual to a biennial election and session and also its own abolition. In place of the board it recommended that in 1880, and every ten years thereafter, the senate by a two thirds vote propose amendments to the house. If the house concurred by a majority vote, that then such amendments be referred to the next assembly. If this concurred by a majority vote in each house, that then a referendum to the voters be made, ratifying by a majority vote. These recommendations were approved by the convention of 1870 so that the board of censors passed out of existence. In 1880 two minor amendments passed the ordeal above mentioned and became part of the constitution.

(4) *New York.* A convention met 1867–68 to revise the constitution, but the revision when submitted November second was rejected, except that Article VI respecting the judicial system, which was submitted separately, was endorsed.

In 1872 the legislature authorized a commission of thirty-two persons to propose amendments to the constitution. A carefully prepared and lengthy list of amendments was submitted by this body to the legislature, which passed them. By the terms of the constitution these had to be approved by the next following legislature and referred to popular vote. The second legislature modified certain of these and submitted the revised set to the voters, who approved them. Those modified by the second legislature were not constitutionally passed, but the others became part of the constitution. The chief changes made provided for a legislative reapportionment, placed further limitations on legislative authority, and made the governor's term three years instead of two, giving him also the item veto.

(5) *Illinois.* This State in 1862 summoned a convention whose constitution when submitted to the voters was rejected. Seven years later another convention met and prepared a constitution which was accepted July second, 1870, on referendum. The new constitution added about six thousand words by additions and enlargements, and included a reapportionment of the assembly, the biennial election, a four year term for the governor and an elected judiciary. A new device came in the form of a three cornered system of minority representation in the election of members to the lower house. Careful attention was given to the article on amendments and revision but the methods of change were made difficult by the vicious requirement of a "majority of those voting at an election" for amendments or the calling of a convention. In 1884 an amendment was added to the constitution giving the governor the item veto.

(6) *Michigan* in 1862 adopted an amendment providing that in 1866 and every sixteen years thereafter the question of calling a convention should be referred to the voters. The referendum was approved in 1866 and a convention called in 1867 whose constitution was rejected. In 1868 and 1870, amendments were passed providing for a biennial session and a reapportionment of membership in the legislature. In 1873, by joint resolution a commission was appointed to recommend changes in the constitution. The commission's report was approved by the legislature of 1873, but rejected, 1874, at an extra session of the next following legislature. In 1882, as required by constitution, a referendum was submitted respecting the calling of a convention but met with a negative response.

(7) *Ohio* in 1873–74 held a convention whose constitution when submitted was rejected at the polls.[1]

(8) *Pennsylvania* in 1872 summoned a convention under its general legislative powers, which submitted a constitution, December sixteen, 1883. This was accepted on referendum and was declared in force by the convention which reassembled, December twenty-eighth. The constitution was more than double the length of the older one, adding some ten thousand words. It included a reapportioned legislature, a biennial election and session, many limitations on legislative powers, a four year term for the governor along with the item veto, and an elected judiciary. In the amending article no provision was made for the calling of a convention for revision purposes.

(9) *Maine* in 1875 determined to try the commission plan and by resolve of January twelfth the governor was authorized to appoint a commission of ten persons, "to consider and frame such amendments to the constitution of Maine as may seem necessary, to be reported to the legislature." Of the twenty-one amendments submitted by this commission, nine were accepted by the legislature and on referendum were adopted. The most important of these gave the legislature the power by a two-thirds vote to call a constitutional convention for revision purposes. By amendment in 1879, biennial sessions and elections were substituted for annual; in 1880 a plurality vote was declared sufficient for gubernatorial elections, and in 1883 Maine's famous prohibition amendment was passed.

(10) *New Hampshire*, in December, 1876, called a convention which submitted amendments to referendum March, 1877. Those adopted readjusted representation,

---

[1] For further details see, pamphlet, Constitutional Conventions of Ohio, by C. B. Galbreath.

provided for biennial instead of annual elections and sessions, and made the date of election November instead of March. The governor and members of the legislature were no longer required to be "of the Protestant religion."

(11) *California* in 1862 had passed several important amendments providing for biennial sessions and elections, the reorganization of the courts, the election of judges and a revised article on amending. In 1878–79 however, a convention was held and a new constitution was submitted and ratified on May seventh. It more than doubled the length of the old constitution, adding over ten thousand words. This was chiefly due to the regulation of the legislature's powers through procedure and limitations, and the elaboration and addition of articles in respect to such subjects as Local Government, Corporations, Revenue and Taxation and the Chinese.

(12) *New Jersey* in 1873 through a commission reported to the legislature amendments to the constitution, the chief of which were the item veto and the placing of limitations on legislative powers. These were referred and adopted. An act of 1881 required the governor to appoint a commission "to prepare amendments to the Constitution of this State"; the commission reported to the next following legislature but no action was taken on the report.

During this same fourth period, eleven of the states confined their changes in constitutions to amendments. Five[1] of these either made no amendments or passed none of special importance. Of the other six, Connecticut reapportioned its house slightly and adopted the November election and biennial elections and sessions. Indiana in 1881 struck out its peculiar Article XIII, which forbade negroes to settle in the state and arranged for the

[1] Delaware, Oregon, Kentucky, Massachusetts, Rhode Island.

colonization of such as were already domiciled. Iowa readjusted its judicial system and changed to the November election. Kentucky modified its legislative apportionment and adopted the biennial session. Minnesota adopted the item veto, the November election and biennial elections, forbade the use of school moneys for sectarian purposes, and inserted precautionary sections in respect to state finances, public debts, and the investment of school funds. Wisconsin adopted the November election, biennial elections and sessions and placed many prohibitions on the passage of special and private bills.

NEW STATES

During this fourth period four new states[1] were added to the Union, each entering with fairly conservative and relatively short constitutions. The process whereby West Virginia became separated from Virginia has already been explained. Its constitution of 1862 was in substance a reproduction in its essential features of the Virginia constitution, omitting its lengthy preamble and shortening its bill of rights. Suffrage was given to white male citizens of the state and provision was made for the gradual emancipation of slaves.[2] An amendment passed in 1866 provided for the disfranchisement of rebels. In 1872 a new convention was held and the constitution it prepared was ratified at the polls. It is evident that the war was over and southern influence once again strong; test oaths were condemned, rebels were no longer disfranchised, and Article I roundly emphasized states' rights and local autonomy.

---

[1] West Virginia, Nevada, Nebraska, Colorado. Kansas, it will be remembered, was included in the previous period.

[2] This section was required by congress instead of one forbidding the admission of slaves into the state for permanent residence.

The influence of the older Virginia constitution was still marked, but local questions were not neglected. The constitution provided for a legislative reapportionment, biennial sessions, and much regulation of procedure, provisions against bribery, and many limitations on local and special legislation. The governor had the veto, differing from Virginia, and also might veto the items of appropriation bills. Judges were elected and the article on Judiciary was enlarged. Voters had to be registered and were to be male citizens. As in many of the revised constitutions of this period, there was a Homestead article, which also secured to married women their rights in property. Corporations, Banks, and Railroads came in for their share of attention. The amending process was simple and provision made for the calling of a convention.

Nevada. At the opening of the civil war, Nevada, with a small population was an organized territory in which slavery was permitted. In 1863 the inhabitants without an enabling act from congress called a convention which submitted a constitution to the voters,[1] who rejected it. On March twenty-one, 1864, congress passed an enabling act which summoned a convention for July fourth, demanding as conditions for admission provisions for religious freedom, against slavery, and in respect to public lands. A constitution was adopted prohibiting slavery and asserting the paramount authority of the Union and its full power to suppress secession. This constitution when submitted was ratified by a large majority and the state was admitted by proclamation, October thirty-first. The constitution thus prepared followed traditional lines. It had a preamble, a declaration of rights, three departments of government and the usual separate articles on Education, Debt and

[1] The population in 1860 was 6,857, in 1870, 42,491.

Finance, Local Government and Public Institutions. Voters were to be white male citizens, registered, and rebels disfranchised. Legislative apportionment was to be made on the basis of the census and biennial sessions held. There was a long list of restrictions on local and special legislation. The governor had a four year term and the veto, and the judiciary was elected by popular vote. The amending process required action by two legislatures and provision was made for a convention. An amendment in 1880 threw suffrage and offices open to all male citizens.

Nebraska. Congress, April nineteen, 1864, had passed an enabling act authorizing a convention, but no definite action was taken at the time in the territory. In February, 1866, an informal joint committee of nine members of the territorial legislature then in session, hastily prepared a constitution. This was promptly passed by the legislature as a joint resolution, and when submitted to the voters, June twenty-first, was ratified by a small majority. Congress, February ninth, 1867, accepted the constitution, on condition that the suffrage provision should state that there would be no denial of suffrage on account of race or color, but providing that this change might be made by pledge of the legislature. This condition was complied with, February twentieth, and on March first the president proclaimed the admission of the new state. A constitution hastily prepared for an emergency without the aid of a convention obviously was not intended to be permanent. It made no provision for amendments but did provide a simple method of calling a convention — a majority vote of legislature and of voters voting on a referendum. Such a convention was called in 1875 and its constitution ratified October twelfth. The document itself presented the well marked features of constitutions of this period : a preamble, bill of rights, a legislative apportionment based on census population but with districts specified in the constitution, a long list of prohibitions on legislative powers and regulations of procedure, and a biennial session with a limitation of payment for forty days only.[1] The governor had a two year term and the veto power including the veto of items of appropriation bills; there was to be an elected judiciary and manhood suffrage. The constitution contained the usual articles on Local Government, Education, Finance and Corporations. The process of amendment and revision was made difficult by demanding on referendum a majority of those voting at a general election.

Colorado did not find the process of admission to the Union an easy one. It became an organized territory in 1861 and March twenty-first, 1864, an enabling act was passed by congress authorizing a constitutional convention. The constitution when submitted, was rejected by the voters. A second constitution prepared in 1865 was ratified by a small majority. Congress passed two separate acts of admission but each was vetoed by President Johnson and neither was passed over his veto. March third, 1875, an act of congress authorized a convention which completed, March fourteenth, 1876, a constitution which was ratified July first and the admission of the state was proclaimed, August first.

The constitution provided for the customary biennial limited session of a legislature based on census population, with legislative powers closely limited and regulated, and many long articles dictating policy on important topics of legislative jurisdiction. The governor had a two year term and the regular and the item veto, judges were elective and the system of courts carefully defined. Suffrage had

[1] Changed to sixty days by amendment, 1886.

the usual provision for manhood suffrage, but with a stipulation that the legislature might after 1890 demand an educational qualification. Along with the constitution was given a referendum on women's suffrage, which met with approval at the polls. The question of prohibition assumed some definiteness by the prohibition of the manufacture or sale of "spurious, poisonous or drugged liquors." Temporarily laws were to be printed in English, Spanish and German. The amending article made simple but excellent provisions both for amending and revising the constitution.

Special References

Burgess, John W.   Reconstruction and the Constitution.
Dunning, William A.   Essays on the Civil War and Reconstruction.
Rhodes, James Ford.   History of the United States, from the Compromise of 1850 to 1877.   Volumes VI–VII.
Thorpe, Francis N.   Constitutional History of the United States. Three volumes.
Columbia University Series.
  Struggle between President Johnson and Congress over Reconstruction, by C. E. Chadsey, Volume VIII.
  Reconstruction in Georgia, by E. C. Wooley, Volume XIII.
  Reconstruction in Texas, by C. W. Ramsdell, Volume XXXVI.
  Reconstruction in Florida, by W. W. Davis, Volume LIII.
  Reconstruction in North Carolina, by J. G. Hamilton, Volume LVIII.
Johns Hopkins Series.
  Reconstruction in Virginia, by H. J. Eckenrode, Volume XXII.
  Reconstruction in South Carolina, by J. P. Hollis, Volume XXIII.
  Reconstruction in Louisiana, by J. R. Ficklen, Volume XXVIII.
  Maryland Constitution of 1851, by J. W. Harry, Volume XX.
  Maryland Constitution of 1864, by W. S. Myers, Volume XIX.
  The Self-Reconstruction of Maryland, 1864–67, by W. S. Myers, Volume XXVII.

CHAPTER VIII

RECENT CHANGES IN CONSTITUTIONS

(1886-1914)

In the year 1886 thirty-eight states were members of the Union and ten others have been added since that date.[1] Of the thirty-eight states eleven[2] have successfully held conventions for the revising of their fundamental laws and Vermont in 1913 succeeded in modifying its constitution with the aid of a commission. Three[3] states attempted to revise their constitutions but without success. Referenda were submitted in five states[4] asking whether conventions should be called, but were negatived; New York, however, voted, April, 1914, to hold a convention in 1915.

In addition to revision, the states have not neglected changes through the amending processes. The procedure of amendment is simple in most states and is enlarged in some through the constitutional initiative; constitutions, moreover, have so lengthened by the insertion of petty

---

[1] In 1889, North Dakota, South Dakota, Montana, Washington; in 1890, Idaho and Wyoming. Utah in 1896, Oklahoma in 1907, New Mexico and Arizona in 1912.

[2] Mississippi, 1890; Kentucky, 1891; New York, 1894; South Carolina, 1895; Delaware, 1897; Louisiana, 1898 and 1913; Alabama, 1901; Virginia, 1902; Michigan, 1908; Ohio, 1912; New Hampshire, 1889, 1903, 1912. The adopted amendments of Oregon since 1902, and of California, are so numerous and fundamental as to amount virtually to revisions.

[3] Rhode Island, 1898, 1899; Connecticut, 1902, 1907; Indiana, 1912.

[4] Maryland, 1907; Iowa, 1900, 1910; California, Indiana, and South Dakota, in 1914.

details and numerous new provisions, that frequent amendments are inevitable, and are multiplying out of all proportion to former notions of fundamental law.   In the fourteen years from 1895–1908,[1] five hundred ninety-five amendments were voted on by the electorates of the states, three hundred forty-seven of these were adopted and two hundred forty-eight rejected.   The number seems large and is large, yet the average per state constitution is less than one a year and would be much less were it not for the "pernicious activity" of several states that apparently are eager to hold the record for amendments.[2]

In the remaining part of this chapter attention will now be directed to the several movements among the states in respect to revision and amendment, and to the constitutions of the ten new states, but without attempting to specify in detail the provisions of the new and revised constitutions. In later chapters, under Part II, will be given the main provisions of all the existing constitutions, as they are at the present time.

Revised and Amended Constitutions in the South

In the south six states during this period revised their constitutions, and several others by amendment modified their suffrage articles, with more or less severity, so as to eliminate the supposed danger from the negro vote.   These revised constitutions will now be taken up in turn, but

---

[1] Since 1910 the American Year Book publishes each year a list of the amendments before legislatures and electorates.

[2] Oregon from 1902–1914 inclusive has adopted twenty-three amendments and rejected forty; California's printed constitution of 1914 gives eighty-three amendments as adopted since 1894; Louisiana from 1900–1912 submitted about eighty amendments, nearly all of which were adopted.   These three states combined submitted in 1914 sixty-eight amendments to referendum, thirty-six of which were ratified.   [Oregon, 21 (4); California, 30 (18); Louisiana, 17 (14).]

the suffrage provisions of these southern constitutions will be considered in Chapter XII. *Mississippi* in 1890 undertook to revise its reconstruction constitution of 1868. The convention adjourned November first, after promulgating on its own authority without referendum a constitution double the length of the one it superseded. This additional length came about largely through the insertion of new wordy articles,[1] numerous restrictions and prohibitions on legislation (about twenty-five hundred words added), and detailed additions to the judiciary article. The secession and paramount allegiance section of the bill of rights was retained, but Section Eighteen was dropped which read, "No property nor educational qualification shall ever be required for any person to become an elector." Under Education was inserted the provision, "Separate schools shall be maintained for children of the white and colored races." Schools of some sort were apparently needed even for legislators, for Section Forty reads, "Members of the legislature before entering upon the discharge of their duties shall take the following oath: 'I, . . . will, as soon as practicable hereafter, carefully read (or have read to me) the constitution of this state,' etc.;" — a theoretically good requirement, for it is doubtful whether five per cent of our seven thousand state legislators could pass a fair examination on the provisions of their respective state constitutions.

The revised constitution radically modified suffrage requirements, made the regular session of the legislature quadrennial,[2] but with a special finance session midway in the term; adopted the plan of numbering its paragraphs

---

[1] That on Corporations has about two thousand words.
[2] But in 1912 went back to the biennial term.

consecutively, a great convenience, and experimented in a curious sort of "electoral college" system in the election of the governor and other administrative officers. The amending article was but slightly altered. Before final adjournment the convention assumed legislative authority by issuing twelve ordinances.

Kentucky in revising its constitution of 1850 increased its length from nine thousand to about twenty-one thousand words through the insertion of the usual many restrictions and prohibitions on the legislature, by greatly enlarging the articles on Suffrage and Elections, and by adding many provisions in respect to local government, revenue, taxation, railroads and corporations. The November election and the item veto were adopted, and registration and the secret ballot in elections. The method of amendment and revision was made somewhat easier. The constitution was approved on referendum and was then promulgated September twenty-eighth, 1891, on the authority of the convention, after some slight changes.

South Carolina held a convention for revision purposes from September tenth to December fourth, 1895, and promulgated its constitution without referendum. This convention also used legislative authority by issuing twelve ordinances. The length of the constitution was increased by about seven thousand words over its predecessor, the reconstruction constitution of 1868. From the Declaration of Rights were dropped the sections concerning slavery, secession, and paramount allegiance, and lengthy additions were made to the article on Suffrage, placing restrictions on the exercise of this right. November elections, January sessions, and the item veto were inserted, with the usual restrictions on the legislature and the wordy lengthening of the article on Corporations. The amending process was slightly modified but still demanded a difficult procedure for changes in the fundamental law.

Louisiana in 1879 had revised its constitution and lengthened it out of all proportion, but the convention of 1898 nearly doubled its length, promulgating on its own authority a constitution of about forty thousand words. The convention devoted itself largely to the article on Suffrage and Elections, which was increased by nearly two thousand words; and to the working out of interminable articles on the judiciary, legislative restrictions, local government (paying especial attention to New Orleans), numerous boards of administration, and on the state's economic problems in respect to taxes, debts, pensions, roads, railroads, river-banks, and agriculture. Naturally, with so detailed and lengthy a constitution, a simple method of amendment had to be provided. The convention promulgated its constitution without referendum.

Since that time every session of the legislature has resulted in a crop of amendments, nearly a hundred in all, until an *impasse* developed in 1913 owing to the necessity of making a new arrangement in respect to the funding of the bonded debt of the state. A referendum was submitted, September eighth, calling for a convention for this specified purpose, and on an affirmative vote, the convention met, November tenth–twenty-second, added a two thousand word Article (number 324) in respect to the funding of the debt, incorporated previously adopted amendments into the constitution, and adjourned after promulgating it without referendum. The constitution is a pamphlet of one hundred twenty-eight pages and contains from forty-five thousand to fifty thousand words.

Aside from the new funding article the interesting changes are: (1) Article 118 on Juvenile Courts (about twenty-four hundred words), adopted 1908, and (2) the continuation of the "grandfather clause," by amendment of 1912. This, however, is not contained in the present constitution in words,[1] but must be followed back to the constitution of 1898. For the revised constitution is, unfortunately, not complete in itself, since it provides in the sixth paragraph of its Schedule that,

> The Constitution of this State, adopted in 1898, and all amendments thereto, are declared to be superseded by this Constitution. But the omission from this Constitution of any Article of the Constitution of 1898 and the amendments thereto or of any other existing Constitutional provision shall not amount to the repeal thereof, unless the same be inconsistent with this Constitution.

Alabama. In 1901 this state held a convention which added about ten thousand words to the constitution of 1875. The convention adjourned September third and referred the constitution to the voters, who November eleventh endorsed it at the polls. The revised constitution dropped from the Declaration of Rights section thirty-five against secession, changed the election month to November, provided for a quadrennial election and legislative session, added two years to the governor's term of office, and devoted some three thousand words to the article on Suffrage and Elections, restricting the voting privilege, and refusing suffrage to "intention" voters not yet citizens of the United States. As usual in this period many limitations were placed on the legislature, and the article on Corporations was much enlarged. The amending process was made simpler and the paragraphs of the constitution numbered consecutively. An interesting addition was made to the section (286) on constitutional conventions, which reads; "provided, nothing herein contained shall be construed

---

[1] See Article 197, Section 5.

as restricting the jurisdiction and power of the convention, when duly assembled in pursuance of this section, to establish such ordinances and to do and perform such things as to the convention may seem necessary or proper for the purpose of altering, revising or amending the existing Constitution."

Virginia in 1902 held a convention which revised its short reconstruction constitution by adding to it about fifteen thousand words. The constitution was promulgated July tenth on the authority of the convention, without referendum. From the Bill of Rights it dropped the slavery, secession and paramount allegiance clauses and also Section twenty, which declared that all citizens of the state should "possess equal civil and political rights and political privileges." The constitution of 1870 had provided (Article VII), "That no amendment or revision shall be made which shall deny or in any way impair the right of suffrage, or any civil or political right as conferred by this Constitution, except for causes which apply to all persons and classes without distinction." Whatever binding effect such a proviso might have on a legislature, it restricts in no way a convention voicing the sovereign will of the people. At any rate the two thousand word article on the Elective Franchise in the new constitution managed to place some rigorous restrictions on "equal" suffrage. In addition, the convention placed limitations on the legislature, gave the governor the item veto, enlarged Local Government, and Taxation and Finance, by some two thousand words each, and inserted a six thousand word article on Corporations, which later was largely copied by the Oklahoma convention of 1907. The difficult amending and revising procedure of the old constitution was retained, except that the provision was dropped which required a referendum every twenty years on the calling of a convention.

Revised and Amended Constitutions in the North

In addition to these six revisions in the south, four others in the north, omitting New England, should be mentioned with some detail.

New York after the fiasco of 1867 continued to worry along with its constitution of 1846, amending it from time to time as best could be done. Finally a convention was summoned in 1894 which, September twenty-ninth, submitted to the voters a constitution which was ratified November sixth. The constitution was carefully revised, article by article, and many changes in detail made but few in general principle. In length the new constitution did not vary much from the older document with its amendments. The membership of both houses of the legislature was enlarged, and a reapportionment ordered to be made after each state census. The judicial system received special attention and provisions were made for civil service rules, the classification of cities and for a state board of charities. The method of amendment was slightly modified but left practically as before. In 1901 by amendment additional limitations were placed on the legislature, and in 1907 a modification of the section respecting the classification of cities. In April of 1914 by a close vote on referendum a convention was ordered for the revision of the constitution in 1915.

Delaware in 1897 revised its short and ancient constitution of 1831, almost doubling it in length. The convention adjourned June 4, 1897, after promulgating the constitution without referendum. The convention surely would never be accused of radicalism. It was distinctly "conservative" in the changes made. The legislative districts of the state were specified in detail, on an undemocratic basis, and no provision made for reapportionment. Naturally there are lengthy provisions aimed at bribery and corruption, in a three thousand word article on (Suffrage and) Elections. Voters were required to pay a fee of one dollar on registering and the ability to read and write was required. The governor was given the veto power including the item veto, and short new articles were inserted on corporations, agriculture, local option and health. The amending and revising process was made slightly easier, but amendments can originate only in the legislature, and must pass two successive legislatures by a two-thirds vote of both houses. Delaware is the only state in the Union that does not submit its amendments on referendum for approval or rejection.

Michigan after many vain attempts to amend and revise its ancient constitution of 1850, managed, April 2, 1906, to secure a referendum vote ordering a convention. This body completed its labors February twenty-first, 1908, and the conservatively revised constitution submitted was ratified at the polls in November. The older constitution had a one line enacting clause but no preamble nor a formal bill of rights. The new constitution contains a preamble of the usual type and a Declaration of Rights of twenty-one sections. Eminent Domain was omitted from this and treated in a separate article. Elective Franchise is brought to the front as Article III, taking the place of Elections in the former constitution. The article on State Officers was omitted, and its provisions placed under the Executive Department. Among the changes made may be noted the addition to the governor's powers of the item veto, the omission of a state census, and significant changes in legislative procedure such as the omission of a time limit on the initiation of bills,[1] ordering the printing of bills at least five days before passage, the insertion of a provision for a legislative yea and nay vote on the demand of one fifth the membership, a prohibition forbidding either house to "adopt any rule that will prevent a majority of the members elected from discharging a committee from the further consideration of any measure," and a prohibition against the passage of any local or special act when a general act can be made applicable.   Salaries for the governor, members of the legislature, and certain other officers were increased, some minor changes were made in the articles on the Judicial Department, and taxpaying women were given a vote on financial referenda.   The most important change was in Local Government (Article VIII).   Laws in regulation of cities and villages are to be general, and home rule charters and local control over franchises secured.   To the amending article a constitutional initiative provision was added, but authorizing the legislature in its discretion to veto initiated measures or to submit an alternative.   This provision came as a compromise after a four days' debate and in April, 1913, was modified by amendment.   The older provision was unworkable, but the amendment gave a definitely popular basis to the initiative.   The older amending process was continued practically as before, except that the powers of future conventions were defined so as to free them from improper legislative restrictions.   The constitution was not materially lengthened in revision and was distinctly improved, though not radically altered, by the few changes made.

---

[1] The original constitution forbade new bills within the last three days of the session.   This was amended in 1860 so as to prohibit new bills after the first fifty days of the session.

Ohio. The constitution of 1851 was difficult of amendment or revision owing to the necessity of securing on referendum "a majority of all the electors voting at said election." So difficult became the amending process with passing years that an affirmative action could be obtained only by the somewhat shady device of omitting from the ballot the "no" of the "yes," "no," placed after the referendum, so that ignorant voters who voted on the amendment would vote affirmatively. Political parties even were authorized [1] to make an amendment part of their tickets, so that voters of straight party tickets might approve such amendments by placing the cross in the circle under the party emblem. By means of this latter device, and the omission of the "no" on the ballot, a convention was finally authorized and held 1912. This body submitted to the voters at a special election, September third, 1912, forty-two separate propositions as the result of its labors. Fortunately for the convention the constitution provided that such amendments might be approved by a "majority of those voting thereon." Eight only of the propositions were rejected, so that thirty-four important changes became part of a revised constitution. One of the chief demands for a convention came from a desire to modify or abolish the old taxation provision "taxing by a uniform rule." On this matter however the convention could not agree and compromise amendments were submitted, retaining the old principle but modifying it somewhat by exceptions.

The propositions adopted are too numerous to specify in this place,[2] but involved modifications in legislative and

[1] The Longworth Act, 1902–08. See Constitutional Conventions of Ohio, by C. B. Galbreath, pp. 44–47.

[2] See references given at end of chapter.

judicial procedure, and in the organization and powers of these departments of government. They modified somewhat the governor's veto, legislated in behalf of labor interests and the conservation of natural resources, improved electional methods, secured municipal home rule, reorganized the taxing system, provided for a carefully regulated liquor license system, and, so far from lengthening the brief article on Corporations, reduced it in size. The recommendations in respect to amendment and revision avoided the blunder of the earlier convention and made the constitution flexible by a simple procedure and the requirement of a "majority of those voting thereon" for both revision and amendments. The most important of the rejected recommendations were; women's suffrage, the abolishment of capital punishment, and provision for the issuance of bonds for a state roads system.

The New England States

Movements for constitutional revision have been prominent in four of the six New England States. *New Hampshire*, which has no process of amending through the legislature, but submits every seven years a referendum in respect to the calling of a convention, has held during this period three conventions. By constitution each convention is to be "proportioned as the representatives to the general court" (the legislature), and recommendations must secure a two-thirds vote on referendum. As the state now has the preposterous number of four hundred and six members in its house of representatives, conventions are entirely too unwieldy to do careful and effective work. Then, too, a referendum vote of two-thirds majority is exceedingly hard to obtain on any really important recommendation, so that few amendments of any consequence ever receive the requisite endorsement at the polls. In 1889 seven amendments were submitted, ten in 1902, and twelve in 1912. The first set was unimportant except for a prohibition amendment. This and one other were rejected and the others accepted. Six of the set of 1902 were rejected and four accepted. These four included an educational qualification for suffrage, taxes on inheritances and franchises, and an anti-trust provision. The chief provisions rejected called for women's suffrage and a much needed reduction in the membership of the house. Of the set of 1912 [1] eight were rejected and four adopted. The only one of consequence among those accepted provided for plurality instead of majority elections. Those rejected involved a readjustment of membership in both houses, and recommendations in respect to taxation, corporations, pensions, and the item veto for the governor.[2]

Rhode Island. This State in 1888 by amendment had relaxed somewhat its suffrage laws by allowing naturalized citizens who owned no real estate a vote in state elections and a modified vote in local elections, and in 1893 it adopted plurality instead of majority elections. Yet, as dissatisfaction at political conditions increased rather than lessened, the general assembly in 1897 authorized the governor to appoint a commission of fifteen persons to report a revision of the constitution. This body was seriously handicapped from the fact that any revision recommended would have to meet with the approval of two successive legislatures.

[1] For brief discussion of this convention, see, *American Political Science Review*, VII. 1. pp. 133–7.

[2] *Parturiunt montes nascetur ridiculus mus*, Horace. Over four hundred delegates had been in session from June fifth–twenty-second at heavy expense to the state, with printing and electional expenses in November, but with no result at all commensurate with the energy and expenditure involved.

Its recommendations in consequence were conservative to the last degree. The revision proposed passed the legislatures without change, but was rejected at the polls November, 1898. This result was far from satisfactory to the party in power, which had the revision repassed with a few verbal changes and again referred June, 1899, but it was rejected by a larger adverse vote than before. In 1912 another commission of nine persons was appointed to report a revision and submitted a report, 1915.[1] Certain recommendations of the first revision have since been passed separately, by the amending process, including modifications in the judicial system, in the house representation, giving to the governor a weak veto power, and providing for a biennial instead of an annual election, though retaining the annual session of the assembly.

Connecticut has in its constitution a difficult amending process and no provision for a convention. In 1901 the legislature under its general powers, after a referendum, summoned a convention but handicapped it by placing limitations on its powers and by having its membership based on the towns, irrespective of population. The constitution prepared made no alterations of real value and made so little concession to the urban centers in representation, that at the polls when referred in June, 1902, it was indignantly rejected. In 1905 the legislature submitted as an amendment a revised constitution, which made no material modifications of any sort, merely incorporating the amendments since 1828 into the main body of the constitution and increasing the salaries of the members of the legislature. This revision also was rejected, November 1907. Since 1886 eight amendments in all have been adopted, the chief of which provided for plurality instead

[1] See, chap. xix.

of majority elections, increased the membership of the
senate, and placed a time limit on the sessions of the
assembly.

Vermont. This State under its constitution as amended
in 1870 considers propositions for amendments at ten-year
intervals, employing a most difficult procedure. In 1880
twenty-three proposals were considered, but two only,
both of small importance, were passed. In 1890 nine proposals were considered, but none was passed. The same
fate befell four amendments offered in 1900. In 1908 by
joint resolution a commission of five was appointed to propose amendments to the constitution. The commission
made in January 1910 a careful report embodied in eight
proposals, and submitted a copy of the constitution so
arranged as to include in the main body all former amendments. Five of these proposals were in substance accepted
by two successive assemblies and by the voters in 1913,
becoming thereby part of the constitution. These included
a strengthening of the governor's veto power, the adoption
of the November election and the January session, and
restrictions on special and local legislation. In place of the
rearrangement of the constitution proposed by the commission a substitute was passed as an amendment authorizing the justices of the supreme court to perform this task.
These reported in September a remodeled constitution
which thereby became the constitution of the state, super-
seding the ancient document of 1793 with its amendments
of one hundred twenty years. In addition to these proposals submitted by the commission seven others were
introduced into the senate but two unimportant ones only
passed the ordeal of the approving vote of two assemblies
and of the electorate.

The other two New England states during this period

have confined themselves to amendments, the most important of which are the following. *Massachusetts* in 1892 removed from the governorship its property qualification, permitted in 1911 the use of voting machines, and in 1913 permitted the legislature to refer legislative measures to the electorate. *Maine* in 1892 adopted an educational qualification for voting and adopted 1908, the statutory initiative and referendum.

Changes in Other States

Indiana. The constitution of this state dates from 1851 and contains no provision for a convention. The amending process requires the action of two assemblies and "a majority of the electors of the state." In consequence of this stringent requirement, few amendments have ever been passed. In 1900 a petty amendment in respect to admissions to the bar was voted on at referendum and failed to receive a legal majority. Later, the supreme court held that under the constitution no further amendments could be submitted until the amendment was definitely adopted or rejected. In consequence, the amendment was submitted once more in 1906, and again in 1910, but aroused so little interest, that it failed to carry. The supreme court then modified its decision so as to permit of the submission of other amendments. In view of this condition, Governor Marshall, now Vice President, having a democratic legislature, in February, 1911, had prepared a revised constitution for the state. This was submitted to a party caucus for modification and endorsement, and then introduced into the legislature for enactment, under the theory that the general powers of the lawmaking body allowed it to submit a constitution to the voters on referendum. Within three weeks the constitution was passed by the legislature, signed by the governor, and referred to the voters at the November election. In view of the difficulty of getting a proper vote on amendments of any sort a statute was also passed,[1] modeled after the Longworth Act of Ohio,[2] providing that pending amendments might be endorsed by political parties, so that straight ticket votes would count towards the passage of an amendment. The legality of the submission of the revised constitution having come before the supreme court, it held (July fifth) that the legislative constitution had been illegally submitted. Finally the legislature of 1913, March fifteenth, under its general powers, voted to submit to the voters, in November 1914, a referendum as to whether a convention to revise the constitution shall be summoned. At the polls this referendum was negatived, since by requirement the referendum had to be approved by a majority of all votes cast at the general election.

Oregon. The constitution of 1857 was in general modeled after the constitution of Indiana (1851), but unfortunately it copied almost verbatim the amending article, so that for fifty years the state found it impossible to pass amendments, owing to the stringent requirements of the constitution. Finally in 1902 the first amendment was passed, an amendment revolutionary in character, since it provided for the constitutional initiative and referendum. At once it became possible to amend the constitution by this easier procedure, so that the succeeding years have seen many attempts, successful or otherwise, to make up for lost time in modernizing the constitution. From 1904–14 inclusive, sixty-three amendments have been acted on and twenty-three of these affirmatively. The consequence is that the constitution has gone through a sort of

[1] Chapter 219. laws 1911.   [2] See, p. 99.

revision, though there is still room for improvement. As is well known, the success of the " Oregon plan " has stimulated a great movement among the states, ushering in virtually a new era in the amending and revising of constitutions.

In Oregon the chief measures introduced into the constitution by these devices are as follows : — The initiative and referendum feature has been made complete, applying to revision through convention, to amendments, to statutes or parts of statutes and to all forms of local laws. It has been supplemented by the recall, applying to every elective office in the state. A large amount of home rule has been secured to city and county, including a partial control under regulation over their franchises, taxes, and debts. The judiciary article has been revised, including modifications of the jury system ; women have been granted the suffrage, "intention" voting abolished, proportional representation made permissive, elections changed from June to November, prohibition adopted, and the poll tax abolished. These amendments unitedly have not materially lengthened the constitution which contains about eleven thousand words.

The State of *California* in amending was not handicapped by any constitutional provision, since amendments may be passed by the usual procedure of a two-thirds vote in the legislature and a referendum vote of a majority of those voting thereon. During the first twenty-five years of the existence of the constitution of 1879 twenty-seven amendments were passed, none of them of an especially radical nature. But during the eight following years, ending with 1912, fifty-six amendments are listed in the revised constitution of 1914, many of which embody the newer radicalism of the times ; nearly half of these amendments were passed at the special election of 1911 and these chiefly embodied the radical and lengthy additions to the constitution. For, the amendments of the last eight years are in some cases not brief, general provisions, but detailed statutes inserted bodily into the constitution. The eighty-three amendments combined have added about thirteen thousand words to the constitution, making a total of nearly thirty-two thousand words. Eighteen of these amendments concern the Judicial Department, all passed since 1904: twenty are under the heading of Counties, Cities and Towns; sixteen are under the heading of Revenue and Taxation; seven under Corporations, all dating from 1908, and seven are under Education.

In enumerating the chief additions made to the constitution, it may be said that the most striking series of changes consists in the many provisions for the use of the initiative and referendum for constitutional and statutory law and local ordinances. This is supplemented by the recall, applying to every elective officer, including the judiciary. Women are granted the suffrage on the same terms as men, and radical primary laws demanded. In local government home rule is secured to cities and counties. Provision is made for a split legislative session, with the hope of eliminating the rush period common at the end of a legislative session, and for larger salaries for members of the legislature and for the governor and other chief administrative officers of the state. The important economic provisions provide for a railroad commission in charge and regulation of all public utilities, a revision of the taxing system as applied to quasi-public corporations, banks and insurance companies, a prohibition of stock gambling and of poll taxes, and provisions for employers' liability, the minimum wage, and the safeguarding of the exercise of eminent domain powers. The amendments on education include provisions for free text books, prepared and printed by the state, and Section twenty-four (Article IV) makes careful provision for the charities of the state.

Changes so fundamental as these emphasize the importance of the study of state constitutions, seeing that a state so inclined may within a very few years profoundly revolutionize not only its constitutional system and political organization, but even to a quite large extent its economic and social life. By modifications in their fundamental law the citizens of states like Oregon and California, whether for good or for bad, have their destiny in their own hands, in marked contrast to conditions in such states as Indiana, Delaware and Rhode Island, where the citizens are held gripped by the "dead hands" of antiquated fundamental law.

THE NEW STATES

Since 1886 ten new states have been added to the Union, completing the statehood of all the national territory except Alaska, Porto Rico, Hawaii, the Philippine Islands, and other minor possessions. On February twenty-second, 1889, an enabling act of congress authorized conventions for the preparation of constitutions for four prospective states; North and South Dakota, Montana, and Washington. These several conventions met July fourth in their several capitals, and prepared and submitted constitutions, which in each case were ratified. Acts were then passed by Congress admitting these territories as states : on November second, North and South Dakota; November eighth, Montana; November eleventh, Washington. Meanwhile, Idaho and Wyoming, envious of the superior lot of their sister territories, on their own initiative held conventions, adopted constitutions, and then submitted these to congress with petitions for admission to the Union. After some delay congress assented to these requests and they were admitted — Idaho, July third, and Wyoming July tenth, 1890. Utah, owing to questions arising through Mormonism, was not admitted with the other territories, but after these troubles had been settled, congress, July, 1894, authorized it to prepare a constitution. This was prepared in the Spring of 1895, ratified in November, and Utah admitted as a state January fourth, 1896. In 1890 the new territory of Oklahoma was formed from part of the lands included in the Indian Territory. By 1905 both of these territories were eager for statehood and the latter even held a convention and prepared a constitution for a state to be called Sequoyah. But in 1906 after much local dissension an enabling act of about five thousand words authorized the two territories to hold a joint convention so as to prepare a constitution for a state combining the two territories. The constitution thus prepared was ratified September 17, 1907, and after some delay, due to the radicalism of certain provisions of the constitution, the state was proclaimed, November sixteenth, as a member of the Union.

In the same enabling act which authorized Oklahoma to hold a convention an additional five thousand words authorized the territories of Arizona and New Mexico to form a joint state. This decision was not satisfactory to them since they each desired separate statehood. This difference of opinion lasted for about four years and ended when congress June 20, 1910, by enabling act, authorized them to hold separate conventions preparatory to statehood. The constitutions were prepared and duly ratified [1] but were not entirely satisfactory to congress. The constitution of Arizona was radical in its provisions and

[1] New Mexico, January 21, Arizona, February 9, 1911.

included a state wide recall. By contrast the constitution of New Mexico was too conservative, since amendment under its provisions would be well nigh impossible. Finally Arizona was instructed to omit from its constitution the recall of judges, and New Mexico to make its amending process more flexible. These conditions were complied with and the territories were then admitted as states, New Mexico January sixth, Arizona February fourteenth, 1912. Once admitted, Arizona promptly asserted her right to deter-mine its own fundamental law by submitting in April as an amendment, the recall of judges; this was ratified at the November election, becoming thereby a part of the constitution.

These ten constitutions in many respects show a marked similarity; barring the radical features of the constitutions of Oklahoma and Arizona, they clearly present the familiar aspects of the average constitution of the modern type. These resemblances are largely due to the fact that their economic systems are based on mining and agriculture; to the influence of older neighboring states under similar environment, and especially are they largely due to the numerous well-defined demands of congress through its enabling acts. From the beginning these territories were under congressional authority. Congressional acts deter-mined their territorial forms of government, after the democratic type lineally descended from the Ordinance of 1787, and congressional enabling acts with their "irrev-ocable compacts" ensured ample guaranties for freedom, education, and a democratic, representative system of government. So powerful has been the democratic in-fluence of congress in reconstruction and in the formation of states out of territories, that one might almost wish that the New England and the smaller middle states would attempt to secede from the Union, so that congress might have the pleasure of reconstructing them on democratic lines, as interpreted by the trend of the last twenty-five years. These states themselves would benefit from the change when once they discovered that the "icy plunge" had had a tonic effect in freeing political systems from antiquated accretions and corrupt bossism.

In general these ten new constitutions start with a combined preamble and enacting clause, insert a bill or declaration of rights, accept (in special articles) the boundaries and conditions set by congress, provide for the threefold separation of powers, specify the organization and powers of each of these three departments, varying, naturally, in detail somewhat, yet all agreeing that many limitations must be placed on the legislature, provide for biennial sessions and elections and for the election (not appointment) of the chief administrative officers and judges of the state, and insert articles on suffrage, local government, education, the militia, impeachment, mines, corporations, and the many other subjects that now regularly find place in constitutions. They end with a procedure for amendment and revision, and a schedule. In length, omitting the constitution of Oklahoma, they vary from sixteen thousand to twenty-one thousand words, averaging about nineteen thousand. Oklahoma's constitution has almost forty thousand words, and if Counties and County Seats [1] is inserted, ten thousand words more should be added. The details of these constitutions will be given in connection with the chapters of Part II yet in respect to the three newest constitutions, it may be said that that of New Mexico is nearest in kind to those of the other western states.

[1] Giving county boundaries etc.; omitted from Thorpe's collection, but contained in the original constitution.

It contains a mild statutory referendum provision and devotes about fourteen hundred words to Corporations and a Corporation Commission. Its amending process, by congressional injunction, was made easy,[1] except that certain sections safeguarding the rights of Spanish-speaking citizens [2] can be amended only by special votes practically impossible of attainment. The constitution of Arizona contains most of the "latest improvements" in the form of initiative and referendum, recall, primary, municipal home rule, and a lengthy article (two thousand words) on Corporations. Its amending and revising processes are simple and changes in the constitution can be made with ease. The constitution of Oklahoma, including the "County" section, has the doubtful honor of being the longest state constitution in the Union, Louisiana being a close second. The document as a whole is poorly prepared, loosely thrown together, and is filled with useless detail. There was some justification for this. The territory had been but lately organized, its population had gathered from every state in the Union and was far from homogeneous, so that necessarily there was but little unity in the territory or its convention, based on common traditions and interests. The inclusion of the Indian Territory into the new state complicated the situation by the mingling of differing races and the confusion of standards incident thereto. Party feeling ran high and there was much rivalry for place and power. The convention lacking unity did not work together easily nor quickly, the more so as there was much dissatisfaction at some of the conditions placed on the convention by the terms of the enabling act. Its intentions

---

[1] A majority of each house, and on referendum a majority of those voting thereon.

[2] Articles VII, 1. 3.; XII, 8. 10.

in the main were excellent, and no one surely could rightly accuse its members of conservatism. The constitution includes the radicalism of the far west, so far as it had developed at that time under the influence of the "Oregon idea." Distrust of the legislature was plainly in evidence in the many stringent restrictions placed on its powers, and in the severe bribery oath required from its members. Suspicions of gerrymandering arise from the undue space given to definitions of legislative, judicial, and county boundaries. An eight thousand word article on Corporations, largely copied from Virginia's constitution was inserted. The constitution ends with a three thousand word schedule and an ill considered amending article, in which for amendments is required "a majority of all the electors voting at such election."

BIBLIOGRAPHY FOR PART I

ALDEN, GEORGE H. New Governments West of the Alleghanies before 1780. Bulletin, University of Wisconsin (Economics, Political Science, History). Volume II, 1.

California. The Establishment of State Government in California (1846–1850), by C. Goodwin. New York. 1914.

CAMPBELL, DOUGLAS. The Origin of American Institutions. Papers American Historical Association. Volume V, pp. 165–186.

CHANDLER, J. A. C. History of Suffrage in Virginia. Johns Hopkins Series. Volume XIX.

Federalist, The. (Edited by John C. Hamilton, 1866. Philadelphia.) See, its Index, under *States.*

HOUGH, FRANKLIN B. Constitution of the State of New York, adopted in 1846, with a comparative arrangement of the constitutional provisions of other States classified by their subjects. Prepared under the direction of a Committee of the New York Constitutional Convention of 1867. Albany. 1867.

MCKINLEY, ALBERT E. The Suffrage Franchise in the Thirteen English Colonies in America. University of Pennsylvania. 1905.

Maryland. State Government in Maryland (1777–1781), by B. W. Bond. Johns Hopkins Series. Volume XXII. Maryland Constitution of 1851, by J. W. Harry. Johns Hopkins Series. Volume XX. (See references to Maryland also at end of Chapter VII.)

Nebraska. Some Original and Peculiar Features of the Nebraska Constitution, by C. S. Lobingier. *Annals.* Volume XV, pp. 433–437.

TURNER, FREDERICK J. Western State Making in the Revolutionary Era. *American Historical Review.* Volume I, pp. 70–87; 251–269.

WILLOUGHBY, W. F. State Activities and Politics. Papers American Historical Association. Volume V, pp. 113–127 (1891). Territories and Dependencies. (First three chapters.) New York. 1905.

SOME COMMENTS ON RECENT CONSTITUTIONS

Alabama, Virginia. Two New Southern Constitutions, by A. E. McKinley. *Political Science Quarterly.* Volume XVIII, pp. 480–511.

Arizona, New Mexico. New States and Constitutions, by George W. Wickersham. Senate Document 62, 62d Congress, 1st session.

Social Principles of the New Constitutions, by A. J. McKelway. *Survey.* Volume XXV, pp. 610–613.

Louisiana. Comparison of the Constitutions of 1898 and 1913, by W. O. Hart. Pamphlet. New Orleans. 1914.

The Suffrage Clause of the New (1898) Constitution of Louisiana, by Amasa M. Eaton. *Harvard Law Review,* Volume XIII, 4.

Michigan. American Political Science Review, by J. A. Fairlie. Volume II, pp. 443–447; Volume IV, pp. 119–123.

Ohio. The Constitutions of Ohio and Allied Documents, by Isaac F. Patterson. Cleveland. 1912.

Constitutional Conventions of Ohio, by C. B. Galbreath. Pamphlet, 63 pages. Columbus. 1911.

The Fourth Constitutional Convention of Ohio. By H. W. Elson. *Review of Reviews.* Volume XLV, pp. 337–340.

Voting Organic Laws, by Robert E. Cushman. *Political Science Quarterly.* June, 1913.

The Ohio Constitution. *North American Review.* Volume 197, pp. 275–280.

American Political Science Review. Volume VI, pp. 573–576, 581–583.

American Political Science Review. Volume VII, pp. 639–650.

The New Constitution of Ohio, by F. C. Howe. *Survey.* Volume XXVIII, pp. 757–759.

Oklahoma. Constitution of Oklahoma, by Henry G. Snyder. Kansas City. 1908.

The Constitution of Oklahoma, by Charles A. Beard. *Political Science Quarterly.* Volume XXIV, pp. 96–114.

REINSCH, PAUL S. In Readings on American State Government, see Chapter IX, Constitutional Conventions.

South Carolina. The Late Constitutional Convention and Constitution of South Carolina, by Amasa M. Eaton. Volume 31, *American Law Review.*

For references already given in Part I, see:

	PAGE		PAGE
Alden, G. H.	18	Hollis, J. P.	88
Bondy, W.	8	Jameson, J. A.	49
Bryce, J.	8	Jameson, J. F.	2
Burgess, J. W.	88	MacDonald, W.	21
Chadsey, C. E.	88	Meader, L. H.	31
Davis, W. W.	88	Moran, T. F.	37
Dodd, W. F.	24	Morey, W. C	9, 24
Dunning, W. A.	88	Myers, W. S.	88
Eckenrode, H. J.	88	Ramsdell, C. W.	88
Ficklen, J. R.	88	Rhodes, J. F.	88
Galbreath, C. B.	82, 99	Thorpe, F. N.	30, 88
Haines, C. G.	8, 28	Webster, W. C.	24, 36
Hamilton, J. G.	88	Wilson, W.	2
Harry, J. W.	88	Wooley, E. C.	88

PART II

PROVISIONS OF EXISTING CONSTITU-
TIONS

CHAPTER IX

THE WRITTEN CONSTITUTION AND ITS BILL OF RIGHTS

THE United States has made many a contribution to the theory and practice of modern politics. Among these by no means the least is the written constitution. Developed during the throes of the Revolution, one hundred and thirty-eight years ago, it, and its maker the convention, have been the chief means through which democracy has made its demands and fixed them in the law of the land. A convention, democratically organized, voices the will of the people. This will, formulated into the fundamental law, is a guaranty of life and liberty, and a surety against governmental injustice and tyranny.

Thomas Jefferson, the apostle of American democracy, used to argue that the constitution of every state should be revised at least once " every nineteen or twenty years," so as to allow each generation to determine for itself its fundamental law. The argument is even more true since his day, for the conditions of life so rapidly change through advancing civilization, that modifications in fundamental law must be made at frequent intervals. These modifications, as Judge Jameson [1] puts it, are regularly made through a

[1] On Constitutional Conventions, pp. 610–611, fourth edition.

legislature and the referendum, when the purpose "is to bring about amendments which are few and simple, and independent;" but a new constitution or a revision of an existing constitution, demands the services of a convention, which "only is appropriate or permissible."

In more recent years, in addition to the legislature and the convention, one must take into account the use of the constitutional commission, and the rapidly growing use of the constitutional initiative in the hands of the electorates of the states.

State constitutions, both past and present, so reflect the changing conditions and varied interests of the United States, that a study of them affords a perfect mirror of American democracy. No one, surely, can arise from this study without a full conviction that American political institutions are established on firm foundations, and that the states are slowly working out a mass of constitutional principles in harmony with morality and intelligence.

The earliest of the state constitutions were far inferior to those of later date. The statesmen of those days, though with the best of intentions, had not a full grasp of democratic principles, nor had they had much political experience in handling great governmental interests. Since their day over two hundred constitutions have been made in this country alone, and the conflicting experiences of the numerous states supply ample material for study. Consequently, it is entirely possible for a state, profiting by past experiences and by a study of present constitutions, to prepare a fundamental law, which shall express the best American political ideals and practices, and prove helpful in the development of the material interests of its people. The real importance of these documents, as indicative of the theories and standards of nearly one hundred millions of population, becomes obvious when it is seen that the citizens of each of the forty-eight states determine their own fundamental law, and have unitedly embodied their demands in forty-eight written organic laws, which in round numbers include about a million words. Such prolixity may not seem desirable and does at times become ridiculous, yet, after all, these constitutions are the expression of popular will, and possibly are developing into a system of flexible legal and administrative principles that some day may rival in historical importance the many excellencies and virtues of the English common law or the basic teachings of the Roman civil law.

CONSTITUTION MAKING

Historically the present state constitutions represent four distinct periods of political development. The first set [1] is composed of the constitutions of the six New England states. These are old-fashioned in type, are based on the outgrown system of town government, and are so difficult of amendment that they retain many obsolete features, and therefore are no longer suitable as models for modern states. The best of these are the constitutions of Massachusetts and Maine. The combination of ultra-conservative rural towns and of a mass of immigrant population as yet ignorant of our political institutions, affords little hope that these constitutions can be modernized without long agitation and considerable difficulty. The second set [2] consists of those constitutions made in the period embracing the twenty-five years before the ending of the civil war. These seven constitutions are

---

[1] Vermont, 1793; Massachusetts, 1780; New Hampshire, 1784; Connecticut, 1818; Maine, 1819, and Rhode Island, 1842. See, chap. xix.

[2] New Jersey, 1842; Wisconsin, 1848; Indiana, 1851; Iowa, Minnesota, 1857; Kansas, 1859; and Nevada, 1864.

democratic in principle and excellent in tone, but do not include the experience of later years, except as this has in part crept in through amendment, so that they are on the whole sadly in need of revision. The third set,[1] thirteen in number, represents in the main the provisions emphasized as the result of reconstruction in the south, and adaptation to economic changes north and south, at the close of the war. The last set, twenty-two in number, consists of two groups, one made up of the ten [2] new mining and agricultural states of the far west, and the other[3] made up of the twelve states that felt compelled to readjust their governmental systems to changed social, economic and political conditions resulting from war and national growth.

Besides these constitutions there is an annually increasing mass of amendments added through legislature and referendum, and through the new device of the constitutional initiative. As a fair estimate of present conditions, it may be said that the states submit every two years nearly one hundred amendments, about three-fifths of which are adopted. The number, however, varies considerably from session to session. Evidently a knowledge of these amendments also is necessary, representing as they do the current contribution of politics toward the supposed defects and shortcomings of existing constitutions.

The *length* of recent constitutions is one reason for so large

---

[1] Maryland, 1867; Tennessee and Illinois, 1870; West Virginia, 1872; Pennsylvania, 1873; Arkansas, 1874; Texas, Missouri, North Carolina and Nebraska, 1875; Colorado, 1876; Georgia, 1877; and Florida, 1886.

[2] North Dakota, South Dakota, Montana, Washington, in 1889; Idaho, Wyoming, in 1890; Utah, 1896; Oklahoma, 1907; New Mexico and Arizona in 1912.

[3] Mississippi, 1890; Kentucky, 1891; New York, 1894; South Carolina, 1895; Delaware, 1897; Louisiana, 1898 and 1913; Alabama, 1901, Virginia, 1902; Michigan, 1908; Ohio, 1912; Oregon, since 1902; California, since 1911.

a number of amendments. The earliest constitutions seldom contained over five thousand words and averaged much less. Now, the shortest constitution (Rhode Island's) contains about six thousand words, the average is about sixteen thousand, and the five largest are codes in themselves.[1] This lengthening of constitutions is to some extent due to a failure on the part of constitution makers to distinguish between fundamental and statutory law, coupled with a natural desire to magnify their importance as lawmakers; but it is chiefly due to two causes: (1) the great popular distrust of legislatures and (2) the growing complexity of modern life and the consequent rise of many new interests that seem to demand attention. Charges of incapacity and corruption against legislators are so common, that conventions incline to limit and regulate in every possible way the powers of legislatures, so as to reduce the possibility of mischief. Time and experience will probably remedy this wordy defect of state constitutions, and, it is to be hoped, will also improve the calibre of statesmanship and the quality of legislation. Constitutions so verbose as the five mentioned in the footnote require frequent amending,[2] and this system so confuses the distinction between fundamental and statutory law, that in such states the constitutions represent a kind of statutory law altered by a somewhat more difficult procedure than that used in the case of ordinary statutes. The real check on a legislature is not secured by turning the constitution into a

---

[1] Alabama uses thirty-three thousand words, Virginia thirty-five thousand, Louisiana, about forty-five thousand, and Oklahoma nearly fifty thousand. The present constitution of California (1914) with its many amendments has about forty thousand words.

[2] The legislature of Louisiana, from 1900–1914, has submitted almost one hundred amendments, most of which were adopted; though some of the earlier amendments had to be superseded by later amendments, as amendments to amendments.

statutory code, but by making use of the experiences of the states and their most successful devices in securing efficient government.

PARTS OF THE CONSTITUTION

A comparison of constitutions shows that a constitution regularly consists of a preamble, an enacting clause, a bill of rights, articles on the several departments of government and their subdivisions, an article defining suffrage privileges, an article of miscellaneous provisions, an article devoted to amendment and revision, a ratification clause, and a schedule containing provisions of temporary importance, such as arrangements for the substitution of the new for the old order of things.

The *Preamble*, which is a statement of reasons and purpose, is regularly included in the same paragraph as the enacting clause (Delaware's is an exception). In general it follows the thought of the preamble of the national constitution, but differs in that some reference to God is regularly found in the preambles of the states.[1]

In thirty-two enacting clauses the wording is: "We, the people . . . do ordain and establish." In most of the others the wording is either "We, the people . . . do ordain," or "We, the people . . . establish." Maryland says, "We, the people . . . declare," three states omit the pronoun *We*, and one state, Tennessee, says, "We, the delegates." A concise statement may be seen in the constitutions of New York, Arizona, and Michigan; a lengthy type, in those of Massachusetts and Delaware.

Twenty-three of the constitutions contain each an article defining the boundaries of the state. This is not a matter over which the state has final jurisdiction, but, as a rule, the

[1] But see chap. x.

article was inserted so as to accord with the demands of an enabling act; it properly is omitted in most of the constitutions. Thirty-three of the constitutions contain a short, but unnecessary article on the Distribution of Powers. Twenty of these use this particular title, but the other thirteen use seven variations of this wording. Seven of the other fifteen constitutions mention the separation of powers in other articles, but the other eight save space by omitting it entirely. A simple form of the article may be found in the constitution of Rhode Island, the ordinary form is that of Indiana, and an exaggerated form is that of Alabama, which seems to have copied the substance of its provision from Massachusetts. In arranging the order of the usual three departments of government, the arrangement regularly is, legislative, executive, judicial; but three states[1] place the executive before the legislative, following the historical order, rather than the order of importance. As the electorate represents the people, there is a marked tendency in many of the constitutions, nineteen in all, to place the article on suffrage among the first, as though to emphasize the precedence of the voters' over the several departments of governments. This article logically should be called The Electorate, or Qualifications for Electors, but as a rule some variation of the term Suffrage is used instead.

A curious feature of some constitutions, old and new, is the insertion by requirement of congress, of an ordinance, which may not be repealed without the consent of congress, Article III in the constitution of Utah[2] for example, or Oklahoma's Article I and its Ordinance, accepting the enabling act. Congress has full power to demand that a territory place certain articles in its constitution as a prerequisite to admission. Once the territory becomes a state,

---

[1] Colorado, Kansas, Maryland.   [2] See, page 19.

however, the obligation to retain such articles is probably moral, not legal.[1] Otherwise, it would be hard to say just how such "irrevocable" articles can be reconciled with any constitutional theory of the equality of states in their local sovereignty. Territories, however, in becoming states have learned not to "look a gift horse in the mouth," and congress in its turn may prefer to ignore the fate of such articles after the lapse of a few years' time.[2]

The *Schedule* is now regularly found in most of the constitutions (35), though almost unknown in the earlier constitutions and not now always essential, if it be assumed that a constitutional convention has ordinance powers. Its place properly is as an addition to the constitution, not as a part of it, since its provisions are of temporary importance only. Nineteen constitutions, however, include it in the constitution itself as one of the articles. In some cases this is due to a failure to keep the schedule for temporary provisions only, matter being inserted which might more properly go under Miscellaneous Provisions.[3] The better place for the schedule may be seen in the new constitutions of Delaware, Alabama and Virginia, though it might more correctly be placed after the ratification clause, so as to keep it entirely separate from the constitution. Its authority could be attested by the signatures of the president and secretary of the convention as in the case of ordinances.

[1] New Mexico provides in its amending article that if congress gives consent, changes in the terms of the contract may be made by a majority vote of the legislature and a referendum. Yet in 1912 it dropped from the Compact article a section (5) which required that the ability to read, write, speak, and understand the English language should be a necessary qualification for office holding.

[2] Oklahoma's amendment adding a "grandfather clause" to its suffrage article, and Arizona's amendment authorizing the recall of judges, were both in violation of conditions set by congress.

[3] This article may be overworked. Texas, for example, has fifty-seven sections in its General Provisions.

So much space is taken up in some constitutions with apportionments of districts and their boundaries, that the question arises why these should not be placed in the schedule, or issued as ordinances, merely specifying in the constitution under what conditions these may be altered by the legislature. The use of the *ordinance* is well illustrated in the work of the conventions that made the present constitutions for Mississippi and South Carolina.

A matter of some little importance is the method of numbering the several sections of the constitution. A cumbersome and old-fashioned system may be found in the constitution of Massachusetts. The others, with some exceptions, use the plan of the national constitution, viz., articles numbered with Roman numerals subdivided into sections with Arabic numerals. Louisiana, Mississippi, Kentucky, Alabama, Virginia and North Dakota much more sensibly imitate the earlier French constitutions, and number paragraphs consecutively with Arabic numerals, inserting titles in their proper places with or without Roman numbers. New Hampshire and Vermont use the same system, except that their constitutions are divided into two parts, and each is numbered consecutively.

BILLS OF RIGHTS

All states contain in their constitution formal bills of rights. Twenty-four prefer the title Declaration of Rights, but twenty-two use the other form. Maryland has the largest number of provisions, forty-five. Louisiana has the fewest, fifteen. Fourteen states have thirty to forty; twenty-three have twenty to thirty, and ten manage to get along with less than twenty. In three of the constitutions,[1] the Bill of Rights comes first after the enacting clause

[1] Colorado, Kansas, Maryland.

or preamble, and before the articles. In thirty-three constitutions it makes the first article, in eleven it is either the second or third article, in one, South Dakota, it is the sixth. A bill of rights properly should contain only broad general principles in regard to the purposes and spirit of government, and general instructions and prohibitions declaring the fundamental safeguards for life, liberty and property. These principles of liberty and democracy are now so thoroughly ingrained in our legal systems as hardly to need explicit statement in a constitution, yet they will doubtless be long retained as assurances against possible legislative tyranny and as mementos of former struggles. They include guaranties of life, liberty, property, and happiness; freedom of conscience, speech, press, petition, and assembly; *habeas corpus*, open courts, a fair trial and the jury in cases of crime; the right to bear arms, to hold free elections, and to "reform, alter or abolish forms of government;" guaranties against unreasonable search, seizure, imprisonment or bail; and provisions in regard to treason, martial law, and imprisonment for debt. Evidently such provisions as these are well worth preserving in our fundamental law. On the other hand one may question whether it is worth while to retain references to the exploded theory of social compact, or to guaranty the right of emigration, or to insert provisions in respect to lotteries, lobbying, dueling, pensions, punishments, slavery, contempt of court, and the tenure of office. Such matters may or may not deserve place in our constitutions, but surely not in a bill of rights. Again, when a simple right of earlier days becomes complex, it might better go into the main body of the constitution under its appropriate heading. Trial by jury, for instance, is frequently modified nowadays by waiving it altogether in certain kinds of cases, or by changes in the traditional number and the unanimous verdict. Such modifications properly belong to the judicial department. Again, the statement that "the property of no man shall be taken for public use without just compensation therefor" (Connecticut), is simple enough, but when this right is hedged about with numerous explanatory clauses [1] it might better be transferred to the legislative department. A similar remark would apply to the subject of libel, which now is generally amplified in constitutions.

In general it may be said that these bills contain too many provisions of doubtful truth, of local or temporary importance, and of details that properly belong to other articles. Many of the newer provisions found in some bills are in others placed under more appropriate headings in the constitution, so that there seems to be a real confusion as to what should or should not be inserted. It is possible that a close study of the great movements of the times might result in the formulation of new sets of rights worth inserting; rights, for instance, of labor, women, children, and of electorates in respect to their definite control over all governmental agencies. There are some new provisions now very generally inserted in the later constitutions that are important enough to become permanent additions to bills of rights. Two at least are so important that a convention failing to insert them in substance somewhere in the constitution should be considered derelict in its duty : — Fourteen constitutions for instance read, "No money shall ever be taken from the public treasury, directly or indirectly, in aid of any church, sect, or religious denomination, or in aid of any sectarian institution"; and seven insert the provision that "Every grant or franchise, privilege or immunity, shall

[1] See for example California, Section 14; or it might even be made into a special article, as in Michigan, Article XIII. Amendments permitting excess condemnation have already begun; e.g., in New York, Massachusetts and other states.

forever remain subject to revocation, alteration, or amendment." [1]

There are two provisions rather generally inserted in bills of rights which, though not so essential as they were once, yet deserve place for historic reasons if not otherwise. They are "The rights enumerated in this bill of rights shall not be construed to limit other rights of the people not therein expressed," and "The provisions of this constitution are mandatory and prohibitory, unless by express words they are declared to be otherwise." In conclusion of this topic it may be said that many states have found the substance of the first eight amendments to the national constitution [2] to be the best basis for their own bills of rights.

[1] There are numerous variations of these two provisions in different articles of other constitutions.

[2] It is understood that these rights in the national constitution are guaranties against congressional action only; each state needs to repeat them in substance in its own constitution, except in so far as they may be considered as secured by the fourteenth amendment.

CHAPTER X

RELIGIOUS PROVISIONS OF THE STATE CONSTITUTIONS

THE principle of religious liberty is one of the most striking features of American democracy. Foreign students of our institutions regularly manifest deep surprise at the practical workings of the theory of the separation of church and state. Chapter CVI for instance of Bryce's American Commonwealth illustrates this attitude of mind. The national constitution took advanced ground when it forbade congress to establish religion or to prohibit its free exercise, and recognized no religious test as a qualification for office or public trust.[1] Some of the states even yet have not advanced so far. There are still survivals in the constitutions of that earlier, more intolerant spirit which now seems so strangely out of place. The religious provisions of the state constitutions may roughly be divided into two classes : (1) those aiming to establish religious freedom ; and (2) those involving some recognition of religion. A statement of each of these in turn may present some interesting features.

RELIGIOUS FREEDOM

All forty-eight constitutions in plain terms provide for freedom of worship but vary considerably in methods of expression. Michigan, for example, states that "Every person shall be at liberty to worship God according to the dictates of his own conscience. No person shall be compelled

---

[1] Amendment I and last clause of Article VI.

to attend, or, against his consent, to contribute to the erection or support of any place of religious worship, or to pay tithes, taxes or other rates for the support of any minister of the gospel or teacher of religion." North Dakota, by contrast, provides that "The free exercise and enjoyment of religious profession and worship, without discrimination or preference, shall be forever guaranteed in this state." Utah, after a similar provision, adds, emphatically, "There shall be no union of church and state, nor shall any church dominate the state or interfere with its functions." Other constitutions again, like those of Massachusetts, Rhode Island, and New Hampshire, have lengthy provisions, the last named state employing two hundred and seventy-three words for Article VI of its Bill of Rights. The additional matter as a rule amplifies the principle in detail by specifying that no preference shall be given by law to religious societies; that no person shall be compelled against his will to contribute toward their support, nor to attend services; that every person shall be free to profess and maintain by argument his religious beliefs; and that every religious denomination shall be protected in the peaceable enjoyment of its own mode of worship. Rhode Island has an eighty word *whereas*, as preface to its provision, and states therein its historic argument for religious liberty. Twenty constitutions however, are careful to say in varying phraseology that liberty of conscience shall not be construed so as to excuse acts of licentiousness, nor justify practices inconsistent with the peace and safety of the state. Many provide that liberty of conscience shall not be construed to dispense with oaths or affirmations, and Idaho, Montana, Utah, Oklahoma, Arizona and New Mexico [1] expressly

---

[1] The last four were instructed to insert this clause by the congressional enabling act.

except polygamous marriage from a guaranty of religious freedom.

The constitutions generally provide that no limitations shall be placed on an individual's rights because of his religious beliefs. Seven states for example prohibit the denial on such grounds of civil rights; ten other states put it "No civil or political rights shall be denied;" and twenty-two states declare that no religious test shall be required as a qualification for any office or public trust. Four states [1] specify that no religious test shall ever be required as a qualification for voting. In judicial matters nine states forbid any religious test as a qualification for jurors, and twenty-one states safeguard witnesses in the same way. Oregon and Washington add to these provisions, "nor be questioned in any court of justice touching his religious belief, to affect the weight of his testimony." On the other hand two constitutions insert a provision inherited from the political theories of Cromwell's time: [2] Maryland bluntly provides that "No minister or preacher of the gospel, or of any religious creed or denomination, shall be eligible as senator or delegate." Tennessee is far more courteous in its similar provision. "Whereas, ministers of the gospel are, by their profession, dedicated to God and the care of souls, and ought not to be diverted from the great duties of their functions; therefore, no minister of the gospel or priest of any denomination whatever, shall be eligible to a seat in either house of the legislature."

Freedom of conscience is also safeguarded by exempting from military duty those who are conscientiously opposed to war. Twenty-three states have provisions of this sort, varying from the quaint phraseology of Maine, "Persons of

[1] Kansas, Minnesota, Utah, West Virginia.
[2] For example, Harrington's Oceana.

the denominations of Quakers and Shakers, . . . and ministers of the gospel may be exempted from military duty," to the businesslike statement of Washington. "No person or persons having conscientious scruples against bearing arms shall be compelled to do military duty in time of peace : Provided, such person or persons shall pay an equivalent for such exemption."

Some of our states by experience have found out that religious sects can be indirectly supported from public funds by grants to religious philanthropic institutions, especially hospitals and orphan asylums. Twenty-four states recognize the danger of this policy and forbid in more or less vigorous terms such grants. A typical provision of this sort (Michigan) reads : "No money shall be appropriated or drawn from the treasury for the benefit of any religious sect or society, theological or religious seminary, nor shall property belonging to the state be appropriated for any such purpose." Montana has a still stronger prohibition ; "No appropriation shall be made for charitable, industrial, educational or benevolent purposes to any person, corporation or community not under the absolute control of the state, nor to any denominational or sectarian institution or association." Lengthy provisions of a similar nature, but with certain provisos, may be found in California, Article IV, sections 22 and 30 ; Louisiana, Article 53, and Virginia, section 67. A kindred provision forbidding aid to sectarian educational institutions may be found in thirty-two constitutions.[1] Article 253 of the Louisiana constitution contains this provision in simple form, "No funds raised for the support of the public schools of the state shall be appropriated to or used for the support of any private or sectarian schools." A safer and far more

[1] Due in most cases to congressional instructions in enabling acts.

emphatic form may be seen in Utah's constitution, Article X, section 13 : "Neither the legislature nor any county, city, town, school district or other public corporation, shall make any appropriation to aid in the support of any school, seminary, academy, college, university, or other institution, controlled in whole, or in part by any church, sect, or denomination whatever." This provision is in nine constitutions enlarged by an injunction against the teaching of sectarian doctrines : Wyoming says, "nor shall any sectarian tenets or doctrines be taught or favored in any public school or institution that may be established under this constitution ;" Wisconsin expressly forbids sectarian instruction in its university, and California also desires its university to be kept "entirely independent of all sectarian influence." Nebraska and South Dakota unite in a provision which in the constitution of the last named state reads as follows : "Nor shall the state, or any county or municipality within the state, accept any grant, conveyance, gift or bequest of lands, money or other property to be used for sectarian purposes." Seven of the mining states,[1] curiously enough substantially agree in providing that, "No religious test or qualification shall ever be required of any person as a condition of admission into any public educational institution of this state, either as teacher or student ; and no teacher or student of any such institution shall ever be required to attend, or participate in, any religious service whatever." (Colorado, IX, 8.). Kentucky has it in the form, "nor shall any man be compelled to send his child to any school to which he may be conscientiously opposed." Mississippi however, in providing for religious liberty expressly says that, "The rights hereby secured shall not be construed to exclude the Holy Bible from use in any public school of this

[1] Colorado, Idaho, Montana, Wyoming, Utah, Arizona, New Mexico.

state." Perhaps, however, the most curious of this series of prohibitions is found in the constitutions of Michigan and Oregon, which provide that no money shall be appropriated for the payment of any religious services in either house of the legislature. The odd part of the Michigan provision is that in the same paragraph forbidding religious services for the legislature it authorizes the employment of a chaplain for the state prison; apparently its inmates were considered more susceptible to religious influences. Mississippi also has the spiritual welfare of its prisoners at heart and permits the legislature to provide for "religious worship for the convicts."

Unless there be a prohibition in the constitution, a legislature under its general lawmaking powers may exempt property used for religious purposes from taxation. For this reason most constitutions are silent in respect to such exemptions. Fourteen states, however, expressly authorize their legislatures to exempt such property. A few states have some curious provisions in regard to this matter. Virginia and West Virginia agree in forbidding a charter of incorporation to any church or religious denomination, but authorize the assemblies to secure the title to church property so as to hold it for designated purposes. Missouri allows religious corporations to be established under general law but only for the purpose of holding title to not over five acres of land (one acre within a city) and buildings thereon, if used for religious purposes. Maryland in a lengthy article in its bill of rights (Article 38) forbids every gift, sale or devise for religious purposes without the prior or subsequent sanction of the legislature, but excepts from this provision land not exceeding five acres and its buildings. Mississippi goes farthest of all in prohibiting every devise, legacy, gift or bequest to a religious body or corporation, and authorizes the heir-at-law to take such property "as though no testamentary disposition had been made." [1] As a final illustration of the regulation of property used for religious purposes, we find Kansas anticipating modern French policy by providing that, "The title to all property of religious corporations shall vest in trustees, whose election shall be by the members of such corporations."

RECOGNITION OF RELIGION

The provisions in constitutions that involve some recognition of religion are simple and comparatively few in number. The most important of these is a formal acknowledgment of the goodness of God. Forty-three constitutions place in their preambles this recognition; three, having no preamble, omit it (West Virginia, New Hampshire, Vermont); and two make no reference to God in their preambles (Tennessee, Oregon). In thirty-three preambles the term Almighty God is used; three use the term God; and three, Supreme Ruler of the Universe. The following terms each occur once only: Creator, Supreme Being, Sovereign Ruler of the Universe, Sovereign Ruler of Nations, and Great Legislator of the Universe. The most common form is a simple acknowledgment of gratitude for the enjoyment of rights and liberty (twenty-three constitutions); thirteen others add to that an invocation or a statement of reliance on Him for blessings and guidance; four use the invocation or statement of reliance only, two use the phrase, "with profound reverence for the Supreme Ruler of the Universe," and Delaware ascribes to Divine Goodness the fact that "all men have by nature the rights of worshiping and serving their Creator according to the dictates of their consciences." The following quotations illustrate the usual phraseology:

[1] Sections 269, 270.

"Grateful to Almighty God for our freedom;" "Grateful to Almighty God, and invoking his blessing on our work;" "Grateful to Almighty God and humbly invoking His guidance;" "Humbly invoking the blessings of Almighty God."

Three constitutions,[1] in their bills of rights quote from the Declaration of Independence, asserting that men are free and equal and endowed by their *Creator* with certain inalienable rights. Similar provisions in other constitutions omit the word Creator.

All of the forty-eight constitutions provide that the officers of the state take oath or affirmation on entering office and as a rule give the oath or affirmation verbatim. In eighteen constitutions the oath ends with the sentence "So help me God" (Vermont and Connecticut use the second person). Seven of these substitute, in case of an affirmation, the phrase "under the pains and penalties of perjury." Four constitutions also provide for an oath or affirmation at registration, or if challenged when voting.

Among the most curious survivals of religious intolerance are those found in eight constitutions regarding qualifications for office. Both Arkansas and Mississippi expressly state that no religious test shall be required as a qualification for office; yet in later articles provide that no person who denies the existence of God shall hold any office; and Arkansas adds, "nor be competent to testify as a witness in any court." Maryland, North Carolina, South Carolina, and Texas likewise refuse office under similar conditions, but Maryland also adds that a witness or juror must believe "in the existence of God, and that under His dispensation such person will be held morally accountable for his acts, and be rewarded or punished therefor in this world or the

---

[1] Alabama, Indiana, North Carolina.

world to come." Pennsylvania [1] and Tennessee, however, go still farther by requiring as a qualification for any office a belief in the being of God and in a future state of rewards and punishments. This provision of Tennessee's constitution must be a lineal descendant of a provision of the constitution submitted by the Rev. Samuel Houston in 1785 for the State of Frankland (Tennessee). It reads as follows:

No person shall be eligible or capable to serve in any office of this state who denies any of the following propositions, viz.: (1) That there is one living and true God, the Creator and Governor of the Universe. (2) That there is a future state of rewards and punishments. (3) That the scriptures of the Old and New Testaments are given by divine inspiration. (4) That there are three divine persons in the Godhead, coequal and coessential.[2]

MISCELLANEOUS PROVISIONS

The constitutions of Virginia and Oklahoma are the only ones to mention the Young Men's Christian Association; the latter authorizes free passes to be given to its traveling secretaries, "and to ministers of religion." Mississippi and Michigan, as already stated, and Washington authorize religious worship for convicts, and the first of these, along with South Carolina, allows ministers of the gospel to register and vote after a shorter time requirement than other classes of persons. New Mexico provides that, "The use of wines solely for sacramental purposes under church authority at any place within this State shall never be prohibited." There are no longer any religious restrictions on the exercise of suffrage. North Carolina recognizes that, "provision

---

[1] See also p. 36.
[2] But see Article xxxii in the Constitution of North Carolina (1776), the parent colony.

for the poor, the unfortunate, and orphan, is one of the first duties of a civilized and Christian state," and Tennessee provides that "No person shall in time of peace be required to perform any service to the public on any day set apart by his religion as a day of rest." Delaware asserts that "it is the duty of all men frequently to assemble together for the public worship of Almighty God; and piety and morality, on which the prosperity of communities depends, are thereby promoted." Vermont goes still farther in saying that "every sect or denomination of Christians ought to observe the Sabbath or Lord's Day, and keep up some sort of religious worship, which to them shall seem most agreeable to the revealed will of God." It also orders its legislature to encourage societies organized for the advancement of religion. Massachusetts in its eleventh amendment asserts that "the public worship of God and instructions in piety, religion, and morality, promote the happiness and prosperity of a people and the security of a republican government." In Chapter V also it declares that "our wise and pious ancestors . . . laid the foundation of Harvard College, in which university many persons of great eminence have, by the blessing of God, been . . . qualified for public employments, both in church and state;" and adds that "the encouragement of arts and sciences, and all good literature, tends to the honor of God and the advantages of the Christian religion." Notwithstanding the recommendations of its last three constitutional conventions, New Hampshire still retains its Puritanic article (6) on evangelical protestantism. The first sentence reads as follows: "As morality and piety, rightly grounded on evangelical principles, will give the best and greatest security to government, and will lay in the hearts of men the strongest obligations to due subjection, and as the knowledge of these is most likely to be propagated through a society by the institution of the public worship of the Deity and of public instruction in morality and religion, therefore, to promote these important purposes, the people of this state have a right to empower and do hereby fully empower, the legislature to authorize, from time to time, the several towns, parishes, bodies corporate, or religious societies within this state to make adequate provision, at their own expense, for the support and maintenance of public Protestant teachers of piety, religion, and morality." [1]

As the foregoing paragraphs include all the religious provisions of American constitutions now in force, our constitutional attitude toward religion is plainly manifest. Freedom of conscience is fully guarantied, and the few intolerant limitations on rights are in fact probably obsolete. Whatever power religion has in the United States over the lives of men is due to its inherent strength, not to a support derived from the state.

SPECIAL REFERENCES

BLAKELY, WILLIAM A. Compiled by, American State Papers bearing on Religious Legislation. New York. 1891.

BROWN, S. W. The Secularization of American Education. 1912. Col. Univ. Teachers College Series, No. 49.

HICKS, F. C. Marriage and Divorce Provisions in the State Constitutions. *Annals*, V. 26. pp. 745–48.

LAUER, PAUL E. Church and State in New England. Johns Hopkins Studies, Volume X, especially Chapters IV, V.

SCHAFF, PHILIP. Church and State in the United States. Papers American Historical Association. Volume II. pp. 391–543. 1888.

---

[1] The word *Protestant* is the one especially objected to by the conventions.

CHAPTER XI

THE AMENDMENT AND REVISION OF CONSTITUTIONS[1]

AMENDMENT

THE amending article of a constitution undoubtedly demands most careful attention. In some respects it is its most important article, since it determines whether the constitution shall be flexible and easy of amendment, or so rigid as to be practically unalterable.[2] Many of our states are thus hindered and have difficulty in finding a way out of their dilemma. In consequence, needed changes in obsolete requirements cannot be made, so that the state's civic and economic progress is retarded. Such blunders in phraseology should be entirely unnecessary in these days, and might readily be avoided, if conventions were familiar with the experiences of many of our states, and with the development of our processes of amendment. An explanation of these processes will now be set forth as briefly as the importance of the subject will admit.

Some of our earliest state constitutions contained no provisions for their amendment. This proved no bar to alteration, for they were amended or revised through ordinary legislative methods or in convention. Gradually provisions were introduced authorizing legislatures to make amendments, but by a more difficult procedure than that required

---

[1] For an excellent recent work on this subject see, The Revision and Amendment of State Constitutions. By W. F. Dodd.

[2] See, Bryce, Flexible and Rigid Constitutions (Bibliography).

for statutes; at a later period it was required that such amendments be submitted to the electorates for approval or rejection.   Then in still later development there came a provision that an entire revision should be made by a convention convoked for that special purpose.   This body was usually called together by the legislature, but in two states, Pennsylvania and Vermont, by a special body known as the board of censors, which was empowered to convoke a convention and to submit amendments.

Forty-seven of the states provide methods of amendment, the exception being New Hampshire, which amends only through a convention.   When constitutions were brief and contained nothing but fundamentals, the process of amendment was properly difficult.   This was attained by the requirement of the action of two legislatures, and large fractions in voting.   But when constitutions became lengthy as at present, the process had to become easier.   This development may be seen in the following statements:

Sixteen states still require the action of two legislatures on amendments, one is sufficient in the other thirty-two.   If sessions were annual as formerly, the requirement of two sessions meant a period of two or three years from initiation to referendum.   But with biennial sessions the time lengthens to four or five years.   One session, therefore, is naturally dropped.   Of the sixteen states that still require the action of two legislatures Delaware alone uses no referendum. South Carolina and Mississippi have the referendum take place between the action of the two legislatures.   Connecticut, Vermont, Massachusetts and Tennessee have peculiar variations in their amending processes and the other ten [1] states have action of two legislatures precede the referendum.

---

[1] Rhode Island, New Jersey, New York, Virginia, Pennsylvania, Indiana, Wisconsin, Iowa, North Dakota, Nevada.

Seventeen constitutions require that amendments be submitted by two-thirds vote of each house, nineteen require a majority only, and seven a three-fifths vote. Four of the states that employ action of two legislatures require one action by two-thirds vote and the other by majority.

The referendum requirement in thirty-three states is "a majority of those voting thereon," but twelve [1] have some variation of the objectionable "majority of electors." Rhode Island requires a three-fifths vote, New Hampshire requires a two-thirds vote, and Delaware, as already said, uses no referendum for amendments. A general election is specified in twenty-five constitutions, but in some states a special election may be ordered. To avoid "rider" amendments, twenty-nine of the states require that each amendment shall be submitted separately. Kentucky adds that each must contain one subject only, and Alabama insists that the substance of each be printed on the ballot. Eight states [2] place limitations on the number of amendments to be submitted at one time, the number varying from two to six. Five states forbid action on a rejected amendment until after a specified period, varying from four to six years (Tennessee). Five others [3] limit the years when proposals

---

[1] See, p. 144. The straits to which a state having this requirement may be driven is shown by legislation passed in Alabama, 1898; Nebraska, 1901; and Ohio, 1902. Those laws in substance provided (1) that if a state convention of a political party declared for or against a constitutional amendment, such declaration should be considered a portion of the party ticket, and that a straight vote for the party should be counted as a vote for or against the amendment; and (2) that the ballot should be so arranged that every failure to vote on an amendment counted as an affirmative vote. How much better not to insert such requirements than to have to resort to such devices!

[2] Arkansas, Colorado, Illinois, Indiana, Kansas, Kentucky, Montana, New Mexico.

[3] New Hampshire, New Jersey, Pennsylvania, Tennessee, Vermont.

can be made, and seven [1] from these two sets are so severe in their limitations that amendments can be made only with great difficulty. While it is fairly well understood throughout the United States by precedent and decision that the executive has no right of veto over legislative actions respecting conventions or amendments, yet Alabama, Kentucky and Delaware make assurance doubly sure by saying so.

Constitutions regularly provide that when legislatures pass amendments the vote must be by yea and nay and recorded. Provision is also made for publication for a certain specified number of weeks or months before the election. Publication is usually required to be through the newspapers, in each county of the state, but may be "after such publication as may be deemed expedient." The length of time and method of publication are frequently left to the discretion of the legislature. But Oregon has set the fashion for a "voter's pamphlet." This system of publication provides that each amendment (or bills subject to referendum) have appended a pro and con argument for the information of the voter, and that the whole series of referred laws with explanations, be printed and mailed to each voter before the election.

REVISION

All but twelve [2] of the constitutions expressly make mention of a convention for the purposes of revision. It is now considered far better to do so. Although the best authorities

---

[1] Illinois, Indiana, New Hampshire, New Jersey, Pennsylvania, Tennessee, Vermont. For a study of the amending attempts of Illinois, see article, *Am. Pol. Sc. Review*, Vol. V. 3. The Working of the State Wide Referendum in Illinois, by C. O. Gardner.

[2] Massachusetts, Connecticut, Vermont, Rhode Island, New Jersey, Pennsylvania, Mississippi, Louisiana, Texas, Arkansas, Indiana, North Dakota.

assert that states can call conventions under general legislative powers, and nearly all have done so one or more times, yet it is far safer to insert the provision expressly, with such safeguards as will allow the use of a convention whenever necessity demands. In one state only (Rhode Island) is there doubt about the matter. Its supreme court in 1883, when requested by the senate for an opinion, in its reply concluded that under the state constitution a convention could not be called. Judge Jameson, however, in his great work, On Constitutional Conventions,[1] in discussing this opinion reaches the opposite conclusion. Seven states provide that the question of calling a convention must be submitted at stated intervals, every twenty years (Maryland, Ohio, Oklahoma, New York), sixteen years (Michigan), ten years (Iowa), and seven years (New Hampshire); but in addition to a set year it is better to insert as four of them do "and also at such times as the legislature may by law provide."

When constitutions authorize a convention, the usual procedure is that the legislatures submit the question to referendum. Seventeen of the states require that the referendum be authorized by a two-thirds vote of each house, fourteen require a majority and one a three-fifths vote. New Mexico makes it three-fourths for twenty-five years and then two-thirds; the New Hampshire referendum goes automatically to the voters without action by the legislature; Maine and Georgia authorize their legislatures to call conventions without referenda. The real difficulty in calling a convention arises from the wording in regard to the referendum vote. No matter how much interest there may be in a state on the question, it is simply impossible to get a much larger vote on the referendum than from about

[1] Fourth ed., pp. 601-15.

one-half to two-thirds of the usual vote at a general election. If therefore a constitution provides that a "majority of the voters of the state," or "a majority of all the voters voting at a general election" must vote for a convention, that state might as well almost give up all thought of ever holding a convention.[1]

Seventeen states have such requirements and in consequence can hold conventions if at all only after years of agitation and expense; seventeen other states more wisely word the requirement a "majority of those voting thereon," and thereby avoid future trouble. Most of the constitutions (23) require that the referendum be submitted at a general election, but eleven leave the time to the legislature or provide for submission either at a general or special election. Experience shows that it is safer to specify the basis of representation in the convention. It should never be the same as the legislature itself, though four states have such a provision, Maryland for example. Seventeen constitutions use the house as the basis; requiring that it be equal in membership to that of the house (Nebraska for example), or double (Wyoming), or based on population (Georgia). Delaware uses the house basis and adds two from each county, but there are three counties only in the state. Three require that it be twice that of the senate (Illinois, Colorado, Missouri); Michigan, three times that of the senate; and New York requires that it be three times that of the senate plus fifteen elected at large. In the earlier years of our history conventions frequently promulgated

[1] See note regarding Illinois on page 142. When these requirements were originally placed in the constitutions, they were entirely proper since voting was *viva voce*, so that every voter naturally voted on all referenda. Since the adoption of the printed and secret ballot, however, and also of lists of registered voters, only those really interested in referenda vote on them, and many, being ignorant or uninterested, ignore them.

constitutions made by them on their own authority, without referendum. After the first generation, however, the contrary held true in the main down to 1890. Since that year six conventions have promulgated constitutions without referenda.[1] Conventions have that power unless restrained by local precedent, statute, or constitution, and for that reason sixteen states require that no constitution go into effect unless ratified by the people. In some cases they also specify the vote, as in the case of a convention, viz., "a majority of those voting thereon" (10) or "a majority of the electors voting at the election" (6).

The Constitutional Commission

In the first century of state constitutions, on rare occasions, and in recent years, more frequently, states have made use of commissions for purposes of constitutional amendment and revision. A constitutional commission is a body appointed by the governor under legislative authority, and therefore is to be carefully distinguished from a joint legislative committee chosen for a similar purpose; like that, for example, in Louisiana which in 1894 submitted a series of about twenty amendments to the legislature. As no state constitution makes provision for the use of a constitutional commission, the recommendations from such a body must conform to the constitution's requirements in respect to amendments. This is a serious handicap, for a commission must work with and under the legislature; unlike a convention, which is coördinate with or superior to a legislature, and either submits its work directly to the electorate, or promulgates it on its own authority. This

[1] Mississippi, South Carolina, Delaware, Louisiana on two occasions, Virginia. Kentucky's convention submitted the constitution to referendum, but later convened and made further changes without referendum.

subjection on the part of the commission to the legislature compels it to subordinate its own wish to that of the body to which it finally reports its work. Commissions therefore have so far proved themselves to be mere conveniences to the legislature, not mouthpieces to the popular will, so that they do their best work when they make no attempt to take the place of conventions for revision purposes. The following commissions have had part in the amending of constitutions since 1870.

New York in 1872, handicapped because of the failure of the convention of 1867, appointed a commission which made selection of some of the most important propositions that had come before the convention and reported these with suitable changes as a series of amendments. Most of these passed the ordeal of an affirmative vote by two legislatures and the electorate, but some failed to receive a complete endorsement.[1] The report of a Michigan commission in 1873 was virtually a revision of the constitution but this was rejected at the polls the following year. Maine in 1875 had a commission whose suggestions were in part adopted and became amendments to the constitution. In 1881 New Jersey made use of a commission but its report was never finally acted on. Rhode Island in 1897 appointed a commission which conservatively revised the constitution. The revision met the approval of two legislatures, but was rejected at the polls, November 1898 and again in June 1899 when resubmitted. In 1912 another commission for the same purpose was appointed and made a report to the assembly of 1915, submitting a revised constitution. This report under the constitution must meet with approval by two assemblies and a referendum vote in 1917. Vermont in 1908 made use of a commission for the suggestion of

[1] See page 80.

amendments, most of which were finally accepted; and North Carolina in 1912 appointed a commission which in the following year proposed fourteen amendments to a special session of the legislature. Ten of these in substance were accepted and were submitted to vote in November 1914 but were all rejected owing to the requirement of a "majority of votes cast at a general election." From these results it is obvious that as an aid to a legislature a commission may have its use, but as a substitute for a convention, for revision purposes, it has so far proved to be a flat failure.

THE CONSTITUTIONAL INITIATIVE [1]

Since 1902 a new device for constitutional amendment has worked its way into some state constitutions and seems destined to become a definite part of American procedure for the process of amendment. This new method started with Oregon in the form of the constitutional initiative and referendum. That state it will be remembered had a constitution impossible of amendment by the procedure fixed by its convention of 1857, but in 1902 by means of a vigorous campaign it managed to pass this measure as an amendment and has been busy ever since in revising its ancient document. Its success stimulated others to make the same experiment, — an excellent illustration of the eager adoption by the states of the best results of political laboratories — so that there are now twelve states [2] having in their constitutions this provision and others that have already taken partial action. From the results of their successes and

---

[1] See pages 215-222.

[2] Oregon, 1902; Oklahoma, 1907; Missouri, Michigan, 1908; Arkansas, Colorado, 1910; Arizona, California, 1911; Nevada, Nebraska, Ohio, 1912; North Dakota, 1914. In 1913 Michigan broadened and simplified the provision inserted by the convention of 1908.

failures is evolving a sort of pattern for future amendments, since it is a safe prophecy to assert that this method has become a permanent addition to American procedure in the amendment of constitutions.

The basis for this system is the insertion in the constitution of a definite provision reserving to the people (the electorate) the right to initiate amendments to the constitution. This right is exercised through a petition presented not later than four months before an election and signed by a definite per cent of voters,[1] who request that there be submitted to the voters as a whole the amendment proposed in the petition. This initiative is *direct*, if it goes to the secretary of state, making it his duty to verify the signatures and to submit the proposed amendment to referendum vote at the next general, or special election. It is *indirect* if it is presented to the legislature for action either in the form of approval, disapproval, or modification. In the last case the legislature may submit an alternative proposition. Provision is then made for an obligatory referendum, the action of the legislature of course affecting the vote one way or the other. Since the direct form omits action entirely on the part of the legislature, it is not so much a petition as an order, or mandate, instructing an official to perform a set task, without the exercise of discretionary power on his part. The indirect form may be considered as voiced in the potential rather than in the imperative mode, since it politely permits the expression of opinion on the part of

[1] This per cent varies from five or eight per cent to fifteen or twenty-five per cent. Eight per cent is favored and California has a requirement of eight per cent for the direct or five per cent for the indirect. Now that California has adult suffrage even these per cents will involve much labor in securing signatures to petitions, since the voting lists include about a million voters. Some demand the per cent in a certain number of districts; Missouri, *e.g.*, five per cent in two-thirds of the congressional districts, but this is not generally favored.

the legislature. As long, however, as there is a compulsory referendum coupled with the indirect initiative, it ultimately leads to the same end as the direct, though it may cause a delay of a year or two if the legislature is at all inclined to be dilatory in action. Properly the governor's veto should not apply to initiated amendments but some constitutions avoid dispute by forbidding him to exercise his veto. An amendment of this sort, prohibiting the governor to veto, or the legislature to repeal initiative and referendum measures, was passed by Arizona, 1914.

The referendum vote is preceded of course by some requirement for publicity, which may take the expensive and inefficient form of newspaper advertising; or on the other hand may be required to be through the so called "publicity pamphlet," or "voter's guide," containing the text of all referenda, with pro and con arguments attached.[1] A copy of this is then mailed to all the voters in the state in time sufficient to enable them to study the proposed amendments (or laws) so as to form a definite opinion on their merits. The ratifying vote may be taken at a special election if so designated, or at the next general election; the usual requirement is that each measure goes into effect when ratified by a majority of those voting thereon.[2] As a rule there is no limitation on the number of amendments to be initiated, though restrictions like that in the Amending Article of Arkansas,[3] should be carefully noted.

[1] This may be required by the amendment or left to legislative discretion; this method of publication is favored and is considered far more effective.

[2] If the referendum must receive "a majority of votes cast at the election," few can ever be ratified, unless the party ballot endorsement system (of Nebraska) is used or a special election designated. Oklahoma has such a requirement and defeats disliked amendments by referring them to a general election, but passes others by calling a special election; the "grandfather" amendment, for example.

[3] "But no more than three amendments shall be proposed or submitted at the same time."

CHAPTER XII

SUFFRAGE AND ELECTIONS

SUFFRAGE

THE states have the right to declare in their constitutions who shall exercise suffrage within their several jurisdictions. The restrictions on this power in the national constitution are simple and few in number.[1] The democratic tendency is shown by the fact that, whereas in the revolutionary period the privilege of suffrage was held by less than six per cent of the population, it is now held by over twenty per cent. The per cent was even larger in 1870, but restrictions have since crept in.

It was once common in thinly settled states to allow aliens who had taken out their first naturalization papers to vote even in national elections. Seven states only still retain this provision;[2] eight have changed within the last few years.[3] Some of the seven would likely change if their constitutions could be amended with ease, for the tendency is to reserve suffrage privileges for full-fledged Americans only.

An educational qualification is rapidly passing into our constitutions through a belief that voters should be intelligent, and that this on the whole is best indicated by the

---

[1] Article I, Section 2; Article IV, Section 2; Amendment XIV, Section 1; Amendment XV.

[2] Arkansas, South Dakota, Indiana, Texas, Kansas, Missouri, Nebraska.

[3] Florida, Michigan, Minnesota, Alabama, Colorado, North Dakota, Wisconsin, Oregon.

ability to read and write.   Such a restriction of course would
be undemocratic if not coupled with provisions for a free
and general education.   Sixteen states now have educational restrictions, and these should be considered in two
sets.   Nine states compose the first set ; [1] two require ability
to read English (Connecticut and Wyoming) ; two to read
and speak English (Washington and Oklahoma) ; and the
other five to read English and write the name.   The other
set consists of seven southern states which have an educational qualification as one of several alternatives.   The
details [2] to these alternatives are too numerous to specify,
but, with the exception of Mississippi and Virginia, which
require the ability to read *or* understand, and Georgia,
which requires the ability to read *and* understand, all require
the ability to read and write, Louisiana making the proviso
that it may be in English or in the mother tongue.   There
are two other states, Colorado, North Dakota, which by
constitution give discretionary powers to their legislatures,
in respect to an educational qualification.

The chief restriction on suffrage in earlier days was the
property qualification.   This still survives in many states
in the form that referenda involving the expenditure of
money shall be voted on by taxpayers only.   Aside from
this, the property qualification by 1890 had entirely disappeared from the United States except in Rhode Island,

---

[1] Connecticut, 1855 and 1897; Massachusetts, 1857; Wyoming, 1889;
Maine, 1893; California, 1894; Washington, 1896; Delaware, 1897; New
Hampshire, 1903; Oklahoma, 1910.

[2] Mississippi, 1890, Sections 241–245, 249, 251.   South Carolina, 1895,
Article II.   Louisiana, 1898, 1913, Articles 197–199.   Alabama, 1901; Sections 177, 178, 180–182.   Virginia, 1902, Article II.   North Carolina, 1902,
Article VI, Section 4 (Amendment).   Georgia, 1908, Article II (Amendment).   Note also the following: Texas, 1902, amendment requiring payment of poll tax by February first; and Oklahoma, 1910, Article III (Amendment).

where there is a property requirement of one hundred and thirty-four dollars for suffrage in financial town meetings and in the election of members of city councils. Five constitutions in their bills of rights formally state their objection in declaring that the holding of property should not be considered as affecting the right to vote and hold office. Since 1895 several of the southern states have introduced this restriction as one of the alternatives for suffrage. It was inserted as a temporary requirement by Virginia in 1902 and is a permanent requirement in the constitutions of South Carolina, Louisiana, Alabama, and Georgia. The qualification is the possession of property valued at the minimum of three hundred dollars, but in Georgia five hundred dollars. Those interested in the famous temporary provisions in certain southern constitutions intended to disfranchise the negroes, should consult the suffrage articles of Louisiana, North Carolina and Oklahoma for the "grandfather" clause,[1] and of Alabama, Virginia and Georgia for the "old soldier" clause.[2]

As women are citizens and all citizens by theory are entitled to the same privileges, women are entitled to the suffrage equally with men unless the constitution is worded or can be interpreted otherwise. Definite agitation for women's suffrage has been carried on since 1848, but in state elections small progress was made up to the last five years. Eleven states and one territory at the present time allow women full suffrage.[3] Illinois in 1913 voted to grant

[1] The " grandfather article " of Louisiana by amendment 1912 was renewed temporarily — until August 31st, 1913.

[2] See also article on Negro Suffrage, by John C. Rose, *Am. Political Science Review*, Nov., 1906.

[3] Wyoming, 1890; Colorado, 1893; Utah, 1896; Idaho, 1896; Washington, 1900; California, 1911; Kansas, Oregon, Arizona, 1912; Alaska, 1913; Nevada, Montana, 1914.

women's suffrage for statutory offices. Five states in 1914 rejected referenda on this question, viz., Nebraska, Ohio, Missouri, North and South Dakota. More than twenty states in addition to the suffrage states allow women suffrage in school and occasionally in other matters.[1] Four states [2] by constitution allow women taxpayers to vote on certain referenda involving expenditures. Obviously conventions in considering suffrage, should decide what privileges, if any, women are to have, and then should state them in express terms.

Registration is now a common form of restriction. The former prejudice against it may still be found in the constitution of Arkansas which declares that registration shall not be a prerequisite for voting. This is the only state retaining the provision, as Pennsylvania removed it in 1901 and West Virginia in 1902. It may be said that now in practically the entire United States registration in some form or other is a prerequisite for voting in state wide elections. For, even if registration itself is not required, the prepayment of a poll tax, for example, is a sort of registration. About twenty constitutions expressly authorize registration, though legislatures could pass such laws under their general powers unless restrained by some provision in their constitutions. The restrictive feature in registration is that the person who claims for himself the privilege of suffrage may be required to present himself in person, by a certain date, and prove his right. The necessity of a personal application will invariably disfranchise a large per cent of the voters, who will neglect to make application. This will prove to be especially true if the date set is several months before an election. The excitement of a campaign would bring out

---

[1] See for example the constitution of Minnesota.
[2] Iowa, Kentucky, Louisiana, Michigan.

many who otherwise will fail to register if the date set is early in election year.   If the proof involves the presentation of naturalization papers, or tax receipts, it may be assumed that another large per cent of voters will fail to appear.   If all these requirements are found, viz., personal application, long in advance of the election, accompanied by proof of citizenship and of the payment of taxes, the list of voters may easily be cut in half.   Add an educational or property qualification, and the task of counting voters will be reduced to a minimum.   Space will not allow further details, but a study of the constitutions of the southern states already referred to,[1] and a comparison of the votes cast in those states before and after the passage of such laws, will abundantly illustrate the utility of rigid registration laws as a means of restriction.   It would be found that the restrictions now in use reduce the voters voting to a percentage ranging from four to ten per cent of the whole population. These same constitutions [2] will furnish illustrations of that other form of registration, in which the name of the person once registered is retained on the lists for life or for a specified term of years, the lists being corrected annually or biennially by the several boards of registration.   It must not, of course, be understood that registration is merely a means of restriction.   It is intended fundamentally as a safeguard against illegal voting, but it is clearly evident that it can be used to cut down considerably the number of voters.

Besides these restrictions there are in practically all constitutions prohibitions of suffrage to minors under twenty-one

[1] In the third paragraph of this chapter.

[2] South Carolina, Alabama, Virginia.   Rhode Island has the same provision in favor of owners of real estate.   Montana, Georgia, Colorado, Oregon and Idaho, and possibly other states, by statute provide for a permanent registration.

years of age, to idiots, insane persons, and persons convicted of crime. Some specify crimes in elections and most forbid the suffrage to those guilty of dueling. There is also always a restriction in the form of a requirement of residence within the state, county and precinct. In the forty-eight states there are twenty-five variations in the times set! On the whole it may be said that the average preference is one year's residence in the state (twenty-nine states), six or three months in the county, and thirty days in the precinct. Seven states require a two years' residence, and eleven states six months. The constitutions also regularly contain a provision defining under what conditions a residence is neither gained nor lost.[1] The prepayment of taxes, property or poll, as a form of restriction has already been mentioned. It exists in a very few states. The poll tax must be prepaid in eight states,[2] usually several months before the election. Six additional states require prepayment of other taxes.[3] The most stringent requirements will be found in the constitutions of Mississippi, Louisiana and Virginia.

ELECTIONS AND POLITICAL PARTIES

Fifteen of the constitutions include elections along with suffrage, under some common title, such as Suffrage and Elections. Two (Rhode Island and Kansas) have separate articles for each subject and the others as a rule scatter provisions regarding elections throughout the constitutions. It would add to clearness if all provisions in regard to

[1] For example see California, II, 4.

[2] Alabama, Arkansas, Louisiana, North Carolina, South Carolina, Virginia, Texas, Delaware, in some cities in Kentucky.

[3] All; Georgia, South Carolina, Tennessee, Mississippi; Pennsylvania a state or county tax; in Rhode Island, personal property voters must prepay, if retained on the property voters' list.

elections and political parties were placed together under some appropriate heading, especially as unusual attention is being paid to such matters at present.

As congress in 1871 provided that elections for members of the house of representatives should take place in even years, on Tuesday after the first Monday in November, states have tended to place their own elections on the same day so as to avoid duplication of expense and work. Four states, however, still prefer to use the odd years,[1] so as to separate state from national issues. The last to change from odd to even were Iowa in 1904 and Ohio 1905. Four states [2] still hold their general elections in months other than November, and one of these by special arrangement holds the national election at the same time (Maine on the second Monday of September). One state retains the old-fashioned annual general election (Massachusetts). New York and New Jersey elect their lower houses annually; two of the newer constitutions [3] (Alabama, Louisiana) provide for a quadrennial election, and all the other constitutions provide for an election biennially.

A system of registration for voters, a system of nomination, including the primary, the election, including the form and method of voting, and the count, are all matters that properly fall under the jurisdiction of the state and may be mentioned in the constitution or left to statutory regulation. The chief requirement found in constitutions (in about thirty-four) is that voting be by ballot. Others authorize it by law. Congress also makes this requirement for national elections. Since the introduction of the Australian ballot system there is a tendency to say *secret* ballot

[1] Kentucky, Maryland, Mississippi, Virginia. Louisiana also holds its session in even years, but has a spring (even year) election.

[2] Arkansas and Maine (Sept.), Georgia (October), Louisiana (April).

[3] Mississippi did so but changed to biennial, 1912.

(ten states). As the voting machine is not a ballot, states desirous of using this mechanism, yet having a ballot requirement, must add an amendment specifying a voting machine or some other device "provided that secrecy in voting be preserved." [1]

On the other hand there has recently arisen a demand that voters necessarily absent from their domiciles,[2] be allowed an opportunity to vote, as for example, was done by many states during the civil war. A legislature may under its general powers [3] provide for the casting of votes anywhere within the state, but if the word "secret" ballot be in the constitution, an amendment may have to be made, so as to permit absentee voting. Such an amendment California rejected and Michigan adopted when submitted to referendum in November, 1914. A few states require that the ballots be numbered and a few others require that the ballot include the party emblem (for example Louisiana) or on the other hand that the names of candidates be arranged alphabetically (Virginia, Wyoming). Colorado by a recent amendment (1912) forbids the use of party emblems on the ballot.

The Australian blanket ballot began as an experiment in Massachusetts, 1889. Not over five states [4] still retain the older methods of voting. The others in their ballot systems divide between the party column ballot (twenty-seven states), and the alphabetical arrangement of the Massachusetts ballot (sixteen states). The former is preferred by

---

[1] See for example Utah, New York, Virginia; and recent amendments to constitutions of Pennsylvania, Connecticut, California, Colorado and Massachusetts.

[2] Soldiers and sailors on service, students in universities, and commercial travelers.

[3] As Kansas (1911), Missouri, and North Dakota (1913) have done. In 1912 about five thousand voters in Kansas made use of this privilege.

[4] Missouri, New Mexico, North Carolina, South Carolina, Georgia.

party organizations so as to encourage straight party ticket voting; the latter is a sort of educational qualification, tending to weed out the votes of illiterate and ignorant citizens. A movement for a non-partisan ballot is developing in the west, in California for example, as a natural supplement to the direct primary. The "short ballot" reform is also making vigorous headway, though two amendments of that sort submitted by Ohio, 1913, were both defeated at the polls.

There are very few constitutional provisions in regard to the primary and the count, such matters are regularly left to legislatures. Michigan's new constitution, Article VI, section twenty, provides for a board of state canvassers having an *ex officio* membership. Illustrations of recent provisions in respect to the primary may be found in California's amendment of 1908 (Article II, section two and one-half) or Oklahoma's constitution (Article III, sections four, five). As is well known, over half of the states now have direct primary laws, aiming thereby to supersede the caucus and the convention, and to bring political parties completely under the control of the state through regulation.

Nearly all constitutions contain some provision against fraud and bribery, but up to recent years legislative ingenuity had not succeeded in making a really effective Corrupt Practices act.[1] In the last ten years, however, most of the states have given this matter careful attention, and over twenty have revised their statutes, somewhat after English models, and at last efficient and excellent laws of this sort can be found among the statutes of the states.

Political parties are voluntary associations and not part of the state's electional machinery. The state under its

---

[1] See Kentucky, Delaware, Maryland for older illustrations of constitutional provisions in respect to bribery and corruption.

police powers has the right to regulate them but should not make the blunder of assuming that political parties represent all voters. If a legislature for instance regulates the party primary or the party ballot, it must arrange that independents also be able to express their choice in nomination and on the official ballot. Any departure from this principle must be expressly specified in the constitution or run the risk of being declared unconstitutional. So far as constitutions are concerned there is very little attempt to regulate party organization, such matters being left to statutes. Louisiana in Articles 200 and 215, or California's Section on the primary, already alluded to, give the gist of what few provisions may be found in other constitutions. A late development, the first of its kind in American constitutions,[1] is Oregon's amendment of 1908 (Article II, section 16), providing for proportional representation through the voter's "expression of his first, second, or additional choices among the candidates for any office." Permission is also given for the application of these principles " to nominations by political parties and organizations." California voted down a somewhat similar amendment in 1914.

[1] Note, however, the Illinois system of minority representation, Article IV. sections 7–8.

CHAPTER XIII

THE EXECUTIVE DEPARTMENT

A FAVORITE American political theory is that of the separation of powers. The several powers of government are grouped under three main heads, each kind placed in charge of a distinct set of officials, and a system of "checks and balances" is used so as to co-ordinate and unify the work of government. In practice these divisions cannot really be separate, so that in national government at least an "unwritten constitution" develops, under which, for example, the executive may have a large determining voice in legislative policy.

Executive powers properly include the war and treaty power, the power of oversight, under which is placed the veto power, and the power of appointment and supervision over the administrative departments. One of the chief defects in our present state constitutions is that these executive powers have not received proper attention. The theory of separation has been disregarded and the legislature has been allowed to share these powers with the executive, with disastrous results. There is at present a strong centralizing tendency in economic and political life, and one effect from this is increased attention to the proper place of the executive in government. This is plainly indicated by a comparison of the articles entitled The Executive Department.

The requirements for the office of governor are practically the same in all the states. The governor must be at least thirty years of age (five states name twenty-five or thirty-five years), a citizen of the United States for a period varying from five to twenty years (Maine requires that he be native born), and a resident of the state for a period of from one to ten years. If the election results in a tie, the procedure is the same in almost all the states, viz., the legislature in joint session selects a governor from the leading candidates. The usual procedure is modified somewhat in five states.[1] Georgia and Mississippi still require a majority vote for election, but all others a plurality. New Hampshire, 1912, changed from a majority to a plurality.

A few states specify his salary in the constitution, others do so but authorize the legislature to change it, and the remaining states wisely leave the matter to the discretion of the lawmaking body. In passing, it may be said that the increase in the cost of living with other reasons, is resulting in a steady increase in salaries paid to state officials. Thirty states now pay the governor five thousand dollars or more, five of these paying $10,000 and one, $12,000; only two states pay less than three thousand dollars. Seventeen states place restrictions on a governor's re-election, the usual form being a prohibition against two successive terms; two states forbid him to be a candidate for the United States senate while in office (Alabama, Utah), and New Jersey forbids its legislature to elect him to any other office "during the term for which he shall have been elected governor." The term of office is four years in twenty-two states, two years in twenty-four states, three years in New Jersey and one year in Massachusetts. The tendency is toward the longer term, not away from it, though New Mexico in 1914 changed from a four to a two year term.

[1] Maine, Massachusetts, Vermont, Georgia and Mississippi; this last state elects its governor through a sort of electoral college.

The governor has certain routine duties common to all states; he represents his commonwealth in its dealings with other states, he may summon the legislature in special session or adjourn it in case of disagreement, he "must take care that the laws be faithfully executed," may commission officers and fill vacancies *pro tempore*, and is the commander of the military and naval forces of the state.[1] He regularly has large powers in pardoning, which he exercises on his own authority or partly in connection with the legislature or senate (thirty-two states) or by the aid of a board (thirteen) or council (three). He regularly has the power to make formal recommendations to the legislature, and may request information under oath, or opinions in writing, from the several officers of administration. Aside from these usual powers, which require no special mention, attention should be given to (*a*) the veto power and (*b*) his power in administration.

The Veto Power

In 1788 two states only (Massachusetts, New York) gave the veto power to the governor; in 1914 North Carolina alone withholds it. The need of an efficient check on legislation simply compelled the change. In the national constitution, a veto is overridden by a two-thirds vote of both houses of congress; this fraction is preferred by thirty-four states, but eight[2] specify a majority, and five a three-fifths vote.[3] This vote must be by yea and nay and recorded.

---

[1] Twenty-six, even some of the inland states, mention *navy;* Massachusetts and New Hampshire have similar quite thrilling and sanguinary paragraphs on the war powers of their governors as commanders-in-chief and admirals of the respective forces of their states.

[2] Alabama, Arkansas, Connecticut, Indiana, Kentucky, New Jersey, Tennessee, West Virginia.

[3] Delaware, Maryland, Nebraska, Rhode Island, Ohio.

Taking warning from experience, thirty-four states now allow the governor to veto items of appropriation bills [1] and three of these also allow him to veto part or parts of any bill.[2] His veto power in theory applies to bills, or bills and resolutions of the legislature, and is not supposed to be exercised against changes in the constitution, or measures initiated and approved by the electorate.[3]

The time given to the governor for the consideration of a bill varies from three to ten days, twenty-two preferring five days, eleven ten days and the others three or six days. If adjournment intervenes between the sending of a bill to the governor and its return approved or vetoed, twenty-four constitutions declare the bill passed and nineteen declare it not passed. Twelve states [4] allow the governor a period of from three to thirty days to decide whether or not to approve such bills; twenty states [5] allow him from five to thirty days to file objections with the secretary of state, if he desires; and eight states [6] require that such bills with objections be referred to the next legislature for its consideration. Alabama and Virginia allow the governor to propose amendments when vetoing.

The constitutions seem to be in doubt whether to consider

[1] The thirteen states not yet granting this power are Connecticut, Florida, Indiana, Iowa, Maine, Massachusetts, Nevada, New Hampshire, Oregon, Rhode Island, Tennessee, Vermont, Wisconsin, all old constitutions. New Hampshire rejected such an amendment in 1912.

[2] Washington, Virginia, South Carolina.

[3] Arizona, for example, provides that "the veto power of the Governor shall not extend to any bill passed by the legislature and referred to the people for adoption or rejection."

[4] Alabama, California, Delaware, Iowa, Michigan, Minnesota, Missouri, Montana, New Mexico, New York, Oklahoma, Virginia.

[5] Arizona, Arkansas, Colorado, Florida, Idaho, Illinois, Indiana, Kentucky, Nebraska, Nevada, North Dakota, Ohio, Oregon, Pennsylvania, Rhode Island, South Dakota, Utah, Washington, West Virginia, Wyoming.

[6] Florida, Indiana, Maine, Mississippi, Nevada, Oregon, South Carolina, Washington.

the veto as executive or legislative in kind ; thirty-two prefer to place it under the executive department and fourteen follow the national constitution in classifying it under legislative. Rhode Island has it among the amendments, and one state, as already said, allows no veto.

This power of veto lodged in the executive, especially when coupled with the power to veto items and to approve or disapprove after adjournment, has become a most effective restraint on legislative action, and has been vigorously used to enlarge executive powers and to conserve public interests.

ADMINISTRATION

Thirty-five of the states have lieutenant governors, and thirty-four of these make that officer president of the senate. In the other states and in Massachusetts the senate elects its own presiding officer, and the constitution arranges the order of succession in case of the death or disability of the governor. An elaborate paragraph on succession may be found in the new Alabama constitution. The officers favored for the succession are either the secretary of state, or the president of the senate. Three of the New England states still retain the old-fashioned executive council (Massachusetts, Maine, New Hampshire), and a modification of it made up of *ex officio* members may be found in North Carolina. Though not provided for by constitution, Iowa has an executive council made up of the chief elective officers of the state and having duties assigned to it by statute.

The power of the executive over administration has during the course of our national history undergone some remarkable changes. This power was in the early constitutions deplorably weak, since in those days legislatures controlled administration also. The present constitution of Rhode Island is an excellent illustration of this old-fashioned type. As governmental business multiplied through the growth of population and wealth, legislatures tried to handle these increasing duties, first, through committees, temporary and then permanent, and finally through the organization of departments, boards and commissions. Most of our states are still in this stage of development. Every new line of activity results in the formation of a special board or commission until these can be counted by the score in almost any state, a joy to the spoils politician, but the despair of every taxpayer.[1] Under such conditions the administration of the state becomes unwieldy, wasteful, and thoroughly unbusinesslike. Each department, board, or commission drifts along under the nominal control of the legislature, united only by the bond of a common affection for the state treasury.

This evil has for some time attracted the attention of the leaders in our several states, so that there is at present a decided movement looking towards a greater efficiency in administration and a centralization of authority. The "short ballot" movement, for example, would seek to lengthen terms of office and to concentrate appointing power in the governor in place of too numerous elections. About thirteen [2] states also have appointed commissions on Economy and Efficiency in state government. The gist of their recommendations unquestionably will be ; improved systems of accounts and auditing ; a demand for the elimination of useless and parasitic boards, a closer coördination

---

[1] The legislatures of thirty-five states in 1913 created 236 boards or commissions, abolished 79, and reorganized 12. See, Article *Am. Pol. Sc. Review*, VIII. 3. pp. 431–436.

[2] Illinois, Iowa, Louisiana, Massachusetts, Minnesota, Mississippi, Nebraska, New Jersey, New York, Ohio, Pennsylvania, South Dakota, Wisconsin. These vary widely in powers and function. See, Rhode Island Legislative Bulletin, Number 7.

of those that remain, and a centralization of authority in the governor rather than in the legislature. The present trend in constitutions is, on the whole, to take administrative power from the legislature and transfer it partly to the electorate but chiefly to the executive, where it properly belongs. The methods by which this has been done will now briefly be indicated.

Attention has already been called to the tendency toward a four-year term and a larger salary for governors. The same point holds true in respect to the heads of the important departments. Their terms are lengthening and their salaries increasing. In the case of the treasurer (seventeen states) and auditor or comptroller (five states) there is the same provision against re-election for successive terms. Heads of departments, instead of being elected by legislatures as formerly, are now almost invariably elected by the people, as may be seen by noting the systems in use in the several states, contained in the American Year Book. In a very few states [1] one or several of these heads are still chosen by legislatures, and by contrast in a few states [2] the governor has that privilege, but the movement sets steadily in the direction of popular election. Nearly all constitutions forbid a state officer to hold a position of trust under the federal government and should forbid him to hold more than one office within the state. (See Florida, Article XVI, 15.) Again, constitutions regularly specify what departments must be organized, and what powers they may exercise. These offices in almost all states include a secretary of state, a treasurer, an auditor or comptroller, an attorney general and a superintendent of public instruction.

---

[1] For examples see Maine, New Hampshire, New Jersey, South Carolina, Tennessee, Virginia.

[2] See Maryland, New Jersey, New York, Ohio, Pennsylvania, Texas.

Another department is common enough, though going under widely varying names. Its duties in general are indicated by 'the term Internal Affairs (Pennsylvania). Besides these departments many constitutions name and define the powers of numerous boards, commissions, or bureaus, intended chiefly for 'purposes of general welfare, and for supervision of the larger economic interests of the state. These are becoming so numerous that a check should be put on so rapid a multiplication of semi-independent boards, bureaus, and commissions. Some are useless and others could be consolidated. By centering responsibility in the governor, efficiency and economy would become possible, but his hands should be strengthened against party demands by the merit system of appointment and tenure.

Conventions by placing such matters in the constitution have deprived legislatures of the power of altering them, and to that extent have developed an administration apart from the law-making body. The newer demand is that this administrative system be wisely coördinated and centralized. The development now in evidence is to require these several departments and officials to report semi-annually to the governor; to make him ex-officio member of the several commissions (Utah for example); to authorize him to investigate thoroughly any department or office at his discretion,[1] especially those handling the finances of the State,[2] and to place in his hands the power to suspend or remove those officers who seem to be derelict in their duties.[3] A few (nine) add to such powers the duty of presenting to

[1] For illustrations of this see Idaho, Montana, Utah, Wyoming.

[2] For curious provisions see Georgia, Kentucky, Maryland, and Mississippi.

[3] See, for example, New Mexico; Article V, Section 5. Note also, Article, Removal of Public Officers. A Ten-Year Review. *Am. Pol. Sc. Review.* Nov. 1914, pp. 621–29.

the legislature at the beginning of each session the budget of anticipated receipts and expenditures. There is also a strong tendency to define more generously his power in removal and to increase his power of appointment in the case of officials other than heads of departments. This power he regularly exercises by and with the advice and consent of the senate, though the wisdom of this requirement may be questioned. It is impossible to specify these details by states in so short a space but a comparative study would show great differences in the extent of executive power. In late years the trend towards centralization may be observed in such states as Oregon, Kansas, Nebraska and Ohio; but compare, for example, some of the newer constitutions such as those of Alabama, Idaho, Montana, New York, Utah and Wyoming; and an older set, such as those of Colorado, Maryland, Missouri, Texas and West Virginia; and a still older set, such as those of Iowa, and Wisconsin; and finally the New England set as an example of executive power at its minimum.

The reason for the longer term and larger salary of the modern governor is now obvious. His duties are so onerous that he must be adequately paid and time be given him to show his capacity as head of the administration. By centralizing administrative responsibility on his shoulders his office becomes powerful, commands respect and is eagerly sought after by capable men. It becomes also a prize in party politics and for that reason should be supplemented by an adequate civil service law modeled after one of the rival systems of either Massachusetts or New York.[1] In short, the loosely coördinated administrative system of the

[1] See Article V, Section 9, New York constitution. Within the last three years over a third of the states have either adopted civil service rules or revised the systems already adopted.

revolutionary period is at last disappearing, and in its place the states are beginning to centralize administrative powers into the governor's hands, as in the national system. Future conventions should pay much more attention to the proper organization of the administration, which might be arranged in a separate article apart from the executive. A beginning in this direction already has been made in eight constitutions,[1] but imperfectly, as these were prepared before present evils had fully developed. A convention that would originate a carefully studied system of reorganized administration, would start a reform that would rapidly pass into the constitutions of other states, since all begin to realize the need of improvement.

THE RECALL

Undoubtedly the most significant trend in state constitutions is the steady growth in the power of the electorate to control and dominate the several divisions of government. In recent years this has taken the form of the initiative and the referendum, and, since 1908, the recall. The citizens of Oregon, in seeking to get control of their government, thought it necessary to assert their right to discharge at discretion from public service any officer, judge, or representative in lawmaking body. An initiatory petition was therefore submitted to the voters and passed, November, 1908, asserting the right of the voters to recall any public officer of the state, and providing methods for so doing. In 1911 California adopted a similar provision but with improvements that make its system superior to the pioneer method of Oregon. In 1912 Arkansas, Nevada and

[1] See Arizona, Article VIII; Article VI, Indiana, Wisconsin, Oregon; Georgia, Article V, Section II; Colorado, Article XII; New Jersey, Article VII; and Tennessee, Article VII.

Colorado adopted the state wide recall; and two other states, Michigan, Idaho, adopted it but excepted judicial officers. In 1914 four other states voted on referenda, providing for the recall, but it passed in Louisiana and Kansas only, both excepting judges.[1]

This remarkable assertion of authority, it is said, is not intended for frequent use or a radical exercise of power, but rather as an extension of the principle of democracy; placing on record in the fundamental law, a definite statement of the authority of the electorate over every public servant, but assuming that the occasions for its use would be few and far between.

The recall, under the systems in use, applies to "every elective officer," or to "every public officer" including therefore those appointed as well as those elected. The provisions inserted in the constitution regularly apply also to county, township and municipality, as well as to state officers; though it may here be said that the use of the recall against local officials antedated its use by the state. The city charter of Los Angeles, California, by amendment in 1893 introduced the recall principle into municipal government and it is now widely in use, especially in connection with the commission form of city charter. The recall takes the form of a petition to be signed by a given fraction of the voters of the state, eight per cent for example, or by a larger fraction of a locality or district, twenty or twenty-five per cent. The petition asks for a referendum and a special election. The referendum is on the question whether a designated officer shall be recalled, assuming that he does not resign before the day set; the election is for the purpose of filling the vacancy if the officer should be recalled. The law usually provides that no petition may be

---

[1] It was defeated in Minnesota and Wisconsin.

circulated against an official until at least six months after he has assumed office, except in case of legislators. The two subjects may be (1) combined into an election, in which the official is a candidate, and is recalled if he fails to receive a plurality over his opponent; or (2) they may be voted on separately but on the same day, with the requirement that each voter must vote on both propositions, the recall and the choice, if his vote is to be counted; or (3) the recall vote precedes the election, which takes place only if the official is recalled. Provision may be made for payment of the official's election expenses, whether sustained or not, or only if sustained. Both the Oregon and the California systems provide for publicity of reasons pro and con for the recall.

CHAPTER XIV

THE JUDICIAL DEPARTMENT

THE judiciary is the department of our government which, up to recent years, has undergone fewest changes and given most satisfaction. The touching confidence of old-time constitution makers in the wisdom and integrity of legislator and judge, may still be seen in the constitutions of the New England states, which dispose of the subject of judicial organization in few words, leaving it almost entirely to the discretion of the lawmakers. Contrast these with recent constitutions and the difference is marked. One of the chief sins of the Louisiana constitution is that it devotes about twelve thousand words to the courts of the state and of the city and parish of New Orleans. It is really a statute under the form of a constitutional article, and yet can be amended only by a slow and tedious process. But, though the chief of sinners in this respect, Louisiana is not alone in this tendency. The rapid multiplication of population and wealth, our democratic fondness for litigation and lawmaking, with social unrest thrown in as a disturber of the peace, all compel movements for the reorganization of the judiciary. The effect of this is seen in the addition to our constitutions of numerous pages devoted to the judicial department; for conventions, filled with distrust of legislatures, realize that a judicial system with organization and functions defined by constitution is beyond the power and control of the lawmaking body.

The American standard of judicial organization is a three-grade system of courts, consisting of a supreme court, an intermediate court usually known as a circuit, district or county court, and courts of the justices of the peace. The jurisdiction of the judges of the highest sets of courts regularly extends to all parts of the state, even though in some cases they are elected by districts.

The supreme court is regularly a court of appeals, usually, if at all, having original jurisdiction only in the issuance of original and remedial writs; this power it regularly shares with the courts next lower in grade. A few states add other jurisdiction.[1] In eight states the supreme court is called the court of appeals,[2] or the court of errors (1), or the court of errors and appeals (2); confusion arises when, as in New York, the supreme court is not a supreme but a district court. In Texas the supreme court has a separate organization for civil and for criminal business. Oklahoma authorizes the same arrangement at legislative discretion; but an amendment in 1914 failed of passage, providing for a single court system. In membership the supreme court ranges from three to nine members, though by exception New Jersey has sixteen. The favored numbers are 3, 5, 7; 9, 13, 11 states having these numbers respectively. Rapid increase of judicial business in many of our states during the last thirty years has burdened their supreme courts beyond reason. Relief comes easily if the constitution permits the legislature in its discretion to increase the membership of the court. Failing this, a temporary makeshift in use is to authorize a supreme court commission, so as to enable the court to catch up with its cases. In recent

[1] For example, California, Illinois, Indiana, Nebraska, North Carolina, Pennsylvania and some of the New England states.
[2] For example in Kentucky, Maryland, New Jersey, New York.

years this has been done by California, Florida, Montana and Nebraska. In New York (amendment 1899) justices of the supreme (district) court, not more than four, may be designated by the governor to serve temporarily as associate justices of the court of appeals. Another possibility is to organize a system of intermediate courts of appeal,[1] but this additional grade, in cases when decisions are conflicting, may add to the expense and time of litigation. Again, there is the system of increasing the number of judges and allowing these to sit in two or more divisions, and *en banc* only when necessary to settle disputes or in especially important jurisdiction. Still another possibility is shown in New Hampshire (1901) and Rhode Island (1903) which have organized each a superior court, having part of the jurisdiction formerly confided to the supreme court. Those constitutions that failed to include some such provision for the relief of the supreme court are rapidly placing it in their constitutions by amendment.[2] Wisconsin has had to change the organization of its supreme court three times by amendment to constitution; in 1877, 1889, 1903.

In view of this national tendency, it would be well if all constitutions hereafter would provide an adequate system for appellate jurisdiction, or leave to the legislature some discretion in respect to the organization of the supreme court.

Little needs to be said in regard to the other grades of court. There are wide differences in organization, and much is left to legislatures. There is little uniformity in name and many differences in jurisdiction. Information

---

[1] For example in Illinois, Indiana, Louisiana, Missouri, New York, Pennsylvania, Tennessee, Texas, and California in 1904.

[2] See for example Kansas, 1900; Florida, 1903; Colorado, Alabama, 1904; Nebraska, North Dakota, 1908; Mississippi, 1914, though a question as to the passage of this amendment has gone to the courts for decision.

on such matters therefore, must be sought from the constitutions and statutes themselves or from some text book on the subject.[1]

TENURE AND APPOINTMENT

Life tenure, and appointment through legislature or executive, was the method in vogue for the higher judiciary at the beginning of the nineteenth century. Only one state, Georgia, at that time elected judges for its higher courts by popular vote. The tendency is entirely the other way at the present time. Three states[2] still retain a "good behavior" tenure, but all others fix a definite term. A long tenure is favored by four other states;[3] the remaining states vary from two years (Vermont) to twelve, twenty-two favoring the six-year term; eight and twelve are the periods next favored. A class system is in use in over two-thirds of the states, the number of classes varying with the period. By this system of retiring a part only of the bench at one time, the opinions of its members are less likely to be affected by political considerations, continuity in decision is maintained, and candidates for election, being fewer in number, receive more attention. The usual practice is to elect these at large, not by districts. The tenure of inferior judges is for a shorter term; if the supreme justices for example, hold for six years, the other two grades of judges hold usually for four and two years. Theorists regularly declaim against the election of a judiciary, yet the practice and experience of our states point the other way. The decisions of the American bench compare most favorably with similar decisions enunciated by appointed judges

---

[1] For example, Governor Baldwin's The American Judiciary.

[2] Massachusetts, New Hampshire and Rhode Island.

[3] Pennsylvania, twenty-one years; Maryland and Virginia, fifteen; New York, fourteen years.

elsewhere, and the results justify the practice. As a sort of concession, however, to this opinion, there are movements in several states[1] looking towards the development of a system of non-partisan nominations and elections for judges.

Chief justices are as a rule so designated by several methods, among which may be mentioned, (1) that justice having the shortest unexpired term, (2) by election, (3) by choice of the justices themselves or (4) by seniority of service. Clerks of the supreme court are regularly mentioned in the constitutions, and in about half of the states are appointed by the courts; in a few states they are elected at large. Judges of the supreme court are still appointed by governor and council in Maine, Massachusetts and New Hampshire; in Delaware, Mississippi,[2] and New Jersey by governor and senate; in Rhode Island, Vermont, South Carolina and Virginia, by the assembly; and in Connecticut by the assembly on nomination of the governor. Georgia in 1898 (assembly) and Louisiana (governor) in 1904, were the last to change to the elective system. The other thirty-seven states elect their judges and show no tendency in the other direction. The usual provision for removal is by vote of the assembly (a majority or two-thirds) or through the governor after action by the assembly, or by impeachment. Four states by constitution fix the retiring age at seventy years, Connecticut, Maryland, New Hampshire, New York.

The salaries of judges are far less frequently specified in the constitutions than those of other civil officers. Those that do, as a rule give the legislature power to modify at discretion. The statutes of our states show a strong tendency to enlarge salaries paid to judges, doubtless because

---

[1] For example, in Minnesota, Idaho, Iowa, Kansas, Nebraska, Wisconsin and Pennsylvania.

[2] An amendment, 1914, changing to election by popular vote probably passed, but is in controversy.

of the broader learning and arduous labor demanded under present conditions of life. The rewards of law practice are now so great that capable judges cannot be obtained except by adequate compensation. The salaries range from $14,000 (New York) to $2,500 (Vermont). About three-fifths of the states pay $5,000 or less; the others, New York excepted, range from $5,000 to $10,000.

THE JUDICIAL RECALL

The most important development of recent years in connection with the judiciary is the movement for the recall of judges and of judicial decisions. Oregon in 1908 started the discussion by providing through amendment for the possible recall of "every public officer," including therefore judges. California in 1911 adopted the same provision, and so did Arizona in making its first constitution. Congress however, compelled Arizona to omit the judicial recall, as a condition for admission to the Union. But when in the following year it became a state, it promptly reinserted the provision in its constitution and went still further by passing an act providing for an advisory recall for judges in the United States' court in the district of Arizona, and for a popular recommendation of suitable persons to the presidency and senate. In 1912 Arkansas, Nevada and Colorado adopted the general recall, and the last named added a further amendment in respect to the recall of judicial decisions. It provides that the supreme court only shall pass on the constitutionality of laws and that such decisions shall be subject to a referendum petition and vote. In respect to the recall of judges it is said that this movement is not directed against judges as such, but rather is an assertion of the general principle that if the voters have the right to elect, they also have the right to dismiss.

The first judge recalled under this system was the judge of the police court of San Francisco in 1913.

THE JURY

It is plainly evident that the time-honored jury system is subject to amendment in these modern days. Several states[1] by constitution or by statute either abolish or authorize the legislature or the court to abolish at its discretion the grand jury. If retained, the number of its membership and of those who must concur is often stated.

Many constitutions arrange that a jury may be waived altogether in petty civil suits, or in more important cases by agreement, or in misdemeanors; or that the jury may be less than twelve, or a verdict may be rendered by a vote that is not unanimous. These modifications are too numerous to specify in detail but many such provisions may be found under bill of rights and judicial department.[2] These modifications in the jury system, though not in themselves so important, yet show a tendency worth noting. A state desirous of modifying its jury system should put a provision to that effect in its constitution, and if its constitution contains some such provision as the following: "The right of trial by jury shall be preserved inviolate," it should add, as Kentucky does, "subject to such modifications as may be authorized by this constitution." It was once rather common in this country to allow a jury to be judge of the law as well as of the facts, the reaction against that older practice is shown by a provision in several

[1] See for example Colorado, Illinois, Minnesota, Missouri, North Dakota, South Dakota, Wisconsin, Wyoming, Utah, Washington.

[2] Most of the constitutions contain such provisions but, as illustrations, see Idaho, Louisiana, Montana, North Carolina, South Dakota, Virginia, Arizona.

constitutions that "judges shall not charge juries with respect to matters of fact but may state the questions of facts in issue and declare the law."[1] Maryland makes the opposite statement, Article XV, 5.

MISCELLANEOUS

It is now common in most of our states to grant legal and equitable relief in one suit, a reform largely brought about through the influence of Justice Field (David Dudley Field). A provision authorizing such procedure is found in several constitutions.[2] "There shall be but one form of civil action, and law and equity may be administered in the same action." Following up this tendency many constitutions provide for tribunals of conciliation[3] whose decisions are not to be obligatory unless by mutual consent.

Certain minor judicial features of our state constitutions may briefly be mentioned as indicative of the present trend. It is quite usual, especially in new constitutions, to define the boundaries of judicial districts. This is purely a matter of detail that might better be placed in the schedule and left to be amended by ordinary statute. Fourteen states expressly authorize the supreme court to superintend and control inferior courts;[4] six states provide that judges may suggest improvements in the law for legislative action.[5] Four of

---

[1] Delaware; also Arkansas, California, Nevada, South Carolina, Tennessee, Washington, Arizona.

[2] Among these may be mentioned Idaho, Montana, Nevada, Utah, and Wisconsin; see also Ohio, Article XIV.

[3] Alabama, Colorado, Kentucky, Louisiana, Michigan, North Dakota, Texas, Wisconsin and Wyoming, for example.

[4] Arkansas, Colorado, Iowa, Louisiana, Maryland, Michigan, Missouri, Montana, New Mexico, North Dakota, Oklahoma, South Dakota, Wisconsin, Wyoming. Oregon gives this power to its circuit courts. See also California, Texas and Washington for modified powers.

[5] Colorado, Florida, Idaho, Illinois, Utah, Washington.

the older states [1] still allow the governor or assembly to ask the supreme court for opinions on important questions of law, or on "solemn occasions." South Dakota and Florida allow the governor this privilege but all the other states wisely prefer to keep the supreme court out of politics and omit the provision.

Idaho and North Carolina authorize the supreme court to hear claims against the state but its decisions are to be merely recommendatory. The senate as a court of impeachment still holds its place in the judicial system, though it is an exceedingly cumbersome and somewhat antiquated method of trial. In New York the judges of the court of appeals are added to the senate in such trials. Oregon only, of all the states (VII, 19), has no provision for impeachment.

An attempt to define libel is a marked feature in many constitutions. This may be found either under Bill of Rights or Judicial Department. Among the most elaborate of these are the provisions found in the constitutions of Michigan, California, Pennsylvania, Alabama, Arkansas, and Oklahoma. Many states make a judicial officer ineligible to any other than a judicial office. Some states refuse him permission to be absent from the state for a longer period than sixty or ninety days.[2] Five states[3] require the court to furnish for record a syllabus of the points adjudicated in each case. A few constitutions use pressure so as to expedite judges in their work. Arizona, for example, requires that every case submitted to the judge of a superior court for his decision must be decided within sixty days. Some of these provide that judges shall

---

[1] Massachusetts, Maine, New Hampshire, Rhode Island. In regard to "Advisory Opinions," see, Thayer's (J. B.) Legal Essays, pp. 42–59.

[2] California, Missouri, Utah, Washington, Arizona.

[3] North Dakota, Oregon, South Carolina, Utah, West Virginia.

not collect their salaries unless they take oath that all controversies finally submitted have been decided.[1] Three states endeavor to define contempt of court.[2] Seven states[3] provide that the publication of decisions shall be free, and two provide that the copyright shall belong to the state (Nebraska, South Dakota).

Alabama authorizes judges to exclude the public from the court room in cases of rape, and Georgia must greatly add to the business of its supreme court by declaring that "The costs in the supreme court shall not exceed ten dollars, unless otherwise provided by law." Florida requires that the legislature "appropriate at least $500 each year for the purchase of such books for the supreme court library as the court may direct." Arizona has a requirement that "No cause shall be reversed for technical error in pleading or proceedings when upon the whole case it shall appear that substantial justice has been done."[4]

[1] For such and similar provisions see California, Georgia, Idaho, Maryland, Montana, Nevada, South Carolina, Utah, Washington.

[2] South Carolina, Arkansas, Louisiana.

[3] California, Missouri, New York, Utah, Washington, Florida, Arizona.

[4] See, for a somewhat similar provision, California's constitution, Article VI, Section 4½. The word "criminal" was omitted from this section by amendment, 1914.

CHAPTER XV

ORGANIZATION OF THE LEGISLATIVE DEPARTMENT AND ITS PROCEDURE

THE most important department in our system of government is that of lawmaking. This power at the beginning of our national existence nearly one hundred and forty years ago was exerted only through legislatures; at the present time the power of making fundamental law has largely passed to the constitutional convention and to the electorate. This latter body, through the referendum, and in some states through the initiative, also shares to some extent the power of making statutes. The relative importance of legislatures is therefore decreasing, not in a few but in all the states, and that, too, in spite of the fact that legislatures are much more democratic than formerly. Under such conditions conventions really have before them a problem well worth considering, viz., shall an attempt be made to enhance the dignity and importance of the legislature so as to make it worthy of the place it theoretically fills in our political system,[1] or, on the other hand, shall the process of minimizing its importance be continued until it becomes an impotent body of small consequence, dragging along a paltry existence, to be finally abolished as useless by some future convention? A powerful executive with ordinance privileges, a convention meeting periodically,

[1] See Vermont constitution, Chapter 2. Section 36. "The House . . . shall consist of persons most noted for wisdom and virtue".

and the use of the initiative and referendum as in Oregon, certainly seem to leave no pressing necessity for a legislature. Under present tendencies it must either pass out of use or be reorganized on a scientific basis. This and the two following articles will contain certain facts obtained from a comparison of our constitutions that may throw some light on this all-important problem.

LEGISLATIVE ORGANIZATION

Name. The lawmaking bodies of our states are generally called legislatures, but that in most cases is not the legal name. In twenty-three states it is known as the general assembly, in twenty as the legislature, in three as the legislative assembly,[1] and in two as the general court.[2] All the states name the small or upper house the senate, and forty call the larger body the house of representatives. Four call it the assembly,[3] three, the house of delegates,[4] and one, the general assembly (New Jersey).

Membership. It is hard to realize that in our state legislatures alone we have 7,347 lawmakers, (1,746 in senate and 5,601 in house, or an average for each state of thirty-seven senators and one hundred and seventeen representatives). Omitting the New England states, the average is thirty-seven in the senate and one hundred in the house. If "in multitude of counsellors there is safety" surely we are safe when our legislatures are in session! If undue size is a political sin, the worst sinners are the New England states, which have in their six lower houses 1,401 members, besides 195 in the senates. This is due to their unfortunate

[1] North Dakota, Montana, Oregon.
[2] Massachusetts, New Hampshire.
[3] California, Nevada, New York, Wisconsin.
[4] Maryland, Virginia, West Virginia.

emphasis on the importance of the town, once the pride but now the bane of New England politics. The five states [1] largest in population average forty-three in the senate and one hundred and fifty-two in the house; New York, the largest state, has fifty-one and one hundred and fifty respectively. Omitting the six New England states the twenty-four next largest states having a population over one million average forty in the senate and one hundred and nine in the house; the remaining thirteen states average twenty-nine in the senate and sixty-three in the house. Of all the legislatures only two senates have a membership of over fifty-one (Alabama fifty-four, Minnesota sixty-seven); two are under twenty (Utah eighteen, Delaware seventeen). Four houses have a membership of less than fifty (Delaware thirty-five, Arizona thirty-five, Utah forty-five, New Mexico forty-nine); and five houses have a membership of over two hundred (Pennsylvania two hundred and seven, Massachusetts two hundred and forty, Vermont two hundred and forty-six, Connecticut two hundred and fifty-eight, and New Hampshire, four hundred and six, almost as large as the national house). An average taken of the ten new constitutions made since 1888 shows the houses to be respectively thirty-three and seventy-four.

Delaware has the smallest legislature, fifty-two members; New Hampshire has the largest, four hundred twenty-six. The population of the latter state is a little more than twice that of the former; or, from another standpoint, New Hampshire has one legislator for every 1000 of the population; Delaware, one for every 4000; and the state of New York, one for every forty-five thousand.

The figures as a whole show that the American tendency is to have a senate from one-half to one-third that of

[1] New York, Pennsylvania, Illinois, Ohio, Texas.

the house in membership,[1] that the legislatures of our largest states should not exceed a joint membership of about two hundred; our average states not over one hundred and fifty, and the legislatures of our small states with a population of one million or less should have a membership ranging from ninety to one hundred ten. Experience shows that it is on the whole best to fix the numbers definitely in the constitution. If the legislature is given the power, the number of representatives becomes too large. It is far easier in practice to increase than to decrease the number.

Representation.[2] Three of the New England states have both houses organized on a basis of population similar in practice to that of the other states. The three other states of this section each have one of their houses fairly democratic, but the other house is based on a town system, regardless of population. These six states, however, are omitted from the comparisons of the two following paragraphs, since they should be studied by themselves.

The prevailing basis of representation in the senate of the forty-two remaining states is population. Thirty-three order a reapportionment after every census, based on population, and three based on voting population.[3] The other six states[4] also base the apportionment on population, but make some modification or exception that renders the senate not quite so democratic in basis as those of the other thirty-six states.

In all of the forty-two states population is the basis of representation in the house. In twenty of these there are

---

[1] This ratio is fixed in some states, for example Iowa, Nevada, Utah, Washington, Wyoming.

[2] See also chap. xix for further details.

[3] Arkansas, Indiana, Tennessee.

[4] Delaware, Georgia, Maryland, Montana, New Jersey, South Carolina.

no restrictions whatever, but in the remaining states there are restrictions aiming to secure representation for each county in the larger house, or to reduce somewhat the proper proportion to be assigned to cities.   These are not excessive in the case of fifteen of the states, but seven are unduly restricted.[1]   Ten of the older states provide in their constitutions a complex ratio for determining representation, but one only of the newer states, Oklahoma, includes a ratio for determining house representation.   The single-member district is the prevailing form in the states, though there are some exceptions, since the county may be used as a general district for the house and its representatives be elected at large.[2]

Terms. Thirty-one states fix on a four-year term for senators and all but seven[3] of these provide for arrangement into two classes, one-half retiring every two years.   New Jersey elects for three years on a three-class system. Fifteen states[4] elect their senators for two years only, and Massachusetts for one year.   For members of the house the term is two years in forty-three states, four years in Alabama and Louisiana, and one year in Massachusetts, New York and New Jersey.

Sessions. In the "good old times" constitutions provided for annual sessions and used to declare that "The legislature ought frequently to assemble."[5]   The states seem not so sure of that now for there are two states that elect their legislatures quadrennially, Louisiana and

[1] Delaware, Georgia, Kansas, Maryland, Missouri, Ohio, Utah.

[2] For example, in Illinois, Mississippi, Missouri, North Dakota, Texas.

[3] Alabama, Delaware, Kansas, Louisiana, Mississippi, New Mexico, Virginia.

[4] Connecticut, Georgia, Idaho, Maine, Michigan, Nebraska, New Hampshire, New York, North Carolina, Ohio, South Dakota, Tennessee, Vermont, Arizona, Rhode Island.

[5] See constitutions of Maryland, Massachusetts, South Carolina.

Alabama, the last of which has but one regular session during that term. All other states hold biennial sessions except Georgia, Massachusetts, New Jersey, New York, Rhode Island, South Carolina which provide for annual meetings. Twenty-six states place no constitutional limitation on the length of the session, but eleven [1] of them provide that pay stop entirely or be reduced in amount, at the end of a specified time. The practical effect of this proviso is to reduce the session to the period of full pay. If all states except the remaining fifteen be considered as having a constitutional time limit we find twenty-one setting a sixty-day limit, six, a limit of from forty to fifty days; and six, at intervals ranging from seventy to ninety days. California formerly had a sixty day limit but now provides for a thirty day session for the initiation of bills, a recess for at least thirty days, and then the continuation of the session without limit. Four [2] states set a limit but authorize the legislature to extend the same if necessary. Special sessions are regularly authorized and eighteen states set limits to the duration of these, the favored periods being twenty, thirty and forty days.

Salaries. Over one-half of the constitutions specify the per diem of their legislators and regularly get it too low. Once fixed in the constitution it is hard to raise the amount by amendment since voters seem to delight in voting down all forms of increase in pay. The per diem amount paid is often barely sufficient for expenses at a cheap hotel and must be eked out from other sources of income. Many constitutions fortunately allow legislatures discretion in regard to the amount of pay and in such states a more

---

[1] Idaho, Kansas, Missouri, North Carolina, Oregon, South Carolina, Tennessee, Texas, Oklahoma, Arizona, Rhode Island.

[2] Arkansas, Georgia, Virginia, West Virginia.

generous provision is made. Yet there is a strong trend towards an increase in the amount paid, but usually taking the form of a stated amount for the term or for the year. There are twenty-nine states paying a per diem which averages about five dollars, fifty cents. The remaining states pay an amount per annum, or for the term or the session. A per diem is usually named for special sessions. The best paid legislators are those of Illinois, who receive $ 2000 per year. The lowest are Oregon (three dollars per day for forty days), Missouri and Kansas, at three dollars per day.[1] Mileage is regularly specified in addition, and in a few constitutions an attempt is made to regulate the amount of incidental expenses.[2]

THE PROCEDURE IN BILLS

Under the legislative department will regularly be found a number of provisions in regulation of the organization and general powers of the legislature. Among these is one authorizing each house to determine the rules of its own procedure. In one respect at least, this power has been taken from the houses. Proper deliberation and an opportunity for free discussion are so important in legislation that the procedure in respect to the passing of bills is now in many of our states regulated by constitution, from the introduction of the bill to its promulgation after passage. This is one of the most important checks on legislative power yet devised. The contrast between the old and the new in this respect can easily be seen by comparing the

[1] All three of these states submitted in 1908 referenda arranging for an increase of pay, but the decisions at the polls were negative. Amendments of this sort were rejected, 1914, in Arkansas, Missouri, North Carolina, Oregon, Texas, Wisconsin, Wyoming.

[2] For example Missouri and Delaware. For California's new provision see its constitution, Article IV, Section 23a.

ancient constitutions of New England with almost any of those made since 1888, especially the constitutions of Alabama, Kentucky, Louisiana, Mississippi. In three constitutions a separate heading has been set aside for such and kindred regulations of procedure or proceedings.[1] A complete list of such restrictions would practically indicate all the evils that have developed in legislative experience, for, of course, each restriction is aimed at some observed defect or evil in the legislative system. In practice the chief difficulty lies in the enforcement of these provisions. Especially are those requiring the reading of bills in full often disregarded by "unanimous consent" or the "suspension of the rules." The courts rarely interfere, since as a rule they do not care to call in question the legality of the actual procedure used by a coördinate department of government in the passing of legislation; so that the two houses virtually have the matter in their own hands.

It is generally provided that no law shall be passed except by bill, and that no new bill shall be introduced within the last few days of the session — three to twenty days — except by consent of a large fraction of the house. Some confine this restriction to appropriation bills. California requires that all bills shall be introduced within the first thirty days of the broken session. Thereafter bills can be introduced only by consent of three-fourths of the membership. The effect of this provision is said to be the introduction of a number of "fake" bills in the early session, to be "amended" in the later session. Nebraska insists that no bills shall be introduced after the first twenty days unless the governor so requests in a special message. General appropriation bills however may be introduced during the first forty days. No bill is to embrace more than one

[1] Mississippi, Missouri, Texas.

subject, which must be plainly expressed in its title, any part not so expressed being null and void. This requirement naturally multiplies the number of statutes to be considered. General appropriation bills, and bills for the revision and codification of laws are excepted from this provision. The time honored provision that revenue bills shall originate in the house only, and be subject to amendment in the senate, is required by twenty-two states. The others either expressly authorize either house to introduce any bill or infer it by silence. It is regularly provided that every appropriation outside of the general appropriation shall be by special bill. Some (Mississippi for example) add that no appropriation bill shall be passed which does not fix definitely the maximum sum thereby authorized to be drawn from the treasury. In others, New York for example, bills appropriating money for local or private purposes must receive a two-thirds vote of all members elected to both houses, and, again, not less than three-fifths of all members elected shall form a quorum for the consideration of a revenue or appropriation bill. No act can be revised or amended by mere reference to its title, but what is amended must be set forth in full; nor is any amendment to a bill allowed which would change the scope and object of the bill.

In view of the great importance of legislative committees it is strange that so few constitutions attempt to regulate them. The task is apparently too great for conventions. The only provisions are the following: Some nine states require that all bills must be referred to a committee. Oklahoma provides that the senate shall elect all of its standing committees by a majority vote. Kentucky states that whenever a committee fails or refuses to report within a reasonable time, any member may call up the bill. Michigan forbids any rule that would prevent a majority of the members elected from discharging a committee from the further consideration of any measure. Three states [1] make provision for a joint committee on local and special legislation, which under its instructions ought to be most useful in handling that distressing part of legislation. Five states provide that voting on reports of committees of conference shall be recorded by a yea and nay vote.

Many of the constitutions authorize a demand for a yea or nay vote on any question; the number who may make the demand varies from one member to one-fifth of the membership. It is generally provided that bills must be read three times, but differences arise as to whether these shall be read in full and on three separate days. The last reading is regularly in full and vote on its passage is recorded by yeas and nays. New York forbids amendment at the last reading. New Mexico requires that "No interlineation or erasure in a signed bill shall be effective unless certified thereon in express terms by the presiding officer of each house quoting the words interlined or erased, nor unless the fact of the making of such interlineation or erasure be publicly announced in each house and entered on the journal." (Article IV. Section 20. See also, Section 21.) Mississippi requires that all votes on final passage shall be subject to one day's reconsideration. It is now a common requirement that bills be printed with all amendments and placed in the hands of members before the final vote.[2] Louisiana authorizes also the printing of minutes each day for the use of members.

A quorum is regularly a majority of all members, and bills

[1] Georgia, Mississippi, Virginia.
[2] As illustrations, Missouri, Pennsylvania, New York.

pass by a majority of those present, but some require[1]
that every bill must receive a majority vote of all members
elected, and New Hampshire requires that when less than
two-thirds of all members are present, a two-thirds vote
is necessary. Kentucky makes the fraction of those present
two-fifths.

All bills of course when finally passed must be signed by
the presiding officers, but this has become a quite formal
occasion; other business is suspended, the bill is read at
length and compared, then the chairman signs in open session and sends on the bill to the other house where the same
procedure takes place.[2] Twelve constitutions allow any
member to make formal protest against a bill and to have
the protest entered on the records.[3] Minnesota allows no
bill to be passed on the last day of the session. Kentucky,
Maine, Mississippi, New York forbid riders on appropriation bills. About one-half of the constitutions define when
the laws shall go into effect. The period set varies from
forty to ninety days, the last being the favorite. A few
prefer to fix a definite date for all bills, as the first day of
June or July, this is usually equivalent to a sixty or ninety
day limit.[4] As a rule provision is made that a bill may go
into effect immediately in case of emergency.

The "emergency" permission is, however, a source of
much trouble, since it is often used to avoid the demand for
a referendum. The legislature, for instance, may attach
the emergency clause to any bill it wishes to put into effect
at once, its wish being the only emergency. In Arizona,
for example, the house in 1912, to avoid the constitutional

[1] Louisiana and Delaware for example.
[2] See Alabama, Kentucky, and Missouri, as illustrations. But as a rule
the reading of the bill in full may be dispensed with by vote.
[3] See Missouri for example.
[4] See Illinois, Iowa, Maryland, North Dakota.

provision, "Every bill shall be read by sections on three different days, unless in case of emergency," placed on its journal a general declaration of emergency and henceforth omitted all but the last reading of its bills. So far, the best safeguard against the wrong use of the emergency clause may be found in the constitution of California,[1] which reads as follows : —

"Whenever it is deemed necessary for the immediate preservation of the public peace, health, or safety that a law shall go into immediate effect, a statement of the facts constituting such necessity shall be set forth in one section of the act, which section shall be passed only upon a yea and nay vote, upon a separate roll call thereon; *provided, however*, that no measure creating or abolishing any office or changing the salary, term or duties of any officer, or granting any franchise or special privilege, or creating any vested right or interest, shall be construed to be an urgency measure." Oklahoma also seeks to guard the emergency clause,[2] and further provides that the governor's veto of an emergency bill must be overridden by a three-fourths vote instead of the usual two-thirds.

It is easy to see that the strict enforcement of the severest of these regulations would prevent much hasty legislation, but it can hardly be said that constitutional conventions or legislative committees on rules of procedure are yet satisfied with existing systems of procedure. Several states already have made studies of these and Nebraska has now, 1914, a legislative committee at work on the subject. Each new convention will doubtless devote much thought to this important problem.

[1] Amendment 1911, Article IV. Section one.
[2] Article V. Section fifty-eight.

CHAPTER XVI

POPULAR REPRESENTATION IN STATE LEGISLATURES [1]

THE famous Northwest Ordinance of 1787, in article second of its compact, declares that, "The inhabitants of the said territory shall always be entitled to the benefits of . . . a proportionate representation of the people in the legislature." This principle of popular representation may now be looked on as a settled American policy and departures from it as exceptions to the general rule. In our state constitutions this principle is embodied in the command that representation in both legislative houses shall be based on population, and a readjustment made decennially, after the taking of either national or state census. Legislatures, to be sure, in carrying out this injunction, may be to some extent unfair in their apportionments, but that is a matter of discretion and expediency, the remedy for which should, in case of gross inequalities, lie in the courts. [2]

While, however, the principle of equal representation is embodied in our state constitutional system, there are exceptions, and some of these are serious departures from the principle. In a few states at least a system of representative democracy does not exist, but rather a form of

[1] Note in Bibliography, Reed's Territorial Basis, especially chaps. vii–viii.

[2] Oklahoma, for example, provides that "An apportionment by the legislature shall be subject to review by the Supreme Court at the suit of any citizen, under such rules and regulations as the legislature may prescribe." Article V. 10. j.

oligarchy. These modifications are generally survivals from an earlier system, once fair enough, but now antiquated and retained for partisan purposes; or retained sometimes as a sort of guaranty for the minority against a powerful majority. In form they are constitutional provisions aiming to secure representation to districts, county or town, irrespective of population; or, on the other hand, to place limitations on city representation as against the representation of the rural population. These provisions are fourfold: there are (1) provisions that each town or county have one or more members: (2) that no city or county have more than a fixed number or fraction; (3) a complex ratio is specified which in effect may discriminate against some in favor of other localities;[1] and (4) the districts are themselves fixed by constitution and limitations placed on legislative power to alter these.

This chapter aims to present in detail the systems of representation in our several state legislatures, from the standpoint of equal popular representation. As a common basis for this study the federal census of 1910 will be used,[2] the county taken as the unit of representation, and an apportionment be considered as "equal," when the population of a district ranges anywhere from a half ratio to a ratio and a half. The ratio, of course, will be obtained by dividing the population of the state by the respective memberships in senate or house. In a few constitutions a different fraction of a ratio may be fixed (two-thirds for instance); or the population taken into account may be the voting population, or the census population less aliens;

[1] For ratio provisions see constitutions of Iowa, Maine, Maryland, Missouri, North Carolina, New Hampshire, New York, Ohio, Pennsylvania, West Virginia, and Oklahoma.

[2] But in New York the state census of 1905.

but these local differences will be disregarded for the sake of uniformity. In New England the town is so obviously the unit that the comparison will be made from both units, town and county.

I. In eighteen of the states the constitutions provide for apportionment in both houses on the basis of population, a reapportionment after each census, and place no restrictions on this basis. These states therefore are broadly democratic in this respect. The list,[1] it will be noted, includes states from all sections of the United States.

II. In twenty-four states, while the census population is made the basis, there are certain limitations on the representation in one, or it may be in both houses, that modify somewhat the principle. These, though on the whole unimportant, should yet be explained in detail:

Alabama. The constitution provides that each county shall have at least one member in the house. There are sixty-seven counties in the state but each of these has a population at least over one-half of the ratio. There are therefore no limitations in fact.

Arizona. The constitution of this state contains a fixed apportionment, which is to hold "until otherwise provided by law." There is no provision for a reapportionment after each census. The apportionment in the constitution is in general based on the population as estimated when the convention was in session.

Arkansas has the same provision as Alabama, but though there are seventy-five counties, each has at least one-half the ratio.

Florida provides that each county have at least one in

---

[1] California, Colorado, Illinois, Indiana, Kentucky, Massachusetts, Michigan, Minnesota, Nebraska, Nevada, New Mexico, North Dakota, Oklahoma, Oregon, South Dakota, Tennessee, Washington and Wisconsin.

the house, and no county more than three. Of its forty-seven counties eight have less than one-half the ratio and hence are over-represented. The two largest counties limited by constitution to three each, are entitled by population to six members each and hence are under-represented.

Idaho requires that at least one member be assigned in the senate to each county, but of its thirty-one counties three only have less than one-half the ratio.

Iowa requires that each county have at least one in the house, and provides a ratio which discriminates against the thickly settled counties. Of its ninety-nine counties sixty-two are below the population ratio, four of these are below the one-half ratio, and of its larger counties six, to which are assigned twelve members, should have by population twenty members. This state illustrates the fact that if the constitution fixes the number of members, over-representation on one side involves under-representation on the other.

Kansas provides that each county shall have at least one in the house, provided it has at least two hundred fifty voters. As its population ratio for the house is 13,528, the smaller districts have too great a representation. The six counties of smallest population have combined only 9248 inhabitants, yet have six members in the house. In fact there are twenty-six districts having less than one half the ratio; these properly should have seven members instead of twenty-six. Hence by necessity the larger districts have too few representatives. The thirteen large districts, having each a population of over 25,000, to which twenty-eight members are assigned, are really entitled to forty-five. This well illustrates the evil of inserting an apparently simple condition without proper consideration of consequences.

Louisiana in its constitution of 1913 provides for a decennial reapportionment on the basis of the federal census, but with the stipulation that each parish (county) and each ward of New Orleans should have at least one member. Of the sixty parishes there are sixteen below the ratio but above one-half, and there are three in which the populations fall below one-half the ratio. As these have a member apiece, two of the large parishes in consequence have to bear the loss, losing two each from their proper quota.[1] The city of New Orleans however, has its full proportion of twenty-four members.

Maine by constitution provides that its senate of thirty-one members be apportioned among the counties in proportion to census population. The present apportionment is in strict accord with this provision.

The constitution also provides for a division of the one hundred fifty-one members of the house among the towns on the basis of census population, but adds a discriminating ratio. This will be explained more fully later; but so far as the house apportionment by counties is concerned, it is exactly based on population.

Mississippi also by constitution provides for reapportionment after each federal census, but with the proviso that each county shall have at least one member in the house. As the state has seventy-nine counties, and two only fall below the half ratio, the requirement does not practically violate the principle of equal representation.

Missouri by constitution provides that its senate be apportioned among districts equal in population and reapportionment made after each federal census.

In the case of the house however each county must have at least one, and a ratio is defined which discriminates in

---

[1] The parishes of Calcasieu and St. Landrey.

favor of the counties of small population. Of the one hundred fifteen counties eighty-four fall below a ratio based on population, and of these fifteen are below the half ratio. The gain in representation to these must be made up of course by a corresponding loss to the counties of larger population. The five counties each having a population of over 50,000, to which seventeen members were assigned, should have had by population twenty-six, and the city of St. Louis, to which sixteen were assigned, should have had thirty members.

Montana provides that each county shall have one member only in the senate. Of its twenty-eight counties nine were below one-half of the ratio and by population are entitled to three members only, and five counties, which by population were entitled to twelve members, had but five. As Montana in area is the third largest state in the Union, it is easy to see through multiplication of new counties the possible development of a "rotten borough" system within a generation or two, unless this condition should be stricken from the constitution.

New Hampshire. The constitution of this state is unique in providing that the senate of twenty-four members be apportioned one each to twenty-four districts, equal in respect to the proportion of direct taxes paid by the said districts. If the districts as set in 1911 be considered as the counties, and their populations ascertained, the result shows that fifteen fall below the ratio, though none below one-half the ratio.[1] By population these smaller districts should have twelve members instead of fifteen, the loss falling on the two largest districts.

---

[1] In population the largest district is the eighteenth, 41,998 inhabitants; the smallest is the twenty-fourth, 9716 inhabitants. The senate ratio by population would be 17,940.

The house ratio is fixed by constitution and is on a town basis. Disregarding this for the present, and considering the ten counties of the state from the standpoint of census population, it may be seen that the nine smaller counties should lose eight members and these should be added to Hillsboro County. As that county, however, had one hundred eleven members in the house, its interests are presumably well guarded, without the help of the missing eight.

New Jersey by constitution makes up its senate by one delegate from each of twenty-one counties. This of course produces great inequality. Fourteen of the counties are below the ratio and nine of these below the half ratio. This necessitates under-representation in the other counties. Essex and Hudson counties should have by population four members each in the senate and Passaic county two.

The constitution also provides that each county have at least one in the house, but as one county only (Cape May) falls below the one-half ratio, the requirement involves no real limitation on popular representation.

New York [1] in Article III, Section 4, of its constitution requires a reapportionment after each state census and places many restrictions about the apportionment of its senators, and in effect modifies somewhat the principle of popular representation in this body. The difference, however, is slight. District two, which is assigned one, is by population entitled to two. Kings county, which has eight, should have nine, and New York county is entitled to fifteen but has twelve. Provision is made that no county shall have more than one-third of all the senators, and no two adjoining counties more than one-half, but these maxima do not as yet apply to New York and Kings counties.

[1] Apportionment of 1907, based on state census of 1905.

Section 5 provides a ratio and other regulations for the apportionment of assemblymen. Among these provisions is found the familiar requirement that every county (except Hamilton) shall have at least one member in the assembly. As the house ratio by population is 53,782 this requirement makes havoc with popular representation. Seven districts fall below the half ratio and twenty-five are between one-half and the full ratio. In addition to these single-member districts, two of the larger districts have a representative each too many. The over-representation of these thirty-four districts necessitates as usual the under-representation of the largest districts. Kings county, which by population should have twenty-five, has twenty-three; and New York county should add nine to its allotment of thirty-five members.

North Carolina modifies equal representation in the house by defining in constitution the ratio, and by the requirement that each county must have at least one representative. Of the ninety-eight counties forty-five fall below the population ratio and eleven of these below the half ratio. This gain for the counties of smaller population is made up by corresponding losses to the counties of larger population. Fifteen counties having one member each assigned, should have two; three having two each should have three; and two having three each should have four.

Ohio also has the familiar requirement that each county shall have at least one member in the house (amendment 1903), and also fixes a ratio in the constitution which complicates the apportionment. In the legislature of 1912 there were one hundred eighteen members, and the five counties that contain a population each over 150,000 should have forty-one members as their proportionate share, but, instead, by apportionment have only twenty-seven members, fourteen less than their proportionate share. Of the remaining eighty-three counties fifty-nine are below the ratio, and ten of these below the half ratio. By population these fifty-nine counties are entitled to just thirty-nine members, but in fact have sixty.

Pennsylvania by constitution provides that its fifty senators be assigned in proportion to population, but with the proviso that no city or county shall have more than one-sixth. This limits Philadelphia to eight members, though by population entitled to ten.

For the house a ratio is fixed by constitution and provision made that each county have at least one member. The constitution sets no maximum to the membership and this by last apportionment was fixed at two hundred and seven. If the population ratio were used, the eleven large counties, having a population of over 150,000 each, including the city of Philadelphia, would have one hundred twenty-one members instead of one hundred ten, nine of these counties sharing the loss. Of the remaining fifty-six counties twenty are below the ratio, and ten of these below the half ratio. These ten by population should have four members only instead of ten.

South Carolina requires that each county have but one member in the senate. Of the forty-three counties twenty-five fall below the ratio, and one below the half ratio. There are seven counties containing each a population entitling it to two or more members, unitedly they should have thirteen members, and hence lose six to the smaller counties. By constitution each county also must have at least one in the house, but all the counties have populations above the house ratio.

Texas has a small senate of thirty-one members, and provides by constitution that no single county may have more than one member. In fact, however, no county has a population in excess of the ratio and there is therefore no real limitation.

Utah has a requirement that each county have at least one in the house. Of its twenty-seven county-districts sixteen are below the ratio and nine of these below the half ratio. These counties by population should have eight, not sixteen members. The more populous districts must therefore lose their proper proportion. Two districts lose one each (Utah and Boxelder counties), and one (Salt Lake) has ten, though entitled by population to sixteen.

Virginia has no constitutional restriction on representation but in its new constitution (1902) accepts the statutory apportionment of April 2, 1902, permits a reapportionment in 1906, and orders one in 1912 and every tenth year thereafter. In 1906 the apportionment of the House was continued without change and no reapportionment was passed in 1912 or in 1914. An examination of the apportionment of 1902 shows it to be substantially in accord with population. The senate of forty is rightly apportioned; in the house of one hundred members five large districts are short one each, to make up for a slight over-apportionment to districts below a full ratio. No district however falls below one-half ratio.

West Virginia fixes in its constitution the method of computing the house apportionment and grants each county one delegate. The last apportionment is on the basis of population; for of the fifty-five counties none fall below the half ratio, though seventeen are between the half and the full ratio.

Wyoming requires by constitution that each of its fourteen counties shall have at least one in each house. In the present apportionment of 1911 this results in the gain to the counties of small population of one in the senate (twenty-seven members), and three in the house (fifty-six members), and the consequent loss of these to the more thickly settled counties. Yet as no county is below the half ratio for either house, the requirement works no real hardship on the larger counties.

III. In six of the states the restrictions placed on popular representation are especially severe. These will now be considered in turn.

Connecticut by constitution divides the membership of thirty-five in the senate among the counties in proportion to population, with the proviso that each county have at least one. The assignment in 1914 is not sufficiently accurate. Each of the eight counties has a population sufficient to entitle it to at least one; Litchfield, Middlesex and Windham counties have each one in excess of their pro rata, and these are lost to Fairfield, Hartford and New Haven counties.

The house is composed of two hundred fifty-eight members and assignment is made on the town basis. If, however, the representation by counties be considered, five[1] rural counties, to which one hundred forty members are assigned, should properly have but sixty-five, and three[2] counties, assigned one hundred eighteen members, should have by population one hundred ninety-three.

Delaware. The apportionment to the three counties of Delaware is fixed by constitution and no provision made for alteration. In the senate, Newcastle, Sussex, and Kent counties are assigned seven, five, five members, but are by population entitled to ten, four, and three members respectively. In the house they are assigned fifteen, ten,

[1] New London, Windham, Litchfield, Middlesex, Tolland.
[2] Hartford, New Haven, Fairfield.

and ten, but should have twenty-one, eight, and six respectively. In Newcastle county the City of Wilmington is assigned two and five members in the houses, but should have seven and fifteen members by population. This injustice in apportionment will grow worse rather than better, owing to the rigidity of the constitutional provisions.

Georgia fixes in constitution its forty-four senatorial districts, but allows a readjustment after each federal census. In the apportionment' of 1906 the seven largest districts by population should have fourteen members instead of seven. This is necessitated by the fact that twenty-six districts fall below the ratio and four of these even below the half ratio. These senatorial districts were set in the present constitution of 1877 and have been continued without modification for over thirty years, except that to eleven of the districts new counties have been added and slight readjustments made. The other thirty-three districts, including the two most populous, have remained unchanged.

As for the house of one hundred eighty-four members the constitution divides the one hundred forty-six counties into three classes, and orders an assignment of three members each to the six largest counties; two each to the twenty-six counties next in size; and one each to the one hundred fourteen remaining. Had the apportionment been in proportion to population, the six largest counties would have had thirty-one members instead of eighteen; the twenty-six counties would have forty-nine; and the hundred and fourteen counties, one hundred and three. But of the counties in the third class five should have had two each, seventeen fall below even the one-half ratio, and fifty-five others range between the half and the full ratio, a plain discrimination against urban centers.

Maryland in its constitution, as amended, provides that each county shall have in the senate one member, and Baltimore city four, making a total of twenty-seven members, since there are twenty-three counties and the city district. This is far from being in accord with population, as nineteen of the twenty-three counties are below ratio, and eleven of these even below the half ratio. By population these should have nine instead of nineteen members. In consequence the more populous districts suffer; Baltimore county should have three, and the city is entitled to twelve.

The same objection lies against the apportionment of the house of one hundred and two members. A ratio is carefully defined in the constitution which discriminates in favor of the smaller districts and fixes a maximum for the city of Baltimore. The effect of this is that twenty-two counties which should have forty-eight members have seventy-two, the county of Baltimore has six but should have ten, and the city of Baltimore has twenty-four but should have been assigned by population forty-four members.

Rhode Island by constitution apportions its thirty-nine senators one to each town or city. By county [1] population this means that the four counties of smaller population should have nine senators only instead of the twenty-three assigned, and that Providence county, the only other county, should have thirty instead of sixteen.

Constitutional provisions in regard to the house require that each town shall have at least one, and no city more than one-fourth of the whole number (100). From the standpoint of county population the four smaller counties should have twenty-two instead of thirty-two members,

[1] The county in Rhode Island is merely a judicial district or districts and has no administrative unity.

and Providence county should gain the ten, making its total seventy-eight.

Vermont requires that its senate of thirty members be apportioned among the counties in proportion to census population, but that each county must have at least one. The county of Grand Isle has less than one-half the ratio, and the member assigned to this county is lost by Washington county, which has three members instead of four.

Representation in the house of two hundred forty-six members is by towns and will be presented later. If the population of the fourteen counties however be considered, it may be seen that the seven smaller counties have twenty-eight members assigned in excess of their population, and this number is taken from the seven large counties

THE NEW ENGLAND STATES

As these states emphasize on the whole the town as the basis of representation rather than the county, their system of representation will now be presented from the standpoint of the town system.

Of these six states *Massachusetts* only apportions the membership of both houses purely on the basis of (voting) population, after each state census. The representation in the lower house is assigned to the counties, and then reapportioned among the towns in proportion to their respective voting population. *Maine* follows the same procedure but specifies a ratio which gives the rural towns an advantage over urban centers. Seven counties only contain urban centers of a population over 7000, and these, eleven in number, are assigned thirty-three members, though by population entitled to forty-one. These eight members are gained by the rural towns in the same counties. Portland, the largest city in the state, is naturally the heaviest loser, having seven members though entitled to twelve.

New Hampshire apportions the membership of the lower house directly to the towns and city wards, on the basis of population, but by a set ratio which discriminates somewhat in favor of the county towns. Its house is the largest in membership among the states, though in population the state ranks as thirty-ninth. The size of the membership varies somewhat from session to session owing to a sort of sliding scale of representation for the smallest districts or towns; but, for the sessions from 1912–1920 the average membership is 406. There are eighty-four of these small districts each having a population less than 600, and these unitedly average fifty-two members. There are also 131 town or ward single-member districts, 41 two-member districts, 20 three-member districts, and fourteen districts with memberships ranging from four to nine members each, totaling 81 members. These larger districts include eleven incorporated cities having a population entitling them to 185 members instead of the 165 assigned. Among these Manchester, the largest city, is entitled by population to 67 members but has 59. These losses of course are gained by the smaller towns. Relatively however to the size of the house these discriminations are comparatively insignificant.

The other three New England states are by no means so equitable in their representation. In theory they seek to make one house popular in basis, and the other representative of the towns irrespective of population.

Vermont, for example, assigns the membership of the senate to the counties on the basis of population, but makes up its lower house of two hundred forty-six members by one delegate from each town or city in the state. Ninety of these towns have a population each lower than one-half the ratio, and, if properly represented, would have but twenty-five members. There are one hundred twenty towns having each a population between one-half and one and a half ratios. These have twenty-two members in excess of their population. There are thirty-six towns and cities having each a population over one and a half ratios, to which should be assigned on a population basis one hundred twenty-three members. The three largest cities combined should by population have thirty-one members instead of three. The largest city, Burlington, should have fourteen members instead of one. Contrast with the three cities the three smallest towns, which have a combined population of one hundred ten persons; these are presumably fully represented by their three delegates in the house!

Connecticut likewise assigns its membership in the senate on the basis of population, and in the apportionment of 1914 divides two hundred fifty-eight members of the house among the towns or cities, assigning one or two members to each. There are seventy-eight single-member districts, and ninety having two members each. This difference in representation is historic, and not based on population. Of these one hundred sixty-eight districts, ninety are towns having each a population less than one-half the ratio. They have one hundred and twenty-four members but should have by population twenty-three. Thirty-four of the ninety towns are two-member districts, and in place of sixty-eight members should have by population eleven members. There are forty-five towns each having a population between a half ratio and a ratio and a half. These have sixty-eight members, though by population entitled to thirty-nine. Twenty-three of these districts have two members each; their representation by population should be twenty-two. The remaining towns, the thirty-three largest towns or cities are all double-member districts and hence have a combined representation of sixty-six members. By population they are entitled to one hundred ninety-six members. The injustice of this may easily be seen by noting the extremes. The four smallest towns have a combined population of 1,358, less than one-half ratio, yet have five members. The four largest cities have a combined population of 407,715 and should have ninety-four members, instead of the eight assigned by constitution. The town of Union with a population of 322 has the same representation in the house, (two members), as New Haven with a population of 133,605.

Rhode Island uses its house as the apparently popular body, and makes up its senate by one member from each town or city. The constitution however requires that each town must have at least one member in the house of one hundred members, and that no city shall have more than one-fourth of the total membership. There are thirty-nine towns and cities in the state, and fifteen of these have each a population less than one-half the house ratio. Instead of fifteen members these towns properly should have four. Eleven towns have each a population between a half ratio and a ratio and a half. Twelve members are assigned to these instead of ten, their proper representation by population. There are seven large towns and six cities to which properly eighty-six members should be allotted, but, owing to the limitations already mentioned, seventy-three members only are assigned. This loss really largely falls on the city of Providence, which by constitution is limited to twenty-five members though its population entitles it to forty-one, a discrimination against urban interests.

The *Senate* is made up of a member from each of the thirty-nine towns and cities.[1] Twenty-five of these fall below the half ratio and should have by population five members only. Eight towns have populations between the half ratio and a ratio and a half, and should have six instead of eight members. The six remaining districts of large population should have twenty-eight senators in place of the six allotted by constitution.

The six cities unitedly have a population of 385,083 or seventy-one per cent of the whole. They should have seventy-one of the one hundred house members and twenty-eight of the thirty-nine senators. In fact they have fifty-seven members in the house, a bare majority, and six in the senate, or fifteen per cent of the whole. By contrast the six smallest towns have a combined population of 5,845, or one per cent of the whole, and yet are represented by six members in each house. The city of Providence which by constitution is restricted to one member in the senate and twenty-five in the house, should by population have sixteen in the senate and forty-one in the house.

By taking into account the towns of smallest population, the majority in each house is theoretically controlled by 7.6 per cent of the population in the senate and thirty-seven per cent in the house. If both houses met in joint session for any purpose, the thirty-two smallest towns containing twenty-six per cent of the population of the state, could cast 72 out of the 139 votes of the grand committee.

Such a system of misrepresentation as this, and those of

[1] In the revision report of the Commission of 1915, a recommendation is made that the senate be reapportioned into forty-three districts, substantially on the basis of population, but fixing a maximum of ten for any one city. Providence, which by population should have eighteen members, would therefore lose eight to the smaller districts. See p. 102 respecting this commission.

Connecticut and Vermont, cannot be justified by any theory of democracy, and are entirely at variance with the great American principle of popular sovereignty. These three, and to a lesser degree, the other three states of class III, are, however, glaring exceptions to the general rule. The remaining forty-two states are practically democratic in their representation, and in due time these six also presumably will conform to established democratic usage.

The National Congress

As a basis of comparison the inequalities in the national congress, chiefly in the senate, may well be stated, though it should be clearly understood that the situation is altogether different in fact. The senate is a federal body, like the German federal *Bundesrat*, and by agreement, through compromise in the convention, is made up of two representatives from each state, regardless of population. Towns and counties within the states have no such sovereign basis for their claims, since they are merely administrative units, bodies politic, entirely subordinate to the state and can claim no undue representation based on inherent right.

The national house of representatives is based on population, except that every state must have at least one member. As only four states are below the ratio and but one of these below the half ratio, there is no real inequality. These four states by population would in any case be entitled to three members, so that one member only is lost to the other forty-four states.

If however the membership in the senate were assigned on the basis of population, seventeen states would be found to be below the ratio and ten of these below the half ratio. The seventeen combined would be entitled to eight members instead of thirty-four. In addition to these seventeen states, the five next larger states would have one senator each, and the fifteen next in population unitedly would have thirty-one. Of the eleven remaining states five [1] would have three each; Texas and Massachusetts would have four each, and New York, Pennsylvania, Illinois and Ohio would respectively have ten, eight, six, and five members. The ten states of largest population have slightly in excess of one-half the population of the states and should have by population a bare majority in the Senate, namely forty-nine members.

[1] Missouri, Michigan, Indiana, Georgia, New Jersey.

CHAPTER XVII

LIMITATIONS ON THE LEGISLATURE

A STATE has original, not delegated, powers. It can legally do whatsoever it pleases within its own borders, subject only to such regulations and prohibitions as may be found in the national constitution. The legislature, as the representative of the people, may exercise all these vast powers at its discretion. The executive and the judicial departments have no such authority. The power to make law includes the power to regulate, alter, or even abolish these departments. In other words in democracies the legislature is legally omnipotent. The legislatures of our states during the revolutionary period really wielded this immense power, but every generation since that time has witnessed the gradual diminution of it. This process has already in part been outlined; the adoption of the theory of the separation of powers brought about the transfer of certain powers, very slight at first, through the written constitution to the executive and judicial departments; then the right to make fundamental law was transferred to the convention and to the electorate through the referendum; now the power over administration is rapidly passing from the legislature to the executive, and judicial organization and powers are quite fully set by the convention, which leaves to the legislature merely the petty details of judicial regulation.

Legislatures would however still remain the most powerful

of the three departments, if their right to make statutes were left untouched, but even this privilege is denied them in part.   Attention has already been called to the fact that conventions, wisely or unwisely, place statutes in recent constitutions.   A twelve-thousand-word judiciary article in the Louisiana constitution, and a six-thousand-word article on corporations in the Virginia constitution, show this tendency clearly.   In fact every detailed command, prohibition, or regulation in a constitution, is in effect a usurpation of the statute-making power of legislatures, so that, in a sense, the length of a constitution roughly indicates the amount of limitation placed on legislatures.

THE STATUTORY INITIATIVE AND REFERENDUM [1]

In addition to this loss of power mentioned above, the electorate, working through the convention and the constitutional referendum, has taken from the legislature large powers in the making of statutes, by the assertion of its right to initiate bills, and to have these or any others referred to it as the final authority in decision.   This famous movement came into prominence through the Oregon amendment of 1902 which reads, "The legislative authority of the state shall be vested in a legislative assembly, . . . but the people reserve to themselves power to propose laws and amendments to the constitution, and to enact or reject the same at the polls, independent of the legislative assembly, and also reserve power at their own option to approve or reject at the polls any act of the legislative assembly.   The first power reserved by the people is the initiative. . . .   The second power is the referendum."   The amendment later provides that the style of all bills shall be: "Be it enacted by the people of

[1] See pp. 147-9.

the State of Oregon" (formerly "by the Legislative Assembly.")

Unquestionably the sudden rise into prominence of the electorate as a prime agent in the work of government is the most remarkable phenomenon in the history of American state constitutions. The potential "sovereignty of the people" has been asserted from the beginning, but chiefly as a theory which the "more intelligent" hoped would never be put into practice. The prevalent profound dissatisfaction with the personnel of legislatures and the quality of work performed by them suddenly came to a climax when the western states began to devise schemes for the *initiative, referendum,* and the later *recall.* This development has resulted in the most important limitation next to the constitutional convention, yet developed against the supremacy of legislatures. The animus of the movement is seen when one notes passing into the constitution, as indicated above, the enacting phrase, "Be it enacted by the *people* of . . ." instead of the more familiar word "legislature." It indicates that the legislature is no longer the repository of lawmaking authority but yields place to the electorate, as the real voice of the people. In Chapter XI attention was called to the growth of the constitutional initiative; the underlying principles and the procedure of the statutory initiative are in many respects the same, but there are differences and these will now be presented, along with the system as a whole, including the referendum.

This legislative limitation consists in the right reserved in the constitution to the people (voters) of determining finally what laws shall be enacted. In its simple form it is virtually a veto, since any particular law passed by the legislature, becomes subject to a referendum on demand or petition of a given per cent of the voters. This may be partly evaded if the constitution provides that bills, which ordinarily would not go into effect until sixty or ninety days after adjournment, may be put into immediate effect by a declaration of emergency. This is met by a requirement that the reasons for the emergency be expressly stated, and voted on separately by a yea and nay vote, and by the provision that even emergency measures shall still remain subject to the referendum.

The next logical step in the development is to provide that the voters by petition [1] may initiate any measure, and this method, as in the case of the constitutional initiative, may be direct or indirect: it is direct when it passes immediately to the secretary of state and by him is placed on the ballot at the next election; it is indirect, when the proposed bill is submitted to the legislature first and is then referred, after some action, or failure to act, on the part of that body. A "campaign of education" follows through the publicity pamphlet or other method of advertising, and on the day set a vote is taken on the referendum, which is adopted if it receives the usual "majority of those voting thereon," or some severer requirement. If to this initiation and referendum of statutory bills is added the constitutional initiative and referendum; and if the same principles furthermore are then applied to the charter and ordinance making of local bodies-politic, such as counties, towns, cities and villages, the process has reached its completion, since the electorate is in control of constitution, statute, and ordinance. A state in its conservatism may venture gingerly into this new field and provide only for the statutory referendum, hedged about with many precautions and severe requirements; but as it becomes

[1] For explanations respecting the petition, see, *Equity*, April, 1914, pp. 80–85.

bolder with experience it broadens out into the statutory initiative, and at last emerges definitely into the full sweep of change by adding on the other provisions, simplifying the methods to be employed, and adopting a state wide recall for every public officer. The amendment to the constitution authorizing these measures may be declared to be self-executing, giving instructions to the secretary of state to put them into effect; or they may require action of the legislature in order to put them into effect, through the detailed specifications of an "enabling act." This latter method has not always proved satisfactory, as may be seen for instance, in the cases of Utah and Idaho.

At the close of the year 1914 nineteen states had adopted some form or other of the statutory initiative and referendum. In view therefore of the importance of this movement a very brief statement will be made about the system adopted in each of these states, noting how the weaknesses of the earlier methods gradually are eliminated.

South Dakota began the reform by providing in 1898 for an indirect statutory initiative and the referendum, allowing the legislature to declare an emergency by a majority vote. It is said that over forty per cent of South Dakota's statutes are now marked "emergency." The amendment further provides that the referenda should be printed in full on the ballot, but in 1910 the publicity pamphlet was adopted, the ballot that year being "six feet long"! In 1900 *Utah* added by amendment a similar system in principle, but left to the legislature the power of putting this into effect through an enabling act. This the legislature has not done, so that Utah does not in fact have the initiative and referendum. *Oregon* in 1902, as already explained, adopted its famous amendment which provides for the direct initiative on (constitutional amendments and) statutes by a petition signed by eight per cent of the voters, and for a referendum on a petition of five per cent. The detail of this provision (Article IV. Section 1) has been quite largely copied, but modified in part by the improvements of the later California system. In 1905 *Nevada* adopted a restricted and useless statutory referendum amendment, requiring, for example, the expensive method of advertising through newspapers, and "a majority of the electors voting at a state election." In 1912 however the state amended by providing for a self-executing indirect (constitutional and) statutory initiative, and a referendum decided by "a majority of those voting thereon."

In 1906 *Montana* adopted the direct statutory initiative and the referendum, both so hedged about with restrictions as to be of small use, owing to the difficulty and expense involved in securing signatures to petitions. *Oklahoma* in its new constitution of 1907 provided for the (constitutional and) statutory initiative and the referendum, adding that a rejected measure might not be again initiated until after at least three years, except by a petition signed by at least twenty-five per cent of the voters. Its chief objectionable feature was the requirement on referendum of a majority of the votes cast at the election. A fortunate provision that the election may be either general or special allows this latter expensive method in case of real necessity. In 1908 *Maine* adopted a good system of statutory initiative and referendum, requiring a two-thirds vote for the declaration of an emergency, and introducing the requirement of a stated number of signatures for petitions, instead of a per cent of the voters. In a rapidly growing state this fixed number would presumably need to be raised at every decennial census. *Missouri* also in 1908 adopted a system of direct (constitutional and) statutory initiative and referendum; requiring newspaper advertising and a prescribed per cent of signatures in each of at least two-thirds of its congressional districts. The referendum vote is a majority of those voting thereon. A numerously signed petition in any case rightly involves much trouble and expense, but excessive additional requirements like that above involve needless trouble and extra expense. In such cases the referendum, like a governor's veto, is a possibility to be taken into account, but presumably will be used in cases of extreme necessity only. An attempt to weaken this law, by amendment, 1914, was defeated.

In 1910 *Arkansas* and *Colorado* adopted each a system of direct (constitutional and) statutory initiative and referendum. It permits the declaration of an emergency, which prevents the use of the referendum, and publicity is secured in Arkansas through advertising in the newspapers. The referendum requires a majority of those voting thereon. The year 1911 added three other states to the list, though these adopted widely varying systems. The convention of *Arizona* inserted into the constitution a direct (constitutional and) statutory initiative and referendum. The emergency clause is to be declared by a two-thirds vote and prevents the use of the referendum. A majority of the votes cast thereon decides a referendum, and for publication purposes the publicity pamphlet was authorized by the legislature. *New Mexico's* convention inserted a referendum provision only, so restricted as to be practically useless. Petitions must be signed by ten per cent of the voters (it is usually five per cent) in each of at least three-fourths of the counties. A majority of those voting thereon is required but it must be at least forty per cent of the vote cast at the (general) election. *California* at a special election added to the constitution (Article IV, Section 1) a lengthy self-executing set of provisions securing both the direct and the indirect (constitutional and) statutory initiative, and the referendum. The referendum, when demanded, suspends the law (or part of law) pending the vote. An emergency may be declared by a two-thirds vote but the measure still remains open to referendum. A publicity pamphlet is the method of publication and a majority of those voting thereon determines the issue.

The year 1912 introduced four other amendments into as many state constitutions. Amendments for the initiative and referendum were submitted also in Wyoming and Mississippi; these received a majority of those voting thereon but not, as required, a majority of the votes cast at the election. *Nebraska* by means of its party ballot method of voting on amendments,[1] authorized the direct (constitutional and) statutory initiative and the referendum. Emergency is declared by a majority vote but does not prevent the use of the referendum. The requirements are excessive, demanding a large per cent of signatures, two-fifths of the counties, and at least thirty-five per cent of the vote cast at the general election. *Idaho* adopted an amendment authorizing a statutory initiative and referendum, the latter of which must be approved at a general election by a majority of the vote cast for governor. The details were left to legislative discretion but no action has yet been taken. *Washington* adopted a statutory initiative and referendum amendment, requiring a per cent of signatures, but not to exceed a number fixed in the amendment. Emergency may be declared by a majority and this prevents the use of the referendum. For passage, a majority of those voting thereon is required, provided

[1] Whereby a party may declare for or against an amendment and straight ticket votes count accordingly.

it is at least one-third of the vote cast. The publicity pamphlet was chosen by the legislature as the method of publication. The convention of *Ohio* among other amendments submitted one which provided for the (direct constitutional and the) indirect statutory initiative and the referendum. The emergency clause, when accompanied by a statement of reasons and passed by a two-thirds vote, prevents the use of the referendum. A petition must have a given per cent of signatures from at least one-half the counties. The amendment included a publicity pamphlet method of publication, and was made self-executing.

In 1913 *Michigan*, dissatisfied with the provision in its new constitution respecting the constitutional initiative, passed a broader amendment providing for (an improved constitutional and) an indirect statutory initiative and a referendum, needing the endorsement only of a majority of those voting thereon. In November, 1914, five [1] other states voted on amendments in respect to the initiative and referendum, but in one only (*North Dakota*) did the amendment pass. This requires for initiation ten per cent, a majority of the counties, and provides for a referendum through the secretary of state in case the legislature fails to submit it. There is the usual emergency clause and the governor is expressly forbidden to use his veto. A referendum may demand the submission of items of bills and referenda are decided by a majority of votes cast thereon. The requirements for the *constitutional* initiative and referendum are so severe that the system is practically worthless.

In ways equally effective, though not so spectacular, the people through the convention have placed in the constitutions requirements that certain kinds of general laws shall

---

[1] Minnesota, Mississippi, North Dakota, Texas, Wisconsin. In Mississippi the matter is in doubt and goes to the courts for decision.

be referred to the electorate for final approval or rejection. Space will not allow a full discussion of this subject, but in brief it may be said that in many states, in addition to the general referendum now contained in many constitutions as the result of the movement for the initiative and referendum, referenda must be ordered in the case of general statutes that involve an increase of state debt above a fixed maximum, an increase in the tax rate when fixed by constitution, or the location of a state capital or important state institution, such as a university or a penitentiary. In statutory local legislation referendum requirements are entirely too numerous to specify. Practically all the states use the referendum more or less in matters affecting counties, towns and cities, or on such questions as the licensing of saloons or an increase in local debt for special expenditures. Even if the constitution contains no specific permission for the use of the referendum in general legislation, yet presumably an assembly may pass a statute, which by its terms is not to become operative unless approved by a referendum vote. Massachusetts in 1913, to make sure of this principle, passed an amendment authorizing its legislature in its discretion to use the referendum for general legislation. Michigan's constitution of 1908 (Article IV. Section 38) puts it in this form; "Any bill passed by the legislature and approved by the governor, except appropriation bills, may be referred by the legislature to the qualified electors; and no bill so referred shall become a law unless approved by a majority of the electors voting thereon." Though in form a provision like this seems to be a *power* and not a *limitation*, yet it involves a sort of necessity for the occasional submission of referenda.

Another limitation, furthermore, is involved in the use of the initiative and referendum. If the electorate initiates and approves a statute on referendum, obviously it would hardly seem fitting that this kind of statute should be subject to legislative change like ordinary statutes. Hence provisions are coming into constitutions stating that in such cases changes are permissible only after a period of two (or three) years, or after a larger fractional vote of both houses (two-thirds or three-fourths), or after a referendum favoring the change.

SPECIAL LEGISLATION

Such restrictions have largely reduced the importance of legislatures in the making of general statutes. These bodies find some consolation, however, if only they are allowed to pass at pleasure special, local or private legislation. Through such measures friends are won, interests placated, and constituencies made secure. An attack upon this privilege seems to add insult to injury; forbid the privilege, and the chief delights of legislative existence pass away. Yet there is great need of some sort of restriction on this kind of legislation. From estimates made, it is safe to say that the legislatures biennially have before them for consideration from fifty thousand to sixty thousand bills, general and special. About a third of these finally become law and of those passed about three-fifths are special, private, or local in kind.[1] Under such conditions general legislation cannot secure the attention it deserves. Really capable men, wearied by numerous demands on their time and patience in the consideration of relatively unimportant matters, drop out of our legislatures and yield place to small men, big with the sense of their own

---

[1] At a recent meeting of the National Bar Association it was asserted that the national and state lawmaking bodies, during the five years from 1909–1913 inclusive, had passed 62,014 statutes.

importance, who delight in special legislation as a means to enable them to hold a position for which they are entirely unfit. Add to this the waste of money through needlessly protracted sessions, and undue multiplication of law, and it is easy to see that conventions have a problem on their hands in devising a remedy for one of the greatest of our political evils.

It now becomes possible to ask what remedies have been devised to check this evil. The most obvious remedy is to forbid special legislation. It is interesting to study the old-fashioned constitutions of New England, almost void of restrictions, then to take up the next older set, and see restrictions creeping in one by one, the more numerous as you go westward, where democracy is more vigorous, and at last to see in the recent constitutions long lists of restrictions, finally as many as thirty-five, each forbidding some particular kind of local, special, or private legislation. To make assurance doubly sure the new Alabama constitution carefully defines terms :

A general law within the meaning of this article is a law which applies to the whole state ; a local law is a law which applies to any political subdivision or subdivisions of the state less than the whole ; a special or private law within the meaning of this article is one which applies to an individual, association or corporation.

These restrictions certainly have some effect. A comparison made [1] between the legislative output of six states whose legislatures were practically unrestricted, and six, quite fully restricted, showed that special legislation was seventy per cent of the whole in the former, and but twenty-eight per cent in the latter states.

The trouble with this remedy is that it may go too far. Our governors in their messages already complain of an

[1] Our State Constitutions, p. 52.

increase of statutes, general in their nature but really special in their application. Special legislation must be had at times, and there should be ways of getting it without subterfuge. Let there be restrictions by all means, but allow some discretion on occasions.

The device of a special committee on local legislation, already referred to as authorized in Georgia, Mississippi and Virginia, is excellent in design but in practice seems not to work well, if one may judge from the amount of special legislation still issued by the legislatures of those states. Such committees should be impartial and judicial in the exercise of their work, like similar committees of the British House of Commons, where the handling of special legislation is a fine art.

Another device found in several constitutions [1] and in the statutes of some others (Vermont for example), is to require that no local or special bill shall be passed, unless notice of the intention to apply for such legislation shall have been published in the locality at least thirty (or sixty) days before the bill is introduced. This is a most excellent plan if properly performed. If, however, the notice is published once, in fine type, in an obscure corner of an obscure paper, little will be accomplished by the requirement.

A much more promising remedy, imitated from the excellent English system of supervision over local government, and now partly in use in many states, under legislative authority, is to authorize by general statute the several departments of administration to apply the principles of such statute to special cases as they arise. For example, the auditor may settle claims for tax rebates, the

[1] Arkansas, Florida, Georgia, Louisiana, Missouri, North Carolina, Oklahoma, Pennsylvania, Texas.

land commissioner many points in titles, the secretary of state issue charters, and the courts, like the federal court of claims, pass on disputed accounts. We have now in many of our states boards of equalization. Such a board might have its powers enlarged so as to pass on very many requests from localities for special legislation. The English Local Government Board, which performs such a service for counties, towns, and cities, is, perhaps, the most successful device in British national administration. This movement is hard to follow from constitutions, because the statutory power of legislatures is ordinarily sufficient for action, but there is a strong trend in this direction throughout the country, and, if supplemented by thorough executive oversight, and civil service rules, should prove a very real remedy for the evils of special legislation. That at least is the conclusion of the best governed of the European states [1] which do not suffer, as the United States does, from such a perversion of lawmaking.

There are however other movements that are powerfully affecting the situation by placing emphasis on the study of comparative legislation and on the wise drafting of bills. There are, for instance, organizations like the National Civic Federation, the American Bar Association and the Commissioners on Uniform Laws; these work steadily and consistently for wiser legislation in the states, based on careful studies of general principles and practices. The many Legislative Reference Bureaus now existent in most of the states as separate organizations or as expansions of state library activities, are exerting a definite and constructive influence on lawmaking through expert advice given to legislators. Such experts aim to familiarize themselves with the laws of their states, the judicial decisions

[1] Great Britain, Germany, France.

interpreting these, and with the legislation and experience of other states and nations. Springing from this is the movement for more efficient bill drafting through the employment of experts and "revisers of statutes," whose duty it is to keep a careful oversight over the statutes of the state and to be able to draft necessary statutes in a thoroughly scientific manner.[1] The need for this expert service is plainly obvious since it is claimed that almost one-half of the (civil) litigation of the country involves the construction of statutes and constitutions and that the greater part of this could be avoided if only statutes were skillfully drawn.

[1] Many states have expert service in bill drafting through their reference bureaus or libraries, but special officials or agencies are employed in New York, Massachusetts, Wisconsin, Connecticut, Colorado, Vermont.

CHAPTER XVIII

CONSTITUTIONAL REGULATION OF IMPORTANT INTERESTS

IT is said that Americans are prone to assert dogmatically their opinions on all subjects of which they are ignorant, and to be diffident in matters with which they are fully conversant. The point of this saying can be appreciated by one who seeks to ascertain how conventions regulate important interests. Most of these interests are in process of rapid development, for, through the multiplication of machinery and wider scientific knowledge, the conditions of life change with wonderful suddenness, as compared with the slow changes of earlier centuries. Yet conventions dogmatically fix in the fundamental law provisions that must be largely superseded in a very few years. The articles on corporations for instance, placed in the constitutions of Virginia and Oklahoma, both of which can be amended only with great difficulty, and Louisiana's lengthy and detailed articles on its judicial organization, no matter how excellent these may all be, yet will surely need frequent amendment. For such reasons the work of conventions in respect to the regulation of social and economic interests is the least satisfactory of all their labors.

There are few specialists, if any, who would with alacrity undertake to write out for a state constitution a detailed system of taxation, of finance, or education; of regulation for corporations, common carriers, or banks; or to define a policy toward labor, or state ownership of monopolies, or control over mining interests. All such matters must of course receive most careful attention from conventions, but the question is rather whether such attention should not confine itself chiefly to the formulation of general principles, to a tentative outline for a system of regulation, leaving details to the legislature, and then to pay much more attention to methods whereby a higher grade of officials and legislators may be secured. If, for illustration, the quality of membership in the legislatures could be raised; if the numerous departments, commissions, and boards were consolidated and unified, the salaries of heads trebled and civil service rules adopted; real economy would result, and efficiency be greatly increased. Conventions should recognize that much of their work is at the best transitory, and that if they persist in preparing lengthy and detailed constitutions, the method of amendment should be proportionately simple. An unchangeable constitution in these days is a haven of safety for spoilsmen, a handicap to progress, and an insult to the spirit of a progressive democracy.

The question now arises, what important interests seem on the whole to have been emphasized in the existing constitutions? The following paragraphs will present these in order.

LOCAL BODIES POLITIC [1]

It seems plain from the constitutions that the town system of New England is dying. It is not imitated outside of that section, and within that section is in a condition of inefficiency and decrepitude. The real unit in the

---

[1] For careful study of local areas in states, see, Reed's Territorial Basis, in Bibliography.

United States is the county, which in thinly settled states is cut up into administrative districts, and these gradually become townships as population multiplies. These townships may become integral parts of the county and have a large share of local autonomy though under the general supervision of the county. The urban center has two distinct organizations, the village and the large city. There is first the village, borough, town or petty city, organized under general law in almost all the states, and having a small compact population under a simple form of government. Lastly comes the incorporated city of large size, either organized by special charter, or in classes by general law, or authorized by constitution to form their own charters, subject to the constitution and general statutes of the states.

When Mr. Bryce in his "American Commonwealth" charged the municipalities of the United States with corruption and inefficiency,[1] there were even then many signs of change. Since that time no field of political activity in the states has received so much attention. Conventions fortunately have not yet ventured to insert in state constitutions drafts of city charters, though California's constitution comes dangerously near to it with a seven thousand word article on Counties, Cities and Towns, but there has been a steady movement looking to the insertion in the constitution of provisions securing to local bodies politic a large amount of local autonomy.[2]

Relatively, state constitutions with occasional exceptions, do not devote much space to local government. In some,

[1] In Vol. I. chap. LI, ed. 1888.
[2] The best studies of recent changes can be made from the constitution of California, Article XI, as amended, 1914; Michigan, Article VIII, and Ohio, amendments forty and thirty-seven, 1912.

the county is not even mentioned, its existence being assumed; Oklahoma by contrast names and bounds in the constitution each county. Between these two extremes there are naturally wide variations. It is common to set a minimum area and population; to regulate changes in county seats and boundaries; to provide for the filling by election of certain designated offices, chiefly administrative and judicial; and to place limitations on taxation and indebtedness. Counties are often given the option of dividing their areas into townships. It is generally provided that counties, townships and villages be organized under general laws and legislatures forbidden to pass special legislation in such matters. California by amendment, 1911, permits each county on petition to elect a board of freeholders authorized to form a charter for the county, which will go into effect on approval of the citizens, and of the next legislature approving as a whole, without alteration. Four states [1] provide that on vote a municipality may become a county, or else that county and city organizations and areas be combined.

Villages if incorporated are regularly incorporated under general law, but the recent changes in Michigan and Ohio [2] permit villages also to form their own charters on petition. In the case of villages and cities there are regularly regulations in respect to taxation, indebtedness, sinking funds and franchises, the newer amendments securing to municipalities a proper control over their franchises and public utilities. This is part of the larger movement aiming to secure to cities a reasonable amount of home rule or local autonomy. This is accomplished by inserting in the constitutions provisions aiming (1) to secure a proper

---

[1] California, Michigan, Minnesota, Missouri.
[2] Articles VIII and XVIII respectively.

classification of cities[1] and general charters appropriate to each class; and (2) to provide that municipalities within certain bounds be permitted to form their own charters[2] and to adopt these on referendum. In Oklahoma the governor also must approve, before a charter goes into effect. The Ohio municipal statute of 1913, based on its constitutional amendment, allows its municipalities three types of general law from which to select, based respectively on the commission system, the city manager plan, and the so-called federal plan of organization. The commission form of municipal government[3] is responsible also for a rapid extension among the states in local affairs of the initiative, referendum, and to a lesser extent, the recall. About three-fourths of the states now have one or more cities under this type of government, so that municipal betterment has obviously made large strides in the last twenty years.

CORPORATIONS

In general the points worthy of notice in constitutions respecting corporations of all sorts are as follows: First, the word is regularly defined and a distinction made between corporations organized for profit, and those for other purposes; these last may be exempted from taxation, if religious, educational, or eleemosynary in character. Second, a distinction is made between domestic and foreign[4] corporations, and this last class regulated so as to secure

[1] Thirteen states make this provision; Arkansas, California, Colorado, Indiana, Kentucky, Missouri, New York, Ohio, Oklahoma, South Dakota, Utah, Washington, Wyoming.

[2] California, Colorado, Michigan, Minnesota, Missouri, Nebraska, Ohio, Oklahoma, Oregon, Washington, Wisconsin.

[3] April first, 1913, two hundred forty-five cities had this form of government, the largest being Denver and New Orleans. *Equity*, April, 1913, pp. 111 and 152.

[4] Those not chartered by the state itself.

investors and the payment of suitable fees or taxes. In respect to corporations organized for profit, constitutions regulate their relations to the state and seek to secure the interests, and to determine the liability of their stockholders. They provide that corporations be chartered by general or special law, that their charters be subject to amendment or revocation, that those already organized must file acceptance of constitutional provisions if they desire to have the benefit of future legislation, and that they be subject to general regulation. This regulation may be loose and allow large freedom, or may be strict or paternal in character. It may include prohibitions of pools, monopolies, and trusts, regulation of the exercise of the power of eminent domain, aiming to secure the rights of those whose property is taken; and prohibitions against the lending of public credit by a state or locality to any private enterprise. In addition there may be regulations of capital stock and its issuance, publicity of conditions and periodic reports to a state commission having powers of supervision and regulation. Such state commissions are found in about one half of the states and may have charge of corporations in general, or may be organized especially for the control of public service corporations and the regulation of public utilities, aiming to secure to the state a just assessment of taxes and to the public adequate service and reasonable rates. Some states [1] forbid corporations to hold real estate out of use after a fixed period of years (five to ten). Illustrations of the above provisions may be found in most of the western and newer southern constitutions, notably Kentucky, Louisiana, Alabama and Virginia. The articles in the constitutions of Alabama and South Dakota on banks are typical of the usual provisions on that subject.

[1] California, Louisiana, Michigan, Missouri, for example.

TAXATION AND FINANCE

There are wide differences in respect to these matters in the constitutions, but a tendency in certain directions is clear. Details must be sought in statutory legislation. Taxes must be uniform, levied and collected under general laws, and for public purposes only; but there is a tendency to allow a classification of subjects so as to permit of exceptions to the uniform general property tax, in the case of property paying specific taxes. A maximum tax rate is fixed, varying with the valuation of the state, and a maximum debt for state and locality, beyond which amount the referendum must be used. The maximum may be fixed by a per cent of the assessed valuation instead of a specific amount. Some authorize an income tax, others an inheritance tax[1] and still others franchise taxes and a tax on the capital stock of corporations; a very few states forbid a poll tax, California, for example, by amendment, 1914; others authorize it for educational purposes only. These special forms of taxation illustrate a strong tendency to seek for the state sources of income apart from those used by localities. State and municipal bonds are regularly exempted from taxation; also personal property up to a stated amount, or the small properties of widows or disabled persons, or property used for religious and philanthropic purposes. Provision may be made allowing to new industries exemption for a term of years (Mississippi for example), or there may be a contrary provision forbidding such exemption.[2]

---

[1] Nine states only do not yet use this form of tax; Alabama, Florida, Georgia, Indiana, Mississippi, New Mexico, Nevada, Rhode Island, South Carolina.

[2] There is a slight tendency to exempt mortgages from taxation (Idaho, Louisiana, Utah, Washington). Louisiana provides exemption for "loans made upon the security of mortgages granted upon real estate situated in this state, as well as the mortgages granted to secure said loans, etc." Article 230.

Georgia lengthily defines the state's sovereign right in taxation.

The system of assessment is justly receiving more attention than formerly, but is a troublesome question and much is properly left to the discretion of legislatures. The chief provisions are, state and county boards of equalization, and in a few states (Louisiana for example) special boards for the assessment of franchise corporations.

In finance careful provisions in respect to bonded indebtedness and sinking funds are characteristic features. The safe investment of funds is a vexed question. Two states at least [1] allow investment of school funds in land mortgages. Prohibitions are common against the receiving by treasurers of profits from the loan of funds in their hands. Our states are mostly in excellent financial condition and this is largely due, in the case of the newer states at least, to the wise pay-as-you-go policy enjoined by constitutions. Wyoming (Article XVI. 7) provided for a state wide system of uniform accounts, which has proved very useful and has been imitated by other states (Ohio, Indiana, for example). Attention has already been called to the governor's control over finance. No state yet has a really good budget system [2] but there are signs of promise. Virginia in its constitution tries an interesting experiment in providing for a standing auditing committee made up of five members of the general assembly. This committee is to have powers of inspection over all officers who handle state funds, may sit after adjournment, and reports to the governor.

Provisions in regard to state ownership of franchises or

[1] Idaho and South Dakota. Missouri allows county school funds to be so invested. Washington by amendment forbids loans of school funds to private persons or corporations.

[2] See, " Columbia Univ. Series " vol. 25, The Budget in the American Commonwealth, by E. E. Agger.

natural monopolies are not common. New York provides that its famous canal system shall forever remain the property of the state, and in another section makes the same provision for its wild forest lands. Utah has a better worded article on forestry. Nebraska reserves ownership in its salt springs. The western mining and irrigating states now have many provisions in regard to the uses of the waters of the state, Wyoming and North Dakota making the waters "the property of the state." Many of the states bordering on the sea and on navigable rivers have articles on tide lands and riparian rights, and declare their policy in regard to the use of the waters.[1] North Dakota provides that "the coal lands, including lignite, of the state shall never be sold, but may be leased," and by amendment of 1914 permits the state ownership and control of grain elevators. States seem not yet to have a clear policy in regard to public lands, whether to sell them in severalty or to retain ownership and lease the lands. Five states place restrictions on the ownership of land by aliens, and Arizona limits the amount of land that may be held by an individual or corporation. Wisconsin and South Carolina both declare that the people "possess the ultimate property in and to all lands within the jurisdiction of the state."

MISCELLANEOUS

The articles on *education* found in the constitutions vary from the simple paragraph of early constitutions to lengthy provisions sometimes several pages in length. This, however, is largely due to the necessity of arranging for the disposition of the school lands so generously voted to the states by congress. These lands are

[1] See for example, Washington, South Carolina, Louisiana, Mississippi.

generally placed under the charge of a land commissioner or board, and provisions are made for the holding or disposing of lands and the investment of school funds. Special attention is paid to the safety and proper investment of these funds, and several states [1] provide that losses through neglect or dishonesty must be made up from other funds. About two-thirds of the constitutions now forbid school funds to be used in aid of sectarian or denominational schools. Many have done this under instructions in enabling acts, and others of their own accord.

Provision is generally made for a state superintendent, a board of education, and similar officials in the counties. Attention also is given to the organization and the support of the higher institutions of learning. Localities are permitted to add to the school funds by special tax, and cities to maintain and control their schools apart from the county system. There are many differences in respect to the length of the term, to compulsory features, to matters of text books and to the organization of separate schools in the south for white and colored.

The growing interest in *labor* questions begins to find expression in the constitutions. Bureaus for the study and preparation of labor or industrial statistics are common. So are courts or boards of arbitration. The eight-hour day for all public work is fixed in eight constitutions,[2] and two require that citizens of the United States only shall be employed on public works. The right of recovering damages for injury is safeguarded, the "fellow-servant"

[1] For example Iowa, Louisiana, Nebraska, North Dakota, South Dakota, Utah, Washington.

[2] California, Idaho, Montana, Utah, Wyoming, Arizona, New Mexico, Oklahoma. Colorado, in 1902, by amendment made eight hours a day's labor in mines.

doctrine modified,[1] the safety of wages guarded for those engaged on public works, and contracts declared null and void which exempt employers from liability. Wyoming by amendment in 1914 provided for a Workingman's Compensation State Fund. Convict labor is regulated so as not to compete with other forms (New York for instance), and boys under sixteen (or fourteen) are forbidden to work in mines. The three new states all have this provision. Wyoming and Oklahoma forbid the employment of girls or women in mines at all, and California by amendment, 1914, authorizes the legislature to provide for the establishment of a minimum wage for women and minors, and for the comfort, health, safety and general welfare of any and all employes. Prohibitions against blacklists and Pinkerton detectives are among the curiosities of this section.

In view of the unfortunate political conditions existing in many states most of the constitutions contain more or less elaborate provisions against bribery, and corruption.[2] This involves much taking of oaths; officials, even legis- lators, must take oath that they have not attained their election by improper means; governors, not to exert im- proper influence on legislators.[3] Free passes are now for- bidden by constitution in at least sixteen constitutions; log- rolling,[4] lobbying, betting at elections, intimidations of electors by employers, and sharing in contracts while in office, are all prohibited in one or more of the constitutions. Dueling, though well nigh obsolete, is forbidden in about

---

[1] There are a few provisions in regard to employers' liability and work- men's compensation (Arizona, for example), but these acts are usually passed under general legislative powers.

[2] See Alabama, Delaware, Kentucky and New York as illustrations. Oklahoma devotes a separate article (XV) to oaths, bribery and free passes.

[3] Ten states require bribery oaths.

[4] The exchange of votes by legislators.

two-thirds of the states, and in most is a disqualification for office. Three states require the duel oath; Texas combines it with the bribery oath. Mississippi requires each legislator to swear to read the constitution, or to have it read to him, and Oklahoma declares that the term "white race" is to include all persons other than negroes. About half of the constitutions now secure married women in their right to separate estates. This provision is often found under Homestead Exemption, for which in some form or other provisions are also common. Many constitutions, especially the newer, pay much incidental attention to matters of social morals, such as the prohibition of lotteries,[1] regulation of intemperance through provisions for local option or prohibition, and authorization of penal reforms.[2] In 1914 four states joined the prohibition ranks (Arizona, Colorado, Oregon, Washington), making a total of fourteen. South Carolina prohibits prize fighting, gambling or betting (to officials) and has a unique provision against lynching. There is a rather general provision for institutions of charity, and for state boards of charity and correction, either with powers of visitation and recommendation, or of control.

Up to 1898 four states[3] had codified their written and unwritten law.[4] Codifications of statutory law are, of course, much more common. Six states[5] by constitution authorize their preparation. Michigan orders a compilation only. There are provisions for the codification of

---

[1] This is found in about thirty-five constitutions.

[2] Note for example; Arizona, XXII. 16; New Mexico, XX. 15; and Louisiana's Article 118 on Juvenile Courts.

[3] Georgia, California, North Dakota, South Dakota. Note also Article on Codification and Revision of Statutes. *Am. Pol. Sc. Review.* Nov. 1914. pp. 629–632.

[4] 27 Am. Law Review, 552.

[5] Indiana, Louisiana, Missouri, South Carolina, Texas, Oklahoma.

procedure in four states [1] and the constitutions of Mississippi and Kentucky each provided for a commission of expert lawyers to prepare such general laws as were necessary to put the new constitutions into effect.

[1] Indiana, Louisiana, Ohio, South Carolina.

CHAPTER XIX

CONSTITUTIONS OF THE NEW ENGLAND STATES

It becomes obvious that in a comparative study of state constitutions, the set in force in New England should be studied separately, because of the numerous peculiarities found in these ancient constitutions. The latest of these has served two generations, and the oldest was written in the midst of the Revolution.[1] Though amended from time to time, they have been amended conservatively and still retain many features long since outgrown by the other states; with all their amendments they rank as the shortest of our state constitutions, averaging about eight thousand words, or one-half the length of other state constitutions.

Three of these place amendments after the main text and thereby compel a perplexing tangle of cross-references and obsolete provisions. New Hampshire incorporates its amendments into the constitution, Vermont did so in 1913,

[1] Massachusetts, 1780, revised through convention in 1820, and twenty-two sets of amendments added since that time up to 1912, forty-one articles in all. New Hampshire, 1784, revised in 1792, and amended 1851, 1876, 1889, 1903, 1912. Vermont, 1793, and twenty-six articles of amendment added through board of censors and convention, 1828, 1836, 1850, 1870, and two additional articles added 1883 through legislative action and referendum. In 1913 seven amendments were added, all amendments incorporated into the body of the constitution, and the entire document rearranged and renumbered. Connecticut, 1818, and thirty-five amendments added up to 1913. Maine, 1819, up to 1875 twenty-one amendments were added and in that year were incorporated into the main text. Fourteen amendments have been added since that date up to 1912. Rhode Island, 1842, and thirteen sets of amendments, sixteen in all, dating from 1854 to 1911.

for the first time incorporating all of its amendments into the constitution, and Maine did likewise in 1875, but adds later amendments as supplements. Three different methods are used to designate the numbering of articles and sections. Three of the constitutions include a short preamble, New Hampshire and Vermont omit- it entirely, but Massachusetts has one long enough (two hundred and sixty-three words) to atone for their shortcomings. Five of the states preface their constitutions with a Declaration of Rights, varying from twenty-one to thirty sections each, but New Hampshire calls it a Bill of Rights, and lengthens it to thirty-eight sections. The religious features of these provisions present marked peculiarities but they have already been presented in Chapter X. All of the states emphasize vigorously the town as the basis of administration and government, and pay relatively small attention to the county or the city. The county in Rhode Island is a mere judicial district, but it plays an increasingly important part in the other five states. This system of administrative districts is in marked contrast to that of the other states in the Union, where the county and city receive special attention, and where the town exists, if at all, in the form of a township. In three of the states there are incorporated villages or boroughs, and in all the states there are organized districts with special powers, for such purposes as fire, water, highways etc. These subdivisions, however, are relatively unimportant.[1]

The six constitutions formally separate the three departments of government but the separation is not made in fact. In each state the legislature is given the mass of power and largely controls administration. In Maine the governor must be a native-born citizen of the United States. Four of

[1] See, Village Government in New England, by Frank G. Bates. *Am. Pol. Sc. Review*, Vol. VI. pp. 367–385.

the states elect lieutenant-governors. In Vermont, Connecticut, and Rhode Island he presides over the senate; in Massachusetts he presides over the council in the absence of the governor. The senate elects its own presiding officer in Massachusetts, Maine and New Hampshire. Three states use the old-fashioned executive council, reducing thereby the governor's powers proportionately. New Hampshire has a council of five, and Massachusetts of eight, both elected from districts; Maine has a council of seven chosen by joint ballot of the legislature. The council as a rule shares with the governor his power in nomination, appointment, and pardon; in New Hampshire and Massachusetts it shares also his control over expenditure through approval or disapproval of disbursements from the treasury. Connecticut, Rhode Island and Vermont provide for the popular election of three of their heads of administration; Massachusetts elects four, Maine and New Hampshire vest the appointing power in the assembly. In Massachusetts the treasurer may not hold office for a longer period than five years; in Maine, six years. The term of executive and administrative officers is two years except in Massachusetts, where elections are annual. The chief power vested in the governor is that of veto, aside from slight supervisory powers, and the usual powers in nomination, appointment, pardon, and war.[1] Four of the states allow their governors five days for consideration of bills, but Connecticut makes it three. The veto may be overridden by a majority of each house in Connecticut, by three-fifths in Rhode Island, but a two-thirds vote is needed in the other four states. If the bill is in the governor's hands when the legislature adjourns, the bill is thereby defeated

[1] The quaint and bombastic phraseology of the New Hampshire and Massachusetts war paragraphs is especially noteworthy.

in four of the states, but is considered as passed in Maine unless returned during the first three days of the next session, or in Rhode Island, unless filed with objections within ten days after adjournment. No one of the six constitutions allows him to veto items of appropriation bills, though thirty-four of the other states give their governors this power.

The legislatures [1] of four states are elected and meet biennially, but Rhode Island has biennial elections and annual sessions, and Massachusetts has annual elections and sessions. All the sessions begin in January, but Maine holds its state election in September and the others in November. There are no constitutional limitations on the length of the session in four of the states, but Rhode Island provides that there shall be payment for sixty days service only, at the rate of five dollars per day; and Connecticut provides that "the General Assembly shall adjourn *sine die* not later than the first Wednesday after the first Monday in June following its organization." Connecticut and New Hampshire fix on a definite compensation for the term, and the other three states fix the amount by statute.[2] The apportionment of the membership of the several legislatures has already been explained in Chapter XVI. The substance of this is that Massachusetts fairly apportions representation in both houses on the basis of population; Maine and New Hampshire practically do so,

[1] In Connecticut, Rhode Island and Vermont, this body is the general assembly; in Maine, the legislature; and in New Hampshire and Massachusetts the general court. Massachusetts calls itself a Commonwealth, not a State. The legal name of Rhode Island is "The State of Rhode Island and Providence Plantations."

[2] Connecticut, three hundred dollars; New Hampshire, two hundred dollars, and forty-five dollars as a maximum for a special session; Maine, three hundred dollars for the term; Massachusetts one thousand dollars, and Vermont, four dollars per day.

but make some discrimination against urban centers in favor of rural communities. Vermont and Connecticut fairly apportion the senate on the basis of population, but in the house grossly discriminate in favor of rural towns; and Rhode Island discriminates against urban centers in both houses and most unjustly so in the case of the senate, whose apportionment is the least popular in basis of all houses in the United States.

The most noticeable feature of the New England legislatures is the slight restriction placed on their enormous powers. Aside from the veto there are almost no regulations of procedure. A roll-call for a yea and nay vote on measures pending in the legislature may be had at the demand of one-fifth the membership (Connecticut, Maine, Rhode Island); or of one member, (New Hampshire); or in Vermont, five members in the house or one in the senate; Massachusetts has no provision in its constitution. There are barely any restrictions on special, local, or private legislation;[1] a few restrictions only on their finance powers,[2] and some general regulation of education and of the militia. Little or nothing is said in regard to such important matters as administrative organization and regulation, local and municipal government,[3] and economic and corporate interests generally. Maine's prohibition amendment of 1884 is the only prominent regulation of

[1] Maine requires the legislature to provide by general law, as far as practicable, for all matters usually appertaining to special or private legislation. Vermont, by amendment of 1913, forbids hereafter special charters of incorporation.

[2] Rhode Island and Maine fix a maximum for state debt; in the former state a referendum may authorize a special debt. Revenue bilis may arise in either house in Connecticut and Rhode Island, but in the house of representatives in the other four states. New Hampshire by amendment (1903) authorized a franchise and an inheritance tax.

[3] Massachusetts has a unique provision that all by-laws made by municipalities shall be subject at all times to be annulled by the General Court.

social interests. Maine, furthermore, has, curiously enough, yielded to the radicalism of the west sufficiently to insert into its constitution, by amendment, 1908, a provision for the statutory initiative and referendum, on demand of a fixed number of voters. The voters already have made good use of their power by placing on the statute books a direct primary law, against the wish of the legislature. Naturally this absence of restriction and regulation gives to the legislatures unusually large discretionary powers in all forms of legislation.

Suffrage qualifications likewise present some peculiar features and variations. In all the states voters must be citizens of the United States. In Maine a residence in the state of three months only is required; in New Hampshire he must be an inhabitant of a town; Rhode Island requires a two years' residence, except in the case of owners of real estate, for whom one year is sufficient. The other three states make the requirement one year. Four of the states have an educational requirement; in Connecticut the voter must be able to read English; in Massachusetts, Maine, and New Hampshire, he must be able to read English and write his name. Rhode Island has a requirement of a tax paid on property assessed at a value of at least one hundred and thirty-four dollars,[1] for suffrage in the election of members of city councils, or for those who participate in financial town meetings, or for taxing referenda of towns or cities. The chief restriction on suffrage naturally is in those three states that by discrimination against urban centers thereby virtually throw the political control of the states into the hands of an easily manipulated rural oligarchy.

The judicial provisions of these six constitutions also present curious features. In general it may be said that the

[1] The old forty shilling franchise.

legislatures have, unlike those of other states, very large powers in defining the organization and powers of the several grades of courts. In Massachusetts, Maine and New Hampshire, the higher judges are appointed by governor and council, in Vermont and Rhode Island by the assembly, and in Connecticut by the assembly on nomination of the governor. The tenure of the justices of the supreme court is two years in Vermont, seven years in Maine, eight years in Connecticut, and during good behavior in the other three states. A seventy-year age limit is fixed in the constitutions of Connecticut and New Hampshire. In Rhode Island, on request of the governor or either house, the supreme court must give opinions on important questions of law. In Massachusetts and New Hampshire, in addition to the two houses, the governor and council, and in Maine the governor or council, have the same privilege, and the phrase "and on solemn occasions" is added to the conditions under which advice may be demanded. Among minor judicial officers it may be noted that Rhode Island alone of all the states in the Union elects its sheriffs through the assembly instead of by popular vote. The other New England constitutions expressly require that they be elected by the people.

AMENDMENT AND REVISION

The amending articles of New England constitutions contain several marked peculiarities. Vermont, Connecticut, Rhode Island, and Massachusetts, make no mention whatsoever of the constitutional convention, and must convoke it, if at all, under general legislative powers inherent in their state sovereignty. New Hampshire uses a convention for purposes of amendment, the power of amendment not being vested in the legislature. By constitution the several towns of the state every seven years vote on the question whether or not a convention shall be called. If an affirmative vote is cast the membership is made up on the basis of the house of representatives, and the results of the labors of this extraordinarily large convention must be submitted as separate amendments to referendum vote and must be approved by a majority of two-thirds. These restrictions are so severe that few amendments have been or can be made to the constitution. Maine authorizes its legislature to convoke, without a referendum, a convention by a two-thirds vote of each house, but this power, given by amendment in 1875, has not yet been exercised. Amendments may be initiated by legislature through a two-thirds vote of each house, and when submitted to referendum vote, must be approved by a majority of those voting thereon, voting at a special election in the September following the submission of the amendments.

New England has been rather partial to the use of constitutional commissions instead of conventions, and three states have made experiments of this sort. In 1875 the legislature of Maine authorized the governor to appoint a commission of ten persons to report to the legislature such amendments as seemed necessary. Nine of the seventeen amendments submitted by this commission were approved by the legislature, referred to the people, and adopted.

The legislature of Rhode Island in 1897 tried the commission plan by authorizing the governor to appoint a body of fifteen persons to report to the legislature a revision of the constitution. The commission was seriously handicapped by the knowledge that its work must satisfy the demands of two successive legislatures. It succeeded in this but failed to satisfy the people, who voted down the revision in November, 1898. This result was far from satisfactory to the party in power, which had the revision repassed with a few verbal changes and submitted to referendum in June, 1899. It was again rejected by a larger adverse vote and thus ended another of the New England experiments of revision through commissions. In 1912 still another commission (nine persons) was appointed to recommend amendments to the constitution, and made its report to the assembly of 1915. No action has yet been taken on this report.

Vermont in 1908 appointed a commission of five to recommend to the legislature such amendments as might seem necessary. The report was embodied in eight proposals most of which in substance were approved by the necessary legislatures and the electorate. All of these reports were strongly conservative and, aside from the Rhode Island rejected revision, involved no matters of fundamental importance. The Rhode Island Report of 1915, however, does make some excellent recommendations; such as the reapportionment of the senate, the abolition of the property qualification, the item veto, the biennial session, provisions for a convention every twenty years, and for a simpler method of amending.

Omitting New Hampshire and Maine, the four remaining states amend through the action of two assemblies but with curious differences. In Vermont, at the end of every decade, dating from 1880, the senate (which represents population) by a two-thirds vote may submit amendments to the house (which represents the towns); if this approves by a majority vote, the amendments are referred to the next assembly, a majority vote of each house must then approve; this is followed by a referendum, and amendments must be approved by a majority of those voting thereon. Massachusetts allows amendments at any time but requires a majority of the senate and two-thirds of the house of the initiating general court, and a similar majority of each house of the next general court, followed by a referendum vote, in which a majority of those voting thereon, approves. Rhode Island requires the action of two assemblies, a majority of each house approving and a referendum; but requires approval by popular vote to be by a three-fifths vote. Connecticut initiates amendments by a majority vote of the house only;[1] these are referred to the next assembly, and must be approved by a two-thirds vote of each house, and then on referendum by a majority of the electors present at the town meetings. Connecticut, under the stress of urgent demands for constitutional reform through a convention, called such a body in 1901 under the general legislative power vested in its assembly. The dominant political interests of the state, however, placed certain limitations on the convention's power of revision, and made assurance doubly sure by making up the membership of the convention by one delegate from each town, irrespective of population. The result was a revision unsatisfactory to all parties concerned, and its consequent rejection in 1902 by referendum vote. The house in 1905 submitted a revised constitution as an amendment. This made no material change, merely incorporating the amendments into the body of the constitution, and increasing the pay of assemblymen from three hundred to five hundred dollars. This revision was acted on favorably by the assembly of 1907, but was defeated at the polls.

These amending articles largely explain the reason why New England constitutions are old-fashioned. The legislative systems of Massachusetts and Maine are popular in basis and allow a fair expression of public opinion. A retention of old-fashioned features in these constitutions,

---

[1] This body represents the towns, not the population.

therefore, implies a conservative policy and an unwilling-
ness at present to initiate any important changes. It
would certainly be a public boon, however, if the general
court of Massachusetts would authorize the secretary of
state to omit from the constitution its obsolete provisions,
and to place amendments each under its proper article.
New Hampshire though popularly organized in its legislature is restricted in amendment by its seven year requirement, its unwieldy convention of over four hundred members, and its preposterous requirement of a referendum
majority of two-thirds. Rhode Island, Vermont, and Connecticut are not organized on a popular basis, amendments
must meet the approval of a rural oligarchy, pass an ordeal
of two assemblies, and in Rhode Island must have a majority
on referendum of three-fifths. Under such conditions urban
enterprise in these three states is suppressed, corruption
in politics is encouraged, and broad progressive policies
for economic and social development rendered impossible.

The question might well be raised in these and a few
other states of the Union whether one generation has a
right to bind future generations by such serious restrictions
on the process of amendment. Certainly no irrepealable
provision would have any binding force on posterity, nor
should an amending article be considered as legally binding
that practically nullifies democratic principles and hinders
economic and political progress. Sufficient precedent and
theory could readily be formulated to justify a legislature
which would disregard such stringent restrictions, and
provide for a system of amendment more in accordance
with a government founded on popular consent.

BIBLIOGRAPHY FOR PART II

BEARD (C. A.) AND SHULTZ (B. E.). Documents on the State-wide Initiative, Referendum and Recall. New York. 1912.

GRIFFITH, ELMER C. The Rise and Development of the Gerrymander. Chicago. 1907.

HICHBORN, FRANKLIN. Story of the Session of the California Legislature of 1913.

Iowa. Applied History Series. Edited by Benj. F. Shambaugh. Two volumes, eighteen numbers. A series of monographs tracing Iowa's legislation in various fields of activity. Iowa City. 1912–1914.

MAGRUDER, F. A. Recent Administration in Virginia. Johns Hopkins Series. Volume XXX.

Michigan. The Michigan Constitution of 1850 (compared with those of other states). 1907.

MUNRO, WILLIAM B. The Initiative, Referendum and Recall. New York. 1912.

New Hampshire. Manual of the Constitution of the State of. Prepared by J. F. Colby. Concord. 1912. (Contains comparative studies).

Ohio. Edited by J. H. Newman. Digest of State Constitutions. (Compared with Ohio provisions.) Columbus. 1912.

PHILLIPS, J. B. Recent State Constitution Making. (Changes from 1895 1903.) Educational Qualifications for Voters. In University of Colorado Studies. Volumes II, III. (First Article, also in *Yale Review.* Volume XII, pp. 389–408.)

SHAW, ALBERT. American State Legislatures. *Contemporary Review,* October, 1889. Pp. 555–573.

For references already given in Part II, see:

	PAGE		PAGE
Agger, E. E.	236	Gardner, C. O.	142
Bates, F. G.	243	Lauer, P. E.	138
Blakely, W. A.	138	Reed, A. Z.	194, 230
Brown, S. W.	138	Rose, J. C.	152
Bryce, J.	139	Schaff, P.	138
Dodd, W. F.	139	Thayer, J. B.	180

PART III

TREND IN STATE CONSTITUTIONS

CHAPTER XX

REVIEW OF DEVELOPMENT SINCE 1776

In the preceding chapters has been traced the growth of state constitutions from the somewhat simple and crude type of revolutionary days to the complex and verbose patterns of this century. Although these modifications are numerous and important, yet no one for a moment supposes that the climax of change has been reached. The states are in the midst of an era of governmental reorganization and already the signs of the times are indicating a drift and trend towards a constitutional system at once democratic in aim and scientific in basis. As a sort of summary of these tendencies, will be set forth in this chapter the several lines of development prominent during the last hundred and forty years; and in the following chapters an attempt will be made to formulate suggestions for improvement in state constitutions, working towards the newer type of fundamental law now in process of development.

A state constitution aims in general to formulate in written law the essential principles of the prevailing theories and practices in respect to governmental organization and powers. In Cromwell's day the notion of a "law paramount" over statutes promulgated by parliament had been evolved, and was embodied in the "Instrument of Government," the modern world's first written constitution. The Restoration, however, obscured for a time this notion of a fundamental law, so that it was only dimly comprehended by the colonists in 1776. The early constitutions, therefore, were in origin and purpose very like legislative statutes, and were chiefly frameworks of government, mere skeletons of organization, leaving by implication very large discretionary powers to the lawmaking body as the representatives of the "sovereign people." The practice followed in separating powers was not so much in harmony with Montesquieu's theory, which in fact has never found favor in the states except in a formal way, but was based on English and colonial custom, supplemented by an acquired dread of executive authority and a determination to curb it in the impending reorganization. The new constitutions, therefore, specified the three well recognized divisions of government; viz., the legislative, executive, and judicial, but took pains to render the last two, and especially the executive, subordinate to the legislative, following the teachings of John Locke. This body, therefore, dominant in the governmental scheme, made up in theory of "men of wisdom and virtue," and having large discretionary powers, naturally had a prominent place in the new system. It however has not been able to retain this position of prominence. The development of the last one hundred and forty years is a long record of a series of steady encroachments on the powers of the legislature, paralleling historically the encroachment of the House of Commons on the powers of the King and his House of Lords, so that, in those states where these tendencies are most fully developed, the question is seriously debated whether state legislatures have any useful function in government that could not be performed more efficiently by a simpler organization of an administrative type, or by a small unicameral lawmaking body.

This process of change is concretely illustrated by the steady increase in the length of constitutions, an increase that apparently has even yet not reached its maximum. It is obvious that every addition to the length of a constitution is in effect a restriction on the discretionary power of the legislature, for these additions in general include detailed instructions as to the organization and powers of the various departments of government and administration, lists of limitations on legislative authority, and lengthy regulations of legislative procedure.

This tendency to enlargement is not without justification. The proper solution of problems arising from the complexity of modern interests, demands more wisdom and knowledge than is usually found in legislatures, which are often incompetent and sometimes venal, so that the democratic demand for legislation through a constitutional convention, is really a demand for legislators of a high grade. Conventions in general are eager to curb legislatures and to minimize their capacity to do mischief, so that to them are left the mere details of legislation, with a minimum of discretion in the formulation of statutes. Broadly speaking therefore the really fundamental trend of change has been from a dominant legislature to a dominant electorate, working through the convention.

If this notion of change through restrictions on legislative authority be taken as a guide in constitutional growth, the whole process may be considered under the six following heads, the sum total of which would represent broadly the trend of change in state constitutions from 1776 to 1914. The headings selected, it may be said, represent a logical arrangement, not the order of historical development.

I. Legal Sovereignty

In every state there is some person or organization having authority to formulate the fundamental law binding on the several departments of government. Attention has already been called to the fact that the earliest constitutions were made by revolutionary conventions, or legislatures that for the most part indifferently passed both fundamental and statute law and by the same procedure. Soon, under the stimulus of the experiences of Massachusetts, there developed the constitutional convention, a body of representatives chosen for the express purpose of formulating a constitution for their state. Then in later development came for convenience' sake the distinction that particular and separate amendments might be passed by the legislature, using a complicated procedure; but that new constitutions, or revisions, should be made by a convention. In either case the older theory was that both legislature and convention exactly voiced the will of the people and hence there was no need of referendum. But with growing democracy there came a demand from the electorate that both amendments and new or revised constitutions should be referred for approval or rejection. In logical development there came a further demand that the process of amendment be simplified, and that the possibility of ordering a revision be made definite by inserting that right in the constitution. Finally, within the last twenty years, has arisen the demand that the electorate of the state be in fact the legal sovereign by specifying its constitutional right to revise or amend the constitution at pleasure through the constitutional initiative and referendum. It is understood of course that not all the states have gone through this entire process of change. Some few still retain methods of amending peculiar to the eighteenth century, and twelve only have so far adopted the constitutional initiative and referendum, but the trend seems to be steadily set in the direction of popular control.

In conclusion of this topic it may be said that few seem to realize the importance of the constitutional convention in American state governments. It is the great agency through which democracy finds expression. In its latest form, that of a body made up of delegates elected from districts of equal population, it is one of the greatest of our political inventions. Through it popular rights may be secured in the constitution, legislative tyranny restrained, and powerful interests subordinated to the general welfare. These objects have not as yet been fully attained, but the convention is the agency through which public opinion can express itself, as it becomes enlightened in respect to the needs of the times.

II. THE EXECUTIVE

In the revolutionary constitutions antagonism to kings took the form of a minimization of executive authority. The governor's chair was honorable through social prestige and men of dignity eagerly sought it, but few powers were attached to the office and its holder even in the exercise of these was under the check of his executive council and of the legislature, which in most states elected him to office. This weakness in executive authority is still characteristic of the states as a whole, but in some respects the governor has gained power at the expense of the legislature. He is no longer handicapped by the old time executive council except in three of the New England states, but on the other hand he has not become the real head of an administrative council, as is the president of the United States. Yet his power of appointment to minor offices is increasing, though regularly shared with the senate, and his longer term of two or four years strengthens his influence. His messages and recommendations to his legislature have greater weight than formerly, because, as the choice of the electorate and the virtual head of his political party, his wishes can no longer be slighted nor ignored. When the national constitution was formed, two states only allowed their governors the veto power; at this time one state only withholds it and most allow their governors, in addition, the right to veto the items of appropriation bills. This veto power of the governor, especially when strengthened by the power to veto items and to approve or disapprove after legislative adjournment, has greatly enlarged the importance of the executive, since it allows him to conserve public interests against an inefficient or corrupt legislature.

III. Administration

Administration is naturally part of the executive function, but in the revolutionary period it was at first controlled and in part carried on by the legislatures. This was done through committees, temporary at first and then made permanent.[1] The work performed by these was gradually transferred to paid officials, who, as functions became specialized, were organized, for the purpose of carrying on the work of administration, into the numerous boards, commissions, and departments of government. Most of our states are still in this stage of development. Every new line of activity results in the formation of a special board or department, the organization and powers of which are

[1] See, The Origin of the Standing Committee System in American Legislative Bodies, by J. Franklin Jameson. Annual Report Am. Hist. Assn. 1893. pp. 393-99.

frequently defined in the constitution. Provision also regularly is made for the election by popular vote of the heads of the chief administrative departments, such as the secretaries of state and of the treasury, the comptroller, or auditor, and the superintendent of education. Their term of office is usually the same as the governor's. As these numerous boards and departments really perform the larger part of governmental business, one would suppose that the several articles and provisions of the constitution in respect to administration would be gathered together and placed under a separate heading entitled, Departments of Administration, and that the functions of these departments would be coördinated, unified, and provisions made for thorough supervision. This is not done, so that the absence of such centralization is perhaps the greatest weakness in state administration. Supervisory control over these bodies by legislative committees tends to become merely nominal, with the inevitable consequences of inefficiency and lack of economy. There is however a tendency in a few states to center such powers in the executive, making him the head of the administration as in the national system. This is done by bestowing on him large powers in appointment and removal, and authority to demand reports and to investigate the management of departments. The several commissions of late years appointed for the purpose of recommending an administrative reorganization, are excellent illustrations of the present trend, which is seeking for efficient and economic administrative systems in state government.[1]

[1] See, p. 165.

IV. THE JUDICIARY DEPARTMENT

The older constitutions disposed of this department in a few words. Discretionary power was conferred on the legislature, and judges, appointed by governor or legislature, usually held a life tenure. The new constitutions completely reverse this practice. The court, in the United States, does not simply decide cases, it interprets finally the constitution, and to that extent is a political factor. For this reason, the existence of complex business conditions and the rise of corporate interests necessitate much more attention to this department of government, if popular interests are to be safeguarded. The newer constitutions therefore regularly outline the grades of courts, define their powers, set the boundaries for judicial districts, and regulate the number and tenure of the judiciary. Similar changes are made in the older constitutions as rapidly as they come up for revision. Three of the original states still retain a life tenure for their highest judges, but all others fix a term of years for judges of the supreme court; the term varies from two to twenty-one years. Six states only retain appointment through the governor, aided by council or senate. Four choose through the legislature, and one nominates through the governor and elects through the assembly. The other states all elect their judiciary and show no tendency in the other direction. The rise of the "recall of judges," and the Colorado experiment in authorizing the recall of judicial decisions, are illustrations of the electorate's determination to get a closer grip on the judiciary rather than to return to the older methods of legislative supervision. Four of the New England states still allow the governor or assembly to ask the supreme court for opinions on questions of law,[1] South Dakota and

---

[1] Massachusetts, Maine, New Hampshire, Rhode Island. See, p. 180

Florida allow the governor this privilege, but all the other states with greater wisdom reject this provision, so as not to compel the court to take sides on questions involving perhaps a political issue. There is a marked tendency in the constitutions to merge law and equity into a common procedure, to modify the jury, and to define libel. These tendencies unitedly show a strong determination to make the judicial system responsible directly to the electorate.

V. The Electorate [1]

By the provisions of the early constitutions, the voting franchise was held by a small per cent only of the population, since there were restrictions based largely on property qualifications and to some extent on religious beliefs. The incoming of democracy swept away these restrictions from one constitution after another, so that at present Rhode Island alone retains a survival of the property qualification, in the election of members of city councils and in the membership of town financial meetings. Male suffrage based on citizenship, therefore, became the rule, but some states enlarged even this by admitting to voting privileges those aliens who had declared their intention of becoming citizens. The civil war added to the electorate the enfranchised male blacks of adult age, and the agitation of over fifty years for women's suffrage is resulting in the addition to the voting lists of women also, so far in eleven of the states.

On the other hand the last sixty years have brought to the front a steadily growing list of regulations and requirements, such as systems of registration, educational qualifications, or an educational qualification with a property

[1] See article by author, Trend of Recent Constitutional Changes, *Am. Pol. Sc. Review*, Vol. VI. pp. 53–60.

qualification as an alternative, or a requirement of prepaid taxes, poll or property; so that the lists of registered voters in some states are in per cent no larger than the voting lists of the revolutionary period. Such fluctuations in the per cent of voting population, varying from an electorate including less than five per cent of the population to those of women's suffrage states where approximately half the population is eligible to the voting lists, indicates wide variations in social conditions and in democratic theory and practice. It should however be said that these are the extremes of variation; taking the population as a whole, from twenty to twenty-five per cent of it can be found on the registration lists of the states unitedly. Furthermore the fact should be noted that the old time requirements of special property qualifications for office holding have almost entirely disappeared, such survivals as exist are allied with property qualifications for suffrage, since obviously an office holder should have the qualifications of a voter.[1] There are still a few religious restrictions on office holding.[2]

This enlargement of the membership of the electorates of the states finds its supplement in the remarkable growth of their powers. When Montesquieu wrote his famous discussion of the separation of powers with its check and balance theory, he failed to see the possibilities of the insignificant electorate of his day as in fact a fourth department of government, destined through democracy to balance and check his three departments, both separately and collectively. In reality the democratic trend of the present is more in accordance with Rousseau's theory, —

[1] There are slight exceptions; for example, women not having suffrage rights, may yet serve on civic committees and commissions.
[2] See p. 135.

that the electorate (the people) should retain in its own possession sovereign lawmaking powers, and should keep the several other departments of government definitely responsible always to the sovereign people.

This trend found expression from the very beginning of national existence. Attention already has been called to the steady growth of popular control over government as a whole, through its power over the fundamental law of the state. This naturally implies an increasing control over the legislative, executive (and administrative), and judicial departments of government. This is shown by the fact that the chief officials of the state and its several local subdivisions, the lawmakers of all grades, and judges, supreme and inferior, are now regularly elected by popular vote and in some states may be recalled by the same process. Since the convention determines the judicial system and its powers, and the electorate chooses judges and serves on jury, judicial decisions tend to be "popular" in their nature. Certainly, also, in those states having effective systems of the initiative and referendum, real lawmaking authority has passed from legislatures to the electorates. The electorates, in other words, by their constitutional powers in the states, are balancing, checking, and dominating the three historic departments of government, so that the older theory of "separation of powers" is rapidly falling into a condition of harmless senility.

In revolutionary days the electorates of the states were largely influenced in their decisions by the personality of powerful leaders, or were manipulated to some extent by cliques of self-seeking politicians. Political parties of the modern type, with their superb organizations, were then unknown. These slowly developed as aids to popular expression and were at first quite responsible to popular demand. Yet as "machine politics" became dominant, there rapidly grew a demand for a fuller and fairer expression of the popular will. In modern constitutions this takes the form of provisions in respect to ballots, primaries, corrupt practices, and returning boards. Through such devices electorates are seeking opportunities to determine nominations and elections apart from the dictation of party organizations, and are endeavoring to evolve systems such that parties may be useful agents but not masters of the voters they in theory are supposed to represent. This aspect of constitutional change is a marked feature of recent constitutions.

VI. THE LEGISLATURE OR GENERAL ASSEMBLY

This powerful body in revolutionary days completely overshadowed the other two departments, and was practically the repository of the sovereign powers in the states. Though the theory of the separation of powers was held, all really important powers were in fact entrusted to the legislatures. This is by no means the present condition. Not only have the other two usual departments been built up and strengthened at the expense of the assembly, but the three other departments of government already mentioned have developed into importance, viz., the administration, the electorate, and that agency, which in every state has the legal right to formulate the fundamental law, the *Legal Sovereign*. These six departments unitedly may exercise every conceivable power included within the term sovereignty.

The revolutionary constitutions differed widely in respect to the organization and membership of their legislatures. Very noticeable, however, is the present tendency to approximate toward a common type. In all the states the legislature is bicameral. Forty-three states elect the members of the house biennially; senators have a four-year term in thirty-one states. A biennial session is required in forty states, and thirty-seven fix actually or practically a time limit for legislative sessions; this in twenty-one states is fixed at sixty days. In twenty states the membership of both houses is made up of representatives from districts of equal population. In nineteen other states there is a requirement that a locality, either county or town, be represented in one or both houses. In these states, however, the requirement modifies only slightly the principle of popular representation, and the districts are practically of equal population. In other words thirty-nine of the states make their legislative houses popular in basis. The nine other states depart from this principle by requiring a disproportionate representation for their rural towns, or counties of small population. The worst offenders in this respect are Delaware, Maryland, Vermont, Connecticut and Rhode Island.[1]

Under the national constitution the powers not delegated to the federation nor prohibited to the states are reserved to the states. This reserved power may be exercised in each state by its legislature, unless the local constitution redelegates parts of this power to the other departments of government, and places restrictions and prohibitions on legislative use of the remainder.

One would think that since our legislators usually come from districts of equal population they would by constitution be entrusted with large discretionary powers in legislation. This, however, is far from being the fact. There is a steadily increasing tendency to restrict in every possible way the enormous powers of legislatures. Every provision

[1] See, chap. xvi.

in a bill of rights limits by so much legislative initiative. The increasing powers of the executive and the rapidly increasing powers of the electorate in appointment, administration, and lawmaking are all at the expense of the assembly; the growth in importance of the constitutional convention subordinates proportionately its rival, the legislature. Every article in the constitution that fixes the organization and powers of a department of administration, or division of government, or defines a policy in regard to important interests, is to that extent a restriction on legislative discretion. Yet in the newer constitutions one may expect to find, as already indicated, lengthy articles on the judicial and administrative departments, and moreover much regulation of taxation, finance, local government, education, elections and the suffrage; land, mines, corporate interests and labor. To these regulations should be added long lists of prohibitions such as those against special or local legislation, and numerous regulations of procedure in respect to the handling of bills. Subtract all these limitations on legislative powers from the totality, and the question naturally arises whether it is worth while to retain large and expensive[1] legislatures to exercise their small residue of petty powers. For it should be remembered that the membership of the state legislatures is unitedly over seven thousand, and that nearly two thousand of these are found in the seven[2] states that have assemblies of over two hundred members. A convention meeting periodically, and well supervised administrative departments with ordinance powers, might perform all legislative functions with entire satisfaction.

[1] In respect to expense, see, p. 279.
[2] Illinois, Georgia, Pennsylvania, Massachusetts, Vermont, Connecticut, New Hampshire.

It seems plain that the really important lawmaking body at the present time is the convention. Its members are of a higher grade and turn out work distinctly superior to that of legislatures, which are really bodies having chiefly ordinance powers. Whenever, through sudden changes in conditions, a legislature unexpectedly develops large discretionary power in statute-making, the next convention in that state usually settles the principle itself and thereby adds another limitation to legislative initiative. This tendency seems to offer every inducement to our legislators to belittle its opportunities and to adjourn as speedily as possible. This is a wide departure from the older belief about legislatures, whose members, as the early constitutions of Maryland and Vermont put it, should be persons "most wise, sensible, and discreet," and "most noted for wisdom and virtue."

In conclusion, attention may well be called to the practical disappearance from our constitutions of some old-time provisions. Among these may be mentioned the annual election, and the annual session, the governor's council, and unequal representation of the people in lawmaking bodies; the life tenure of judges, and the advisory capacity of the supreme court. Religious restrictions on office-holding, and the property qualification for suffrage, with very slight exceptions, have gone; the town system of New England is dying in that section and does not exist outside of it. The real local units of administration now are, (1) the rural county with its districts, its townships, and its villages, and (2) the incorporated city. These local bodies politic, once entirely subordinated to the legislature, are now rapidly securing for themselves, through constitutional provisions, rights of self-government through guaranties of local control over franchises and a determinate voice in the making of their own charters. In passing, it may be said that the initiative, referendum, and recall features are in more vigorous use in local even than in state government.[1]

If general tendencies in the making of constitutions may be condensed into a sentence, we may say that the governmental powers of the states are centering into their electorates, which voice themselves through the ballot and the constitutional convention.

[1] See Article, Municipal Initiative, Referendum, and Recall in Practice, by C. F. Taylor, *National Municipal Review*, October, 1914.

CHAPTER XXI

THE ELECTORATE, LEGAL SOVEREIGNTY AND THE LEGISLATURE

THE trend of change indicated in the previous chapter suggests an interpretation of these tendencies, so as to formulate suggestions looking towards a series of suitable modifications in existing constitutions. It would of course be feasible to work out from the figments of one's imagination an ideal constitution, which like Plato's "Republic" would be best suited for a utopia inhabited by perfect citizens. Or by contrast one might cull from the constitutions of foreign states those features that would likely blend best with the principles of American democracy, and then attempt to synthesize the whole into a model constitution.

The commonwealths of the United States, however, are somewhat conservative by nature, not prone to experiment overmuch, and prefer to make modifications based on American experiences, sanctioned by proofs of successful working under the usual conditions of political existence in this country. In the following pages, therefore, under the same six headings used in the previous chapter, will be indicated the possibilities of improvement in existing constitutions, basing these suggestions in the main on definite tendencies manifest in American economic and political experiences.

I. THE ELECTORATE

It seems obvious that under present conditions and in the long run the principle of adult or equal suffrage will prevail over manhood suffrage. Yet it is also clear that a large per cent of women are adverse to the acquirement of suffrage rights and would therefore be likely to refrain from registration and voting, thus adding to the already large fraction of "stay-at-home" voters. Furthermore, there is the problem of the negro vote in the south, the vote of naturalized foreigners in northern urban centers, and generally the problem of a voting population made up in part of illiterates, economic "ne'er-do-wells," and citizens of all classes who are ignorant of or indifferent to the duties involved in the suffrage. Yet as long as political parties are on a keenly competitive basis, emphasizing perhaps loyalty to party above the public weal, such masses of ignorant and indifferent citizens are a boon to politicians, since from their ranks can be called out to party support, under the stimulus of cajolery, bribes, or parasitic employment, an army of voters who often outcount the more intelligent and patriotic part of the body of citizens. On the other hand, it seems evident, from the enormous interest shown in legislation in respect to primaries, ballots, and corrupt practices, that the state electorates are determined to compel political parties to subordinate partisan politics to general welfare; or as an alternative to insist on non-partisanship in state and municipal politics. As this object becomes achieved, it will become easier and more possible to standardize the electorates of the several states by emphasizing uniform principles in law, suited to the usual conditions prevalent in all states. These for example, might adopt adult suffrage as a fundamental, but should insist with varying degrees of emphasis that the suffrage is not so much a right as a privilege, the enjoyment of which is dependent on the fulfilment of certain requirements and qualifications as a test of interest and intelligence. Among such tests might be specified; the ability to read and write English with some ease, a registration in person during a period ending at least three months before a general election, and the payment by each registering voter of a small registration fee, such as the dollar poll tax collected in many states.[1] The necessity for a personal application and payment of a fee would automatically disfranchise those whose interest in voting depends on the excitement of a campaign or a bribe, and would place on the voting lists those who had at least sufficient education to enable them to acquire information from the printed page, and sufficient interest in voting to register before campaigning began and to pay a fee for the privilege.

If, as a matter of policy, personal interest and intelligence were rigidly demanded as qualifications for the suffrage, citizens lacking these would tend to feel that they were lower in status than those who had registered as voters, so that there would be a constant incitement in their own minds inducing them to meet the requirements, so as to have the *privilege* of voting. States and their municipalities also would realize more fully than they do at present the obligations resting on them to reduce illiteracy to its minimum, and to develop civic interest by proper instruction in such matters, not only in the schools but more especially among immigrants within their boundaries. On the other hand, under this system women who preferred not to vote would

---

[1] Under such a system poll taxes preferably should be abolished. Corrupt practices acts would of course see to it that registration fees were not paid from party funds.

simply refrain from registering, and their sisters who wished the ballot might enjoy that privilege by registering within the stipulated time and paying their fee. By emphasis on some such requirements, suffrage would cease to be deemed an inherent right, automatically going to each adult citizen as he attained his majority, but rather a right earned by showing an intelligent interest in civic life, yet liable to be forfeited by neglect. A moderately sized voting list of interested citizens would surely prove to be preferable to an unwieldy mass of voters having among its membership a dead weight of inert citizenship.

The powers of the electorates in the several states presumably will under present tendencies increase to such an extent, that in fact as well as in theory each electorate will hold in its hand the sovereign power of its state by controlling through the ballot the several departments of governmental organization. How this may take place in detail will be discussed in the later headings of this and the succeeding chapter. It is evident however that as aids to the effective use of the ballot, electional systems must be so ordered as to permit the average citizen to vote intelligently and to express his real will. Hence the lengthy "circle" ballot so dear to all politicians should be superseded by a "short ballot" on the "alphabetical" plan. Furthermore, the state must publish for each election a "voters' guide," furnishing information not simply in respect to projected legislative referenda, but also brief statements of the records and qualifications of candidates. These "publicity pamphlets"[1] have fully justified their usefulness, and might well become part of a series of state publications supplying information to voters about matters of health,

---

[1] The best pamphlets of this nature are issued by Oregon, California, Nebraska, Washington, Wisconsin and Arizona.

education, employment, economic possibilities and proposed legislation. These, by act of congress, might be mailed either free of postage or at newspaper rates. Such a method of publication would be vastly more efficient than the present usual method of advertising in newspapers, would involve much less expense, and would prove to be a great educational agency for the promotion of interest in matters of civic policy.

II. Legal Sovereignty

If it be assumed that the powers of legal sovereignty will in most of the states soon be vested in the electorate by constitutional provision, this body to some extent at least will delegate the making of fundamental law to representatives, whether in constitutional convention or legislature. This can safely be done if the constitution definitely asserts the right of the electorate to initiate amendments, to demand a convention for revision purposes, and to have referred to it all amendments and revisions. Popular control over fundamental law through the use of the direct constitutional initiative may in the first enthusiasm of reform be carried too far, as in some states at present; but as a permanent proposition these measures are likely to be used conservatively, as a sort of last resort, or as a veto check on venal or ill-considered legislation. As legislatures become more trustworthy, and make use of legislative reference and bill drafting departments, presumably the electorate might better initiate the fundamentals of their propositions, stating simply the essentials of the desired legislation, and leaving the elaboration of the details to the legislature. Yet as a safeguard against neglect, provision might wisely be made authorizing the secretary of state to submit a drafted bill, in case the legislature failed to take action on the initiated measure.

As for amendments initiated by the legislature, the states obviously are agreeing that the procedure for these should include action by one legislature only, by a two-thirds vote, without reference to the governor, but with a reference to the electorate, who make final decision by a majority of those voting thereon. Amendments should be separated on the ballot, but restrictions on the number to be submitted at any one time are of doubtful utility. A proper interval of several years, however, might well be required between the defeat of an amendment and its resubmission. Preferably amendments should be submitted by legislative rather than by popular initiative, provided that the legislature really represents the will of the electorate.

The constitutional convention may rightly be considered as the best type of lawmaking body yet devised in the United States. As a body especially chosen for the formulation of fundamental law, as the voice of the people it represents, and as the collective wisdom of the state seeking to embody principles for future political organization and policy, it occupies a commanding place in American democracy. For this reason the convention should never be made supplementary or subordinate to the legislature, to which it is superior in power and prestige. Its composition therefore should be different from that in the legislature, and should be determined by the constitution, not by the legislature, since this body might be inclined to gerrymander districts or to provide a membership so composed as to assure no reforms of material consequence.[1] By usual practice the convention's membership is elected from districts of equal census population, or in part by general ticket; preferably the members should be elected by nonpartisan methods and should be few, not

[1] As Connecticut did in 1901; see, p. 251.

many in number.[1] Rarely if ever should the legislature be allowed authority to place limitations on the powers of the convention, or to determine the length of time for its sessions, or the time and manner of referendum. The constitution should contain provisions fixing such matters, so that the convention may be left free from dictation by the existing departments of government, so as to work out in its discretion what may seem best for the state, subject only to a compulsory referendum to the electorate.

As far as possible, preliminary information should be prepared in advance of the assembling of the convention, so as to save time and expense. This might be accomplished by the collection of material through the legislative reference bureau or the state library. This information might be digested by a small, appointed commission, not necessarily members of the convention,[2] authorized to prepare a draft of a constitution to be submitted to the convention, in which case the members of the commission, if not elected as members of the convention might be given a right to the floor for purposes of discussion. Or again, should some of the delegates be elected at large, these by arrangement could serve as a committee to draft a constitution, calling the convention as a whole at a later date, when the committee was prepared to report. If, however, it should seem best that the convention have full control over this matter, it might on assembling appoint such a committee and then adjourn for thirty or sixty days awaiting a report.

---

[1] It might be remembered that the convention that made the national constitution had in attendance fifty-five members only, forty of whom signed the constitution.

[2] New York uses such commissions to prepare material for its constitutional conventions; note especially the Commissions of 1891 and 1914.

III. THE LEGISLATURE

Of the three historic departments of government the lawmaking body necessarily is the most important. Whatever powers a state has under the national constitution, inhere in the legislature except in so far as they have been forbidden to it or otherwise delegated by the convention in formulating the constitution. These two lawmaking bodies unitedly deserve the blame for defective legislation and inefficient administration. No system of reorganization in state government therefore, would be effective that failed to take into account the possibility of improvement in present legislative organization and procedure. Unfortunately the present popular attitude towards the legislature is destructive rather than constructive. This attitude in general consists in assuming the dishonesty and incompetency of the lawmaking body and yet the necessity for its continuance in its present form; varied with occasional threats of annihilation, or a threat to substitute for it a commission after the municipal plan. Thus, in the constitutions are inserted provisions against bribery, corrupt practices and duplicate officeholding, and attempts are made to reduce the legislature's power of mischief by lengthy prohibitions on legislative activity, by fixing in the constitution policies which the legislature may merely amplify, and by adding numerous regulations of its powers such as those in respect to the passing of bills. By contrast, similar conditions in the cities have resulted in carefully revised charters providing for new forms of organization such as the "federal," "commission," and "general manager" systems, civil service rules, and a rapid extension of the use of experts in municipal service in place of the old time spoils-seeker. Unquestionably similar changes will soon be demanded in state systems, so that one may anticipate a breaking away from the older traditions towards experiments in improved governmental machinery.

Fortunately the principles that ultimately should prevail are rapidly becoming familiar through experimentations in local government, in cities and in counties, so that the experience of these will throw light on the problems of their states. In municipal reform, for illustration, the principle has become well established that in place of the old time double chamber there should be a single legislative house or even a board or commission. At present no one of the forty-eight states has adopted the plan of a unicameral legislature, yet the movement in that direction has definitely begun in several states,[1] and undoubtedly it is a mere matter of time before the experiment will be made. Presumably a bicameral system is suited to an aristocracy where class distinctions are emphasized; or to a federation in which a second house may represent the constituent states or commonwealths; but a democracy naturally expresses itself through a single house, elected by and responsible to the electorate. The eighteenth century demand for "check and balance," which was then satisfied by evolving the governor's council into a legislative senate, can now be met by the governor's message and veto, and by the statutory initiative and referendum. In all the states with the few exceptions mentioned in Chapter XVI, the senate and the house both are practically based on equal population districts, so that they represent the same kind of interests. In experience the two-house system has not worked well in the United States, neither in the cities nor in the states. It

---

[1] For example, in Oregon, Ohio, Oklahoma, Nebraska and Kansas. Amendments of this sort were voted on, 1914, in Oregon and Oklahoma, but were defeated.

results in political bargaining, deadlocks, a lack of legislative responsibility and a multiplication of useless legislation. Furthermore the labor and expense are entirely out of all proportion to the returns. Bulletin Number Four of the Nebraska Legislative Reference Bureau gives a summary of the expenses of the last sessions (1913–1914) of the several state legislatures. The expenses of thirty-eight states are given in approximate figures, under- rather than over-stated. If the average of these is taken as the expense of each of the remaining ten states, and the proper additions and subtractions made for states having annual or quadrennial sessions, it would seem that the biennial expense of our legislative sessions is about fourteen and one quarter millions of dollars. No one for a moment supposes that the states get their money's worth in return for this enormous expenditure. Unquestionably better results might be secured at half the cost under a more efficient system. Yet to this heavy drain on the treasury of the states should be added the additional expense of useless and wasteful administration and the burden of needless litigation necessitated by defective laws.

A single-house system, however, of itself would be of small importance. It should be supplemented by careful attention to the personnel of its membership. This need not necessarily be composed of experts in legislation, but should in any event be made up of intelligent men of character and experience in affairs, so that they can give proper consideration to the important duties entrusted to them. Such men who can give time to public affairs are not numerous, so that even the single house should not be too large; preferably the senate rather than the house should be retained.[1]

[1] Yet an Ohio amendment reducing the size of the membership of both houses was decisively rejected, 1913.

These members should be elected from large districts made up on the basis of census population, not necessarily single-member districts, for a useful system of minority or proportional representation may sometime be devised. Possibly as an alternative, a part might be elected at large and others from districts. In that case those elected at large would presumably be leaders and chairmen in the work of legislation. The age qualification should certainly be that of the senate not the house, for older men of experience are best in counsel, though younger men might prove more capable in administration. If members were elected by the class system, one half or one third at a time, continuity would be secured and permanent policies might be pursued. The reduction in number and the scaling down of useless expenses would allow the payment of larger annual salaries, so generous as to enable legislators to live honestly and comfortably on their salaries. Every attempt should be made to have the position of legislator become one of dignity, so that the office would appeal to a more capable set of citizens than those who ordinarily serve in legislatures. In this intense age a legislator should have more than a good heart and patriotic intentions, he should have also a wise head and a trained conscience, so that he will represent, not the average man, but rather what the average man aspires to be — an intelligent, reliable citizen who does his duty with honesty and industry. Every inducement should be made therefore to persuade such citizens to offer themselves as candidates: — good pay, civic dignity, and long tenure, subject of course to the recall in case an unworthy choice should by chance be made. If annual or sessional salaries were granted, as they should be, the time limit on legislative sessions, now so common, should be removed. A small body of well paid, capable men would naturally adjourn when they had completed their tasks, and could reassemble whenever there seemed to be need of their services.

Such a reorganization as that suggested above would necessitate a complete readjustment of rules of procedure, committees, and methods employed in the legislative consideration of bills. Unquestionably local, private, and special legislation should be handled separately from general bills. Much of that sort of legislation should become administrative and be delegated to the proper departments for settlement. The services of experts could be used advantageously in preparing material for legislative consideration and in the drafting of bills; administrative officers voiced through the governor could prepare a budget of estimated receipts and expenditures for the consideration of the legislature; and, if it were deemed wise, these administrative heads might on set days be given the privilege of the floor for purposes of questioning and explanation. The present steering committee, or the committee on rules, might well be recognized as the leadership of the house or houses in legislation.

Furthermore states should make it a matter of pride to elect their legislators on local issues and platforms, barring the use of national party names from state parties. Now that presidential electors and the membership of both houses of congress are elected by popular vote, there is no reason aside from partisanship, why national policies should be confused with state and municipal issues, so that the ultimate separation of national from state and local elections, using alternate years, will become inevitable. States must soon realize the importance of concentrating the attention of their electorates on their own domestic problems, apart from consideration of national issues.

These also would gain in comprehension if electorates should study them apart from state issues.

Numerous constitutional restrictions on procedure prove often to be a serious handicap in legislating, so that a system of "unanimous consent" or "suspension of the rules" becomes inevitable. Rules should be observed and committees should be efficient and report their bills promptly and after due consideration, yet it is doubtful whether any provisions in a constitution can remedy the evil.[1] This is deep rooted and is the result of partyism, bossism, the spoils system and inefficient governmental organization. The politician simply pits his brain against the law and evades it. In the national congress each house determines its own rules of procedure and is not hampered by constitutional provisions. States might well do likewise if only they would first reorganize their legislatures and aim to elect as legislators citizens who would forget partisanship and take a real interest in the welfare of the state.

A little reflection would show that a body of one hundred and fifty to one hundred and seventy-five men of opposite parties, largely new in legislative experience, limited to a sixty day biennial session, working through two houses and numerous committees, cannot give careful attention to some fifteen hundred to two thousand bills introduced by the members, and to the complex details of finance and appropriation bills; studying these in committee, debating, explaining, or amending them on the floor, or listening to citizens at public hearings. Of necessity most bills are hastily and wretchedly worded; if reported favorably they are often passed without debate, in a perfunctory way, without

---

[1] For legislative reports on a revised procedure, see New York's report made in 1895 through a commission; and Bulletin Number Four, Nebraska Legislative Reference Bureau.

adequate explanation or examination, sometimes in a wild rush at the end of the session, in the midst of a confusion too great even for the clerks to record properly what is taking place. It is not strange that under such conditions the governor's veto comes in as the final umpire, — vetoing after adjournment the worst of the bills and dropping from appropriation bills those items that in his opinion are without justification. The growth of the governor's veto has kept step with the growing recognition of legislative incompetence.[1]

Assuming that statutory legislation will slowly develop in quality under the present demand for improved laws, there should come an insistence that legislation be based on thorough studies made through experts and framed so carefully that each particular piece of lawmaking may stand out as a model of legislative capacity. Legislators should take as much pride in the scientific accuracy and applicability of their laws as an Edison might in the improvement of his inventions. Surely no greater honor can come to a man than the privilege of formulating and fathering a law that voices the constructive trend of the times and benefits the state in which his life is spent!

[1] Mr. Tom Finty of the Dallas *News* thus summarizes the work of the thirty-third (Texas) legislature:

"Many measures of considerable merit failed of passage; others were passed in imperfect form, either through lack of effort to perfect the same or by reason of amendments offered in ignorance or malice. The really big things, such as riddance of the statutes of useless laws, the removal therefrom of errors committed by former Legislatures and the adjustment of codes to meet changed conditions, were not even undertaken, except in one instance. Hundreds of bills were rushed through pell mell and without opportunity for anyone to understand them. It has developed that some of these were useless; others defective and still others harmful. How many bills were thus objectionable is not yet known — if not many, then it must be that the Thirty-Third Legislature has a lucky star. The writer believes that in the circumstances the Legislature has done well, and that it deserves the epitaph inscribed for Mark Twain's cowboy: 'He done his durndest, angels could do no more.'"

In respect to the statutory initiative and referendum it would seem advisable to have these powers reserved by constitution to the electorate.   Yet the electorate should not take the place of the legislature in lawmaking and the initiative and referendum should be used merely as a last resort.   Measures initiated should properly be worded by the state's drafting department, submitted to the legislature for action, and given a fair and careful consideration.   An intelligent legislature would do so, but in case of no action, the secretary of state might be instructed to refer the bill to the electorate.   Laws made by the electorate presumably should be altered or repealed only with its consent, yet this would introduce into legislation another kind of procedure in lawmaking; — to constitutional provisions and legislative statutes would be added laws made by electorates.   This is unfortunate but temporarily necessary. When legislatures again return to popular favor, the third sort will probably rarely be formulated.   Even now such laws are relatively few in number,[1] and the exceptions are mainly in those states, like Oregon and California, where bossism had long prevailed and a sort of house-cleaning had to be made.   As needed readjustments are made, there will be less and less necessity for the use of the initiative and referendum in statutory legislation.   It is to be hoped also that as scientific management and the efficiency movement make headway in business circles, applications of these principles will be made to government, so that one may confidently anticipate in the near future real improvements in legislative and administrative systems.

[1] See, *Equity*, January, 1913, pp. 34–47.

CHAPTER XXII

THE EXECUTIVE, THE ADMINISTRATION AND THE JUDICIARY

I. THE EXECUTIVE

ALTHOUGH for many years the state executive has been growing in popular favor and political importance, his power in administration is still weak by comparison with his power over legislation. The national theory of an executive, who is likewise head of the administration, has not on the whole found favor in the states. It may be that these are wiser in this than the national government, and that the burden of administration is too heavy a load to place on the shoulders of a conscientious governor. There is certainly need of centralizing administration under a responsible head, but possibly that might best be accomplished by developing a premiership from among the heads of administration, leaving to the governor general supervisory powers, including the right to suspend from office and to order investigations of suspected branches of administration.

Aside from a supervision over administration the governor has many other duties to perform. As the voice and personification of the personality of the state he has a large social function which in some states is a heavy drain on his nervous energy. As the head of the state militia his duties might become really onerous in case of riot or war. His serious task however arises from his connection with the legislature. Through his message and veto he must keep in close touch with the needs of the state and with proposed or possible legislation, serving in a sense as the exponent of the popular will. For this reason it would be only a natural expansion of his power to allow him the privilege of introducing along with his message bills embodying his recommendations and those of heads of departments, with the understanding that a proper time would be set apart for the discussion of such bills and that the administrative heads would have the privilege of the floor during the discussions, so as to allow opportunity for question and explanation. A governor who wisely performed his legislative functions only, would surely have duties sufficient to task his energy and strength, without the additional burden of the responsibilities of administration; for necessarily he would also continue his social duties as head of the state, and presumably should exercise a general supervisory power over administration, so as to enable him to check corruption and inefficiency.

II. The Administration

To those at all familiar with the workings of government it is clearly obvious that the administration of the state is sadly in need of reorganization. In every state exist scores of loosely coördinated, virtually independent departments, boards and commissions, each nominally supervised by the legislature, or governor, or both, but all largely neglected because of the many other duties and responsibilities devolving on these. The result is that each particular part of the administration seeks for itself the largest possible appropriation; conducts its business in a somewhat leisurely fashion, chiefly concerned lest it should unfortunately fail to use up its allotment;

and endeavors to "stand in" with the powers that be, so as to feel assured of a permanent tenure in office and a large appropriation. There are of course many conscientious officials who work hard and honestly for the state, but the system is against them since it puts a premium on time-serving and sycophancy. Few realize to what an extent boards and commissions control the most important interests in the state, such as corporations, charities, and health; or how numerous are the boards to which are entrusted subordinate functions, administrative, regulatory or semi-judicial in kind. Seldom is there any attempt to adjust these properly into the system so as to ensure their honesty, efficiency and economy. Many of these boards have long outlived their usefulness, are parasitic by nature, and should be abolished. The remaining boards should be unified and brought into definite relationships with the fundamental departments of government, and no new board should be created unless its powers, duties and duration are carefully defined, and its relation to some existing department made emphatic.

It is possible, as already suggested, that the responsibility for efficiency in administration might be placed on the governor, as the "willing horse," but it is plainly impossible for him to give proper care both to administration and legislation. Conceivably the lieutenant-governor might be removed from his sinecural position as presiding officer in the senate and made head of the administration, as a sort of "business manager" for the state, subject to the governor's supervisory powers, and having in administration an authority like that exercised by the president in his cabinet of administrative heads. Such responsibilities would certainly dignify this somewhat useless officer, and would afford him excellent training for a later promotion to the governor's chair.   But, whether under the governor, lieutenant-governor, or a premier selected from among the heads of administration, there is urgent need that the loose-jointed system of the present be superseded by a strongly centralized group of from five to ten departments, among which should be divided the functions now performed by the existing numerous boards and commissions. The heads of these departments should serve as an advisory cabinet so as to unify policy and to induce economy and efficiency.   The chief heads of administration should preferably be elected, but for long terms and subject to removal and recall.   Yet if the "business manager" system should be adopted, presumably even the heads of departments should be appointed so as to ensure expert service, though as a concession to democracy they might be made subject to the recall.   Subordinate heads of administration might better be appointed during good behavior but subject to removal by the usual means.   Civil service rules for employes should be insisted on, and promotions made only after a proper examination of record and capacity.

It is unfortunate that many conventions have felt it necessary to fix in constitution the salaries and per diems of the officers of the state.   Such provisions are hard to change by amendment, since electorates are inclined to be penurious when the salaries of office-holders are concerned. Yet a fair compensation at one time may be grossly unfair a few years later.   Again it is coming to be recognized in business, and partly in government, that skill and capacity are worth large salaries, and that it is poor economy to pay beggarly pittances to those in important positions. Expert knowledge, qualities of leadership, and an open-minded attitude towards new ideas are hard to find, and when found in business readily meet with adequate pecuniary compensation. The dignity of state office is a partial reward for services, so that the state may secure the services of capable citizens at smaller salaries than can business corporations. Yet in order to get really efficient officers the state must be able to offer dignity, social prestige, long tenure and a compensation adequate for proper support. There is a growing recognition of this fact in municipal administration, and in the states also the compensation paid to administrative heads, legislators, and judges, is steadily increasing. This is more true of governors and legislators than of judges and administrative heads, who have been neglected, so that too many receive salaries inadequate to the services demanded from them.

In conclusion it should be kept clearly in mind that inefficient administration is in the long run too costly a luxury. Efficiency not only considerably reduces the expenses of government but also performs a far more useful service to the people of the state. Many matters now neglected in such functions as, for example, health, sanitation and civic education, could be carried on effectively without an additional burden of taxation. Especially might the legislature be relieved from much routine labor by transferring to the administration the duty of preparing a budget and estimates as the basis for state policy in finance and taxation; or by authorizing the administration to make decisions as to the advisability and proper wording of private, local and special bills; or to redistrict judicial, legislative and administrative districts on the basis of a new census. Through a legislative reference bureau also might be secured comparative and historical data as the basis for new legislation; and through experts in scientific drafting, bills might be so worded as to be free from ambiguity and useless phraseology, comprehensible to the judiciary, and in harmony with existing statutes and the constitutions of state and nation.[1]

III. The Judiciary

It is significant that at the present time the judiciary system as a whole is absorbing a steadily increasing space in the constitution and that it is somewhat constantly under adverse discussion. There is still much dissatisfaction, notwithstanding the fact that both judiciary and judiciary system are rather completely under the control of the electorate, since judges are regularly elected and conventions pay much attention to the courts in revising constitutions. But the "short ballot" movement has brought to attention the fact that popular elections may be carried so far as to result in excessive partyism and the absence of a real democracy. Just as in administration, so in judicial organization there is great need that authority be centralized and agencies developed for the purpose of making improvements in law and judicial procedure. Thus criticisms of the existing judicial system usually take two forms: — (1) against the popular election of judges, and (2) against the needless complexity and ambiguity of law, the technicalities of procedure, the consequent multiplication and protraction of litigation, and hence in general the difficulty of securing justice.

The demand for the election of judges came originally as the result of a growing democratic desire on the part of the electorate to control all governmental offices; and also because of the unsatisfactory character of many judges appointed by governors or chosen by legislatures. It is not likely that the voters would be willing to surrender their control over judges, but it might be possible to substitute

[1] Under General Bibliography, note name of Kaiser, J. B.

the right of recall for the right of election, and then to authorize the supreme court of the state to appoint the judges of circuit or district courts and these again to appoint inferior judges, justices of the peace, and notary publics. If deemed advisable, these appointments might be referred to the governor as recommendations for formal appointment. Under such a system the judges of the supreme court might be elected at large, by classes after the usual system, so that they might feel their responsibility to the electorate. Or they might be appointed by the governor on recommendation from the State Bar Association, subject to the right of recall on the part of the electorate. There should also exist the power of removal for cause in the courts recommending or appointing inferior judges, and in the legislature over the judges of the supreme court. A tenure during "good behavior" or for a lengthy term of years for the more important judgeships, and adequate salaries, would enhance the dignity and desirability of the office and hence would call to the bench a more capable body of judges. Popular interests would be fully safeguarded by a definite power of removal and the judicial recall, the latter of which, however, would probably seldom be brought into use.

If the bench as a whole be improved in quality, the next problem of simplifying law and procedure would be easier. It must be admitted that the statutory laws of most of our states are so hopelessly entangled that judges rather should be commended far more for what errors they avoid, than blamed for the errors they commit. Unquestionably, by general opinion both popular and professional, there is great need of simplifying, coördinating, and synthesizing law and procedure, both civil and criminal. Commissions from time to time do report to legislatures revised codes, statutes, and procedure, but these bodies are usually sporadic and their members are not always the most suitable persons for expert revisions. Possibly the newer movement arranging for permanent "revisers of laws" will provide a good substitute for the old-time commission. Or, as an alternative, the courts might be required to submit biennially to the governor bills embodying their conclusions as to changes needed in the existing law. These should be given a preferred place on the calendar, like other administrative bills, and explained at the proper time by the state's attorney. Or, again, the legislative reference bureau with its corps of bill drafters might refer to the attention of the courts, or to the governor, such incongruities as would come to their attention while pursuing investigations; or it might make suggestions of improvement, based on the experiences of other states. From social and economic experts likewise might readily be secured suggestions of change based on their experiences; such as the introduction of newer methods of procedure and of special courts, both trial and conciliation, for the disposition of such cases as juvenile and first offenders, drunkards, domestic relations, and labor disputes.

If judicial reorganization were definitely undertaken, and a system of revision established as a permanent policy, presumably the agitation for the recall of judicial decisions would prove to be temporary in nature since there would be no need to recall decisions that could not be amply satisfied by an amendment to the state constitution. In any case the possibilities in the radicalism of this form of recall are greatly limited by the fourteenth amendment to the national constitution, the final interpretation of which lies beyond the jurisdiction of the states.

MISCELLANEOUS

Lengthy constitutions are at present unfortunately too common. This tendency is largely due to the prevalent distrust of legislatures, so that should these once again win public confidence, constitutions presumably would diminish in size. As things are, it is useless to reiterate the desirability of a brief constitution, composed of fundamental principles, to be elaborated in detail through statute and ordinance by the several divisions of government. The national constitution shows the possibility of a workable short constitution, but the states must be willing to reorganize in a somewhat radical way their governmental systems before the short constitution will become really feasible. Yet all signs point to the speedy coming of a time when some future convention will reconstruct the governmental organization of its state so as to ensure efficient administration and careful legislation.

Much of the undue length of modern constitutions is due to the insertion of numerous details which of necessity must be frequently altered by amendment, as illustrated by the experiences of Louisiana for the last twenty years. Then, too, large space is given to the setting forth of detailed policies in respect to corporations, banks, public utilities; finance, taxation and debt; local government and education. This tendency is growing out of all bounds, so that whole statutes relating to such matters are passing into the constitutions, thus destroying the proper distinction between a constitution and a statute. Should legislatures remain as they are, it may be assumed that this distinction really will break down through the intrusion of statutes and initiated measures into the constitution. The effect of this will be an approximation to the "unwritten constitution" idea of England, since a constitution will be merely a loosely cohering mass of statutes, easily amended by a special procedure, and differing slightly if at all from the subject matter of general statutes. On the other hand should legislatures be reorganized so that they once again gain the confidence of the electorate, there is no reason why the constitution of a state including a bill of rights might not once more become a fairly brief document of a few thousand words. A bill of rights may well be retained in the constitutions of the states, even though some of its provisions are duplicated in the national constitution and safeguarded by the fourteenth amendment. Yet it is surely time that a revised and modern bill be inserted in some constitution as a model for the twentieth century, as that of Virginia was for the eighteenth century. "Natural rights" are obsolete, the civil war is over, slavery will never return, many rights once worthy of mention have now lost their importance, and newer rights as they come into prominence deserve to be incorporated. Certainly also a bill embracing some twenty or twenty-five provisions should allow ample space for the enumeration of all rights worthy of mention.

If the constitution as a whole be considered, much improvement in form and matter is possible. As a convenience, each paragraph should be numbered as in the Louisiana constitution. Amendments preferably should be carefully incorporated into the body of the constitution, not made as addenda to the constitution. The recent improvement made in the constitution of Vermont by this process contrasts well with the confused provisions of the Massachusetts constitution, where the amendments of the last one hundred and thirty years, the amendments to amendments, and the amendments even to these, are still printed as supplementary to that hoary document. Again the habit of inserting lengthy sections defining the boundaries of counties and of judicial and legislative districts should be discouraged. Such districting is usually redolent of gerrymandering and is unworthy of a convention. If at all necessary under prevalent conditions, such matters might better be passed as ordinances, but with the proviso that alterations made by the legislature must be followed by a referendum. In fact for precaution's sake statutory matter now too often inserted in constitutions, might better be passed as ordinances, yet be subject to change by ordinary legislative processes but with an obligatory referendum. The schedule, sometimes mistakenly inserted in the constitution, properly should be separate and classed as an ordinance, since its provisions are temporary in kind. In general, finally, the help of a body of drafting experts would aid in freeing the constitution from its wordiness, ambiguities, and useless provisions, and in condensing such lengthy lists as, for example, the numerous sections of legislation prohibited, into a generalized paragraph expressed in few words.

In conclusion it may be said that if the states should succeed, as they might, in reestablishing their governmental systems on firm bases, the present drift towards the centralization of powers into the federal government would be checked.[1] The enormous powers entrusted to the states by the national constitution are most important for the general well-being of the citizens; but as long as state governments prove incompetent to handle wisely these great interests, especially those pertaining to health, morals, and corporations, almost inevitably there will come an

[1] See, Article by Woodrow Wilson, The States and the Federal Government, *N. Am. Review*, Vol. 187, pp., 684–701.

insistent demand for federal intervention and an assumption of larger authority through interpretation or amendment. An enlargement of centralized control over domestic affairs would be a result greatly to be regretted. As the United States grows in population and wealth, in commerce and in manufactures, there will be an ample field for federal constructive statesmanship in managing the international policy and in regulating the interests of the nation as a whole, preferably leaving to the states even a larger jurisdiction than is enjoyed at present, in proportion as they show evidence of a spirit of civic efficiency and cooperation among themselves. After all, the United States of America is not an empire but a federation of republics : — "an indestructible Union composed of indestructible States."

BIBLIOGRAPHY FOR PART III

BRADFORD, GAMALIEL. The Reform of our State Governments. *Annals.* Volume IV, pp. 883–903.

KALES, A. M. Unpopular Government in the United States. Especially Chapters XIV–XVI inclusive.

CROLY, H. D. Progressive Democracy. Chapter XIV, Visions of a New State.

MATHEWS, J. M. The New Stateism. *North American Review*, June, 1911. Pp. 308–15.

Oregon Plan, The. See American Year Book :
  1910. Pp. 153–155.
  1912. Pp. 67–70.
  1913. Pp. 81–82, and *Equity*, July, 1913, article by W. S. U'Ren.

TYNG, T. S. A Draft of a Frame of Government. *Political Science Quarterly.* Volume XXVII, pp. 193–214.

WHITE, F. H. The Growth and Future of State Boards and Commissions. *Political Science Quarterly.* Volume XVIII, pp. 631–656.

In "General Bibliography" note references under *Annals*, and *Proceedings* of Academy of Political Science.

GENERAL BIBLIOGRAPHY

(See lists also on pages 88, 113–5, 138, 253, 296.)

AMERICAN COMMONWEALTHS SERIES. (Nineteen states to 1908.) Edited by H. E. Scudder. Boston.

BALDWIN, SIMEON E. Modern Political Institutions. Especially, Chapters III, XI. Boston. 1898.
The American Judiciary. New York. 1905.

BEARD, CHARLES A. Readings in American Government and Politics. New York. 1909.
American Government and Politics. New York. 1910.

BEARD AND SHULTZ (B. E.). Documents on the State-wide Initiative, Referendum and Recall. New York. 1912.

BIERLY, W. R. Police Power, State and Federal. Philadelphia. 1907.

BINNEY, CHARLES CHAUNCEY. Restrictions upon Local and Special Legislation in State Constitutions. Philadelphia. 1894.

BIZZELL, WILLIAM BENNETT. Judicial Interpretations of (American) Political Theory. New York. 1914.

BONDY, WILLIAM. The Separation of Governmental Powers. Columbia College Series. Volume V. Note also, The Separation of Powers, by Thomas R. Powell. *Political Science Quarterly*, June, 1912, and March, 1913.

BORGEAUD, CHARLES. Adoption and Amendment of Constitutions in Europe and America. New York. 1895.

BRADFORD, GAMALIEL. The Lesson of Popular Government. Especially, Chapters 22, 23, 32, of Volume II. Two volumes. New York. 1899.

BRYCE, JAMES. The American Commonwealth. Especially, Volume I, Part III. Two volumes. Edition 1910. New York.
Flexible and Rigid Constitutions. In Studies in History and Jurisprudence. Volume I, Essay III, pp. 124–215.

CLARKE, R. FLOYD. The Science of Law and Lawmaking. New York. 1898.

CLEVELAND, FREDERICK A. The Growth of Democracy in the United States. Chicago. 1898.
Organized Democracy. New York. 1913.

Constitutional Conventions. The best collections of Journals and Debates of Conventions may be found at the Library of the New York Bar Association, the Harvard Law Library, the John Hay Library of Brown University, and at the Library of Congress.

CROLY, HERBERT DAVID. The Promise of American Life. New York. 1909.

Progressive Democracy. New York. 1914

DAVIS, HORACE. American Constitutions. Johns Hopkins University Studies. Series of 1885. Pp. 467–81.

DAVIS, HORACE A. The Judicial Veto. Boston. 1914.

DEALEY, JAMES Q. Our State Constitutions. *Annals*, March, 1907. Philadelphia.

The Development of the State. New York. 1909.

Ethical and Religious Significance of the State. (Pamphlet, 48 pages.) Philadelphia.

DODD, WALTER F. The Revision and Amendment of State Constitutions. The Johns Hopkins Press. Baltimore. 1910.

FAIRLIE, JOHN ARCHIBALD. The Centralization of Administration in New York State. Columbia University Series. 1898.

Local Government in Counties, Towns, and Villages. New York. 1906.

FINLEY (J. H.) AND SANDERSON (J. F.). The American Executive and Executive Methods. New York. 1908.

FREUND, ERNST. The Police Power. (Constitutional Rights and Public Policy.) Chicago. 1904.

HAINES, CHARLES GROVE. The American Doctrine of Judicial Supremacy. New York. 1914.

HITCHCOCK, H. American State Constitutions. New York. 1887.

HOWARD, GEORGE E. Introduction to the Local Constitutional History of the United States. Baltimore. 1889.

HOWE, FREDERIC C. Wisconsin, An Experiment in Democracy. New York. 1912.

ILBERT, COURTENAY. (Clerk of the House of Commons.) Legislative Methods and Forms. Oxford. 1901.

The Mechanism of Law Making. New York. 1914.

JAMESON, JOHN ALEXANDER. On Constitutional Conventions. Fourth Edition. Chicago. 1887.

JONES, CHESTER LLOYD. Statute Law Making in the United States. Boston. 1912.

JUDSON, FREDERICK N. Power of Taxation, State and Federal, in the United States. St. Louis. 1903.

The Judiciary and the People. New Haven. 1913.

JUDSON, HARRY PRATT. The Essential Elements of a Written Constitution. Chicago University Decennial Publications. Volume IV. 1903.

KAISER, JOHN BOYNTON. Law, Legislative and Municipal Reference Libraries. Boston. 1914. See, especially, Chapter II, Legislative Reference Libraries. List of publications by these, pp. 379–387. Bibliography of Legislative Reference Work, pp. 388–401.

KALES, ALBERT M. Unpopular Government in the United States. Chicago. 1914.

LEGISLATIVE REFERENCE BUREAUS. See in Bibliography, Kaiser, J. B.

LINCOLN, CHARLES Z. Constitutional History of New York (State) to the Year 1905. Five volumes. Rochester. 1906.

LOBINGIER, CHARLES S. The People's Law. New York. 1909.

MCCARTHY, CHARLES. The Wisconsin Idea. New York. 1912.

MACDONALD, WILLIAM. Jacksonian Democracy. New York. 1906. Documentary Source Book of American History (1606–1898). New York. 1913.

MCLAUGHLIN, ANDREW C. The Courts, The Constitution and Parties. Especially, Chapter V, The Written Constitution. Chicago. 1912.

MACY, JESSE. Party Organization and Machinery. Revised Edition. New York. 1912.

MERRIAM, C. EDWARD. Primary Elections. Chicago. 1908.

OBERHOLTZER, ELLIS PAXTON. The Referendum in America. New York. 1911.

OSTROGORSKI, M. Democracy and the Organization of Political Parties. Two volumes. New York. 1902. Democracy and the Party System of the United States. New York. 1910.

PIERCE, FRANKLIN. Federal Usurpation. New York. 1908.

POORE, B. P. Compiled by, Charters and Constitutions. Two volumes. 1877.

POWELL, THOMAS R. See in Bibliography, Bondy, W.

REED, A. Z. Territorial Basis of Government under the State Constitutions. Especially, Chapters VII–VIII. Columbia University Series. Volume 40.

RANSOM, WILLIAM LYNN. Majority Rule and the Judiciary. New York. 1912.

REINSCH, PAUL S. Readings on American State Government. Boston. 1911. (See, especially, Bibliographical note by William L. Bailey. Pp. 465–70.) American Legislatures. New York. 1907.

SCHERGER, GEORGE L. Evolution of Modern Liberty. New York. 1904.
SCHOULER, JAMES. Constitutional Studies. State and Federal. Parts I, III. New York. 1897.
Ideals of the Republic. Chapters II, VI. Boston. 1908.
STIMSON, FREDERIC JESUP. The Law of the Federal and State Constitutions. Boston. 1908.
The American Constitution. New York. 1908.
Popular Law-Making. New York. 1910.
STINESS, JOHN H. State Constitutions and Statutory Laws. Chicago. 1912.
STOREY, MOORFIELD. The Reform of Legal Procedure. New Haven. 1911.
SUMNER, HELEN L. Equal Suffrage. New York. 1909.
THORPE, FRANCIS NEWTON. Constitutional History of the American People. Two volumes (1776–1850). New York.
Constitutional History of the United States. Three volumes (to 1895). Boston.
Federal and State Constitutions. Compiled and edited by. Seven volumes. Washington. 1909. Note lengthy Bibliography.
(For criticism of this set, see *American Historical Review*, October, 1909. *American Political Science Review*, February, 1910. See, also, Bibliographical Note in Reed (General Bibliography), pp. 242–250.)
WILCOX, DELOS F. Government by All the People. New York. 1912.

American Historical Review, issued quarterly from October, 1895. Also, *Annual Reports* of the American Historical Association. Organized 1884.
American Political Science Review, published quarterly by the American Political Science Association since November, 1906. Also, *Annual Proceedings* of the Association, organized, December, 1903.
American Year Book. A Record of Events and Progress. From 1910. (See especially headings, Popular Government and Current Politics, State and County Government.)
Annals of the American Academy of Political and Social Science. Issued bi-monthly from July, 1890. Note especially, numbers of
July, 1910. Administration of Justice in the United States.

September, 1912. The Initiative, Referendum and Recall.
May, 1913. County Government.
March, 1914. Reform in the Administration of Justice.
May, 1914. State Regulation and Public Utilities.
Columbia University. Studies in History, Economics and Public Law. Fifty-eight volumes from 1891 to 1914 inclusive.
Cyclopedia of American Government. Edited by Andrew C. McLaughlin and Albert Bushnell Hart. Three volumes. New York. 1914.
Cyclopædia of Political Science, Political Economy, and of the Political History of the United States. Edited by John J. Lalor. Three volumes. New York. 1888.
Equity. (Formerly *Equity Series.*) Issued quarterly at Philadelphia, since January, 1899.
Johns Hopkins Studies in History and Political Science. Annual Series, from 1883.
New International Year Book. Edited by Frank Moore Colby. Since 1907. (Old series, 1898–1902.) New York.
Political Science Quarterly. Edited by the Faculty of Columbia University, and issued since March, 1886. Also, *Proceedings* of the Academy of Political Science, issued quarterly at Columbia University, from October, 1910. Of the *Proceedings*, note especially the following numbers:
July, 1911. The Reform of the Criminal Law and Procedure.
January, 1913. Efficient Government.
October, 1914. The Revision of the State Constitution (chiefly New York).
Public Affairs Information Service. White Plains, New York. 17 bulletins from October, 1914, to February 20, 1915.
Yale Review. Edited by the Professors in Political Science and History. Issued quarterly since May, 1892.

INDEX

The numbers refer to pages. Authors' names will be found in the Bibliographies